Controlling
SOFTWARE PROJECTS

MANAGEMENT
MEASUREMENT
& ESTIMATION

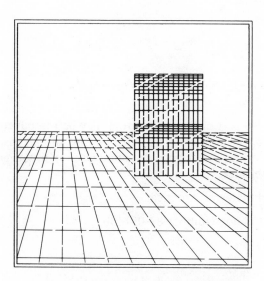

TOM DeMARCO
FOREWORD BY BARRY W. BOEHM

Yourdon Press
1133 Avenue of the Americas
New York, NY 10036

Printed in the United States of America

Library of Congress Catalog Number 82-051100

ISBN: 0-917072-32-4

This book was set in Times Roman by YOURDON Press, 1133 Avenue of the Americas, New York, N.Y., using a PDP-11/70 running under the UNIX® operating system.*

---

*UNIX is a registered trademark of Bell Laboratories.

For
Allan V. DeMarco
and
Murray O. Smyth

It is no will-o'-the-wisp that I have followed here.

Contents

Acknowledgments

At the end of a book publishing project, there is a traditional gathering of all participants for a glass of champagne. I am always surprised at such affairs to see what a great number of people have been involved in the project. The job of running this huge and unwieldy team falls to the editor. So, in addition to being a skilled semanticist, grammarian, and diplomat, the editor must also be a manager. Our editor has been Janice Wormington. She has managed each of us with such gentleness and calm efficiency that we seldom realized we were being managed at all. Yet the remarkable smoothness of the project proves, in retrospect, that a true professional was in charge. I am also indebted to Janice for her role in shaping and refining the manuscript.

My technical reviewers were Mark Wallace (of Quasar), David Bulman (of Pragmatics), and Tim Lister and Al Brill (of Yourdon). Each has had a strong, positive effect on the result.

My thanks to Susan Moran and Lorie Mayorga for copyediting and production work, to Dan Murray for cover art, and to Andrea Diaz for help in research and assembly of the manuscript. Thanks also to Wendy Eakin for her advice and guidance.

There is a formal convention for citing the source of each borrowed graphic and quote, but there is not even an informal convention for acknowledging people who have shaped the author's thinking or who have suggested useful abstractions or illustrations to improve the presentation. For such difficult to categorize services I am indebted to Tim Lister, Steve McMenamin, Capers Jones, Gary Schuldt, Ed Yourdon, Barry Boehm, and Sally Smyth.

Foreword

Tom DeMarco's book, *Controlling Software Projects: Management, Measurement & Estimation,* is a very timely, helpful, and enjoyable book.

It is timely because most software organizations are currently running short of money, or people, or both. If your organization fits one of these descriptions, this book can help you bring your software costs under better control, and help you avoid many of the common sources of lost effort on software projects.

The book does this by providing a number of helpful methods to estimate the costs of future software projects, and to track a project's progress with respect to its estimates. Better cost estimation methods help us to understand the relative costs and benefits of a proposed future system well enough to be able to reduce its scope or to eliminate portions whose benefits do not justify their estimated costs. Better cost and progress tracking helps us identify potential project trouble spots in time to avoid large sources of wasted effort.

It is worth providing some evidence that the benefits of such quantitative approaches to software engineering are real; that they are achievable; and that they are already being achieved by a number of organizations.

For example, at TRW we have operated an Office of Software Cost Estimation for several years, and we feel it has repaid our investment many times. It currently consists of three full-time people who operate, maintain, and refine our software cost estimation model; who help project people develop realistic cost estimates and cost-effective system architectures; and who provide an invaluable corporate memory on our software costs. This latter function has provided us with a number of significant insights on how to improve our software planning and control capabilities. Most recently, it has helped us structure a program of corporate investments designed to improve the productivity of our future software projects.

Other organizations with a large stake in reducing software costs, such as IBM, SDC, and portions of the U.S. Department of Defense, have established similar programs with significant payoffs. And advanced business and banking organizations are beginning to reap benefits from such programs also.

One of the major strengths of Tom DeMarco's approach to software cost estimation and control is that it builds directly on his successful and widely used methods of software system specification and design. His recommended software sizing and costing estimates are based on objectively measurable properties of the function models, retained data models, state transition diagrams, module hierarchies, and data structures that form the basis of the methodology in his previous book, *Structured Analysis and System Specification.* This direct connection makes it relatively easy to go from a system specification or a design specification to a quantitative estimate of the costs required to implement the specified system.

At this point, you can legitimately raise a few objections (or cite me chapter and verse from my own book on software engineering economics) that such imprecisely defined terms as functional primitives, data elements, modules, "tiny," and so on, do not provide a rigorous basis for precise software cost estimation. And I would have to agree. Such terms still leave a good deal of room for personal interpretation or even rigging of estimated quantities.

But this is *not* a good reason for invoking the Perfectionist's Procrastination Principle and saying, "I'm not going to bother with these software cost estimation techniques until they're absolutely precise." Rather, there are at least three good reasons to begin learning and using the estimation methods in this book:

1. They are a lot better than the purely "off the cuff" estimation methods used in most places today.

2. Given that no precise estimation methods exist today, it is best to use as many methods as you can to cross-check the validity of your estimates.

3. DeMarco's framework of methods provides a good foundation on which to gather and analyze data to build a more precise set of estimators tailored to your own environment.

Of course, it won't all be easy. Learning to develop and use objective software cost estimates is a lot like learning to ride a bicycle. It's a bit awkward at first, but after a while you get the feel of it and it comes fairly naturally. And it develops some general skills of balance that turn out to be very useful in related pursuits.

Finally, this book is fun to read. It's one of the few software books I could recommend to take along for an enjoyable read at the beach. DeMarco's sense of humor and vast fund of corroborative anecdotes make it a pleasure to learn from him. In the words of W.S. Gilbert,

> For he who'd make his fellow creatures wise
> Should always gild the philosophic pill!

Not many people can do this well, but fortunately for us in the software field, Tom DeMarco is one of them.

Barry W. Boehm
Chief Engineer
Software Information Systems Division, TRW

August 1982

PART I
Chaos and Order
in the Software Development Process

Most software engineering technologies are inherently *qualitative*. They address questions like, What requirement? What design? What approach to coding and testing? But the problems of software development are not exclusively qualitative. There is, as well, a host of *quantitative* problems: How much time? How much money? How much risk? For a typical software development manager, the quantitative unknowns are usually the more troubling and the more urgent. Failure in a quantitative sense can lead to utter chaos. Successful management of a project's quantitative parameters leads to control.

Part I proposes a set of quantitative methods specifically intended to help the software manager stay in control.

1

THE ISSUE
OF CONTROL

You can't control what you can't measure. In most disciplines, the strong linkage between measurement and control is taken for granted. But I fear the idea may be news to many software managers, otherwise rational men and women who harbor an illusion of control, even though they never measure anything.

This book is, most of all, about measurement. It will endeavor to show you how to organize software projects so they are measurable, what to measure and how, and how to use measured indications to effect meaningful control over the software development process.

The issue of control is a rather delicate one. The manager of almost any software project would bridle at the insinuation that his/her project might be out of control. Let me make that statement much more personal: *You* would be very annoyed at the suggestion that *your* software project was out of control. Of course your project is under control; it's your function as manager to see that it is. And, of course, you're doing your job and doing it well. But there are some disquieting facts to be considered:

- Fifteen percent of all software projects never deliver anything; that is, they fail utterly to achieve their established goals.
- Overruns of one hundred to two hundred percent are common in software projects.

The manager of an effort that fails to deliver any result at all, or that overruns budget and schedule by a hundred percent or more, appears in retrospect never to have been in control. But, almost certainly, when those projects were at the stage that your project is at now, the managers *believed they were in control.* What surprises did the future hold for them, and might it have similar surprises in store for you? When you find yourself walking a battlefield that's littered with corpses, you have to wonder, "What did they learn at the end that I still don't know?"

1.1 The state of the art of software management

I believe that the modern-day software manager is walking on such a battlefield. So many software projects fail in some major way that we have had to redefine "success" to keep everyone from becoming despondent. Software projects are sometimes considered successful when the overruns are held to thirty percent or when the user only junks a quarter of the result. Software people are often willing to call such efforts successes, but members of our user community are less forgiving. They know failure when they see it.

In my first book (naturally stuffy people often write this way), I discussed the user-developer gap, along with some of its causes and cures [DeMarco, 1978]. I advocated some ways to communicate more fruitfully with people on the other side of the gap, ways that I still endorse and practice. But the user-developer gap is not entirely a communication problem. One of the major reasons that the user community distrusts and dislikes software developers is based on performance: *Users are accustomed to achieving goals in their own fields with a consistency that is unheard of in the software world.* A construction engineer who contracts to have some software built is very inclined to judge the result by the same standard that his/her customers apply to construction work. A construction job is considered a debacle if it overruns by six percent. By that measure, there have been awfully few successful software projects.

1.2 The anatomy of project failure

A lot of software projects fail, but we software developers are not such dummies that our sheer incompetence can account for them all. Software managers are no less adept at managing their people and their subject areas than are managers in other disciplines. In my years of auditing software projects, I have seen many total failures where lack of competence and drive could never have been considered the cause. I have known project managers who excelled in those characteristics that I associate with good management:

- strong motivation of project staff members
- clear understanding of the issues
- adequate grasp of relevant technologies
- evident capability in the political sphere

Yet their projects failed. Why? They didn't design poorly or code slowly or introduce too many bugs. In most cases, they simply failed to fulfill original expectations. I am convinced that most project failures are of this very nature, and, in most cases, it is not the fault of the project team at all. It is rather the fault of *inflated and unreasonable expectations.* The sad consequence of unreasonable expectations is that projects are dubbed failures without regard for the quality and quantity of work actually done.

1.3 The meaning of "to control" a software project

You control a project to the extent that you manage to ensure the minimum of surprises along the way. The best-controlled project is not necessarily the one that does the best or most work, but the one that best lives up to its predictions. When there are deviations from what the project originally proposed to deliver, those deviations are minor and they are *signaled early*.

The worth of a project manager is largely a function of how well that manager stays in control. This leads to the following paradox: If Manager A plans mediocrity from beginning to end of his/her project and delivers exactly that, while Manager B predicts great wonders and delivers wonders of a slightly lesser order, then A is a better manager than B. I am not deliriously happy about this conclusion, but it seems correct. Smooth operation of any but the smallest enterprise depends more on control than on the occasional wonder. Of course, the two need not be mutually exclusive.

Staying in control means making sure that results match up to expectations. That requires two things:

1. You have to manage the project so that performance stays at or above some reasonable and accepted standard.

2. You have to make sure that original expectations are not allowed to exceed what's possible for a project performing at that standard.

Neither requirement alone guarantees control.

But where did that "reasonable and accepted standard" come from? How do we calculate what limitations such a standard must entail? How do we track performance over time? What steps can we take to see that deviations are noted early in the project? There are no easy answers to such questions. Any attempt to answer these questions at all leads us into the area of measurement.

1.4 The importance of measurement

"I hope you'll be able to help me with my estimating. As it is, I'm a terrible estimator."

"How terrible?"

"Just *awful.*"

The manager who was asking for help had recently been through an estimating fiasco. But when pressed, he was unable to say exactly what the extent of the fiasco had been. He had not kept records of the actual time and cost expended on the project. And as for his original estimates, well, he just couldn't put his finger on them — they had been lost in the shuffle.

Estimating is a complicated business, and the reasons we do it badly are very involved (more about that in Chapter 2). But even if this manager's problems were as trivial as always being off by a fixed factor, he would never learn. By not measuring the result and comparing it back to the estimate, he was missing his only chance to improve.

Missing the only chance to improve estimating skills is something that software project managers do all the time. For example, it is nearly unheard of to conduct a software project post mortem. Except in the most successful projects, everyone scurries off at the end without even taking note of the actual total cost. Estimates for the next project are made as though the last project never happened, and no one benefits from past mistakes. If aircraft manufacturers were so cavalier about analysis of their failures (crashes), the public would be outraged. But in our field, ignoring the lessons of the past is the invariant rule. Of course it ought not to be that way; we ought to go poring over the wreckage of our failures, analyzing and looking for patterns, in just the way that airplane crash investigators do.

The only unforgivable failure is the failure to learn from past failure.

This rule particularly applies to estimating. Not learning anything from a bad estimate is unforgivable.

We learn from the post mortem, which is as much a necessary part of each project as analysis, design, and coding. But it is not enough. Standing in the shambles of a poorly completed or aborted project, we may be unable to answer even the fundamental question, Where did the time and money go? We have to institute a policy of careful measurement and record keeping *during* the project in order to assure that all the crucial data is available at the end. This measurement and record keeping is what I call the Metric Function.

I have stressed here the importance of measurement to building estimating skills. Other project skills could benefit equally from careful measurement. The Metric Function should be able to provide answers to questions like these: How good was our design? (our specification? our test package? our code?) Did that new method for _____ help us or hurt us? How much time and effort were lost, and why? Have we seen any benefit from our training investment?

Any aspect of the project that cries out for control cries out equally for measurement. Control is impossible without feedback; that's why you can't control what you can't measure. If you accept that idea, a guiding principle of this book, then you ought to be aware of two of its corollaries:

- The extent of control is a function of the precision of measurement.
- Anything you don't measure at all is out of control.

In order to keep the software process in control, you have to institute a policy of careful and effective measurement. If you don't measure, then you're left with only one reason to believe that you are still in control: hysterical optimism.

1.5 The goal of this book

The goal of this book is to help you to set up a Metric Function in your organization and make it work. When it is working, you should expect to reap these benefits:

- better control of software projects; fewer and smaller overruns; earlier indications of failure
- better original estimates
- better management of original expectations
- better capacity to improve and fine-tune the software process
- improved relations with your client community

Measurement is always a recording of past effects. The uses we will want to make of our measurements nearly always involve some predictive quantification of future effects. Yet we know that the past cannot dictate the future. This seeming paradox is not peculiar to this book; it is the paradox underlying any use of the science of statistical inference. Statistics cannot predict, but they can imply. They can give you a bounded confidence in the likelihood of some event happening in the future as a function of measurement of similar events in the past. The first proof I offer that the goal of this book can be achieved is the very existence of the science of statistics.

Measurement and statistical inference are used in many fields to project future performance. In the area of home construction, for instance, the estimating function is based rigorously on statistics collected from past activity. An estimator in the construction trade works with a "bluebook" or estimator's handbook, full of tables like this:*

Table 1-1
Labor Hours Required for Finishing Concrete Surfaces

LABOR HOURS REQUIRED FOR FINISHING CONCRETE SURFACES	
Type Of Work	**Labor Hours Per 100 S.F.**
Troweling Floor, Sidewalks	2.0 to 3.0
Troweling Plain Base And Cove	2.0 to 3.0
Troweling Fancy Base And Cove	5.0
Corborundum Rubbing, Floor And Walls, Typical	7.0
Corborundum Rubbing, Sill, Base, Cove, Typical	9.0
Machine Grinding, Typical	6.0
1-Inch Granolithic Or Terrazzo Laid After Concrete Has Hardened, Incl. Mixing And Placing	11.0
1-Inch Granolithic Or Terrazzo Laid Integral With Concrete, Incl. Mixing And Placing	9.0
Removing Fins, Patching Rock Pockets	2.0 to 3.0
Scrubbing Surface	3.0
Washing Surface With Acid	3.0
Sand Blasting Surface	4.0
Cement Or Other Kind Of Surface Work, Per Coat	3.0

For the princely sum of $8.25, you can buy an estimator's bluebook for wood-frame house construction. If such a book were available for software estimating, I hope you would have had the good sense to buy it instead of the one you are now reading. Still, a software estimating bluebook is not out of the realm of the possible. Even

---

*T.F. Winslow, *Construction Industry Production Manual* (Los Angeles: Craftsman Book Company of America, 1972), p. 49. Reprinted by permission.

today, many of the tasks of software development (particularly those near the end of the life cycle) are being projected by bluebook methods. Companies that began two years ago to implement the Metric Function are now producing substantially better estimates based on carefully collected local empirical data.

2

THE ESTIMATING
DILEMMA

As we discovered in Chapter 1, managing expectations is as essential as managing performance. When expectations exceed any possibility of delivery, projects are doomed. In such cases, it is our estimating that has done us in. Estimating is at the very heart of the difficulty we have in controlling software projects. For this reason, I think it is useful to examine, all in one place, the various problems that have plagued estimating efforts in the past.

Software engineers are notoriously poor estimators. This is my list of the chief causes of poor software estimating:

1. We don't develop estimating expertise.
2. We don't make adequate provision to offset the effect of our biases.
3. We don't have an adequate understanding of what an estimate ought to be.
4. We don't cope well with political problems that hamper the estimating process.
5. We don't base our estimates on past performance.

I'll treat each of these causes in its own numbered section below.

Figure 2-1. The estimating dilemma.

2.1 Lack of estimating expertise

While traipsing around the country and the world giving lectures, I get to meet a lot of software managers. Recently, I've been asking them to assess their estimating capabilities. Oddly enough, I find that the average software manager rates himself/herself *substantially below average* as an estimator. If you also consider yourself a mediocre-to-poor estimator, I have this observation for you: You probably aren't a great zither player either. The reason for the first is the same as the reason for the second: lack of practice.

How many estimates have you made over the past year? A typical software project calls for estimates at the beginning of the project, and regularly thereafter (say, once a month). If you make all these estimates yourself, you will probably spend a total of three percent of your time estimating. I don't think this is enough to gain expertise. When we look in detail at how that three percent of your time is spent, the situation looks even worse: Most of what we call "estimating" is not estimating at all. Software managers may not have learned much about estimating, but they have non-estimating down to a science. The five most prevalent kinds of non-estimate are treated in Subsections 2.1.1 through 2.1.5.

2.1.1 Next estimate = last estimate

Once an original estimate is made, it's all too tempting to pass up subsequent opportunities to estimate by simply sticking with your previous numbers. This often happens even when you know your old estimates are substantially off. There are a few different possible explanations for this effect:

"It's too early to show slip."

"I know I'm behind, but I don't yet know how much."

"If I re-estimate now, I risk having to do it again later (and looking bad twice)."

"Publishing a new estimate now that shows two months' slip is no better than just slipping two months without ever advertising it."

As you can see, all such reasons are political in nature. But their effect is very practical: They force the manager to pass up an opportunity to do some subsequent estimating. He or she misses a chance to build estimating expertise through practice.

Sometimes we fail to re-estimate for a slightly different reason: We allow the previous estimate to take on the significance of a goal. Once in this frame of mind, we find it distasteful to abandon the previous estimate; we'd rather strive to make it come true. Over the past four years, I've been running controlled experiments in estimating in some of my manager-oriented classes. Here is one that points out the reluctance to re-estimate:

Estimating Experiment 1

First part: Estimate as precisely as you can the total monetary value of all coins in the pockets and purses of people in this lecture hall. (There are typically fifty to one hundred people in the hall.) Take fifteen seconds to come up with your estimate, and write it on a piece of paper.

Second part: Estimate the same total again. This time take ninety seconds to estimate. Write your estimate on a piece of paper.

To date, more than a thousand managers have taken part in this experiment. The sample of results is large enough to show a marked pattern: The second estimate is substantially better than the first. Almost everyone gets closer to the actual result on the second try. Of course, this is to be expected — fifteen seconds is too little time to come up with any sort of reasonable answer. In ninety seconds, you have time to count the people in the room exactly, to count your own change, and perhaps to find out from a small sample of people around you how much change they have. You might make a separate count of women and men in the room and factor in whatever difference you expect between the amount of change the average woman carries compared to the average man. No surprises so far. The surprising result that comes out of the experiment is that *fully fifteen percent of the managers refuse to make a second estimate.* They write a question mark in the second space or leave it blank or merely copy their first answer. They are done within a few seconds of the beginning, and are often slightly annoyed at being asked to redo something they have just done. The quality of first estimates for those managers who refuse to make a second try is no better than the first estimates of the other managers (that is, they're poor). But having once made a bad estimate, they prove unwilling to change it.

As a project manager, you may find yourself obliged to publish a regular endorsement of the current (totally unreasonable) estimates. You may even be obliged to call what you're doing "estimating." I hope you can see, though, that you don't build any estimating skills in the process.

2.1.2 New estimate = last estimate + permissible slip

Even when you do decide that politics dictates or permits a revised estimate, you might still not do any real estimating. Your revision might be entirely based on what others are willing to hear, rather than on your true assessment. If you feel you're substantially behind, but know that the client will only put up with a twenty percent slip, why go through the bother of estimating? You show twenty percent slip and hold on for dear life. Another chance to practice your estimating skills is lost.

2.1.3 Past slip = future negative slip

When project phase N is two weeks late finishing, the project manager is sometimes inclined to "re-estimate" phase $N + 1$ to show that it will finish two weeks early and thus cover any past slip. It's not worth making a case against this practice: Everybody knows what its problems are. I point out only that it isn't estimating; you don't develop estimating expertise by doing it.

2.1.4 Original estimate = expected right answer

So far, I've been talking about ways in which project managers often dodge the task of re-estimating. But in many cases, the original project estimates don't involve any true estimating either. Whenever there is an "expected right answer" conveyed to the estimator, the estimating process is likely to be stifled. Suppose your boss asks you for a set of estimates and, each time you produce one, checks it against a little black notebook that you aren't allowed to see. Suppose further that your boss shows evident displeasure at some of your numbers because they don't compare favorably with the numbers in the book. If you're a political animal, you catch on quickly — soon you aren't estimating the work at all, you're just trying to guess what's written in the little book. Your reward is to be considered a team player. But you didn't build any estimating skills.

There are many variations on the theme of the little black book. In some cases, upper managers convey their displeasure with raised eyebrows or by actually *negotiating* estimates. I have sat through sessions in which estimates were haggled as at a bazaar: "Fifteen months." "No more than nine." "I can't do it in less than a year, no matter what." "My final offer is eleven months." "You got it."

I have trouble keeping a straight face at such sessions. But I'm usually the only one; all others are deadly serious. They think what they're doing is "estimating," and probably believe it helps them to hone their abilities. I think of it as low comedy.

2.1.5 Your estimate = expected right answer + X

If you've ever played the guess-what's-written-in-the-little-black-book game, you have probably discovered that you can push the numbers a bit to your later advantage. You figure out what kind of a deviation your manager will put up with and add that to your best guess for what's written in the book. Good luck to you, but this isn't estimating either.

There are probably more ways to dodge the estimating process, and it might be amusing to consider them all. (It would be more amusing if it weren't so painful.) But I think the point is made: Most project managers don't do very much estimating. Some don't do any. The result is that they don't build much expertise.

2.2 Biases in estimating

You might think that a bias would be the easiest kind of estimating problem to rectify, since it involves an error that is always in the same direction and of reasonably constant magnitude. But your own biases are, almost by definition, invisible to you; the same psychological mechanism that creates the bias works to conceal it. The following simplistic experiment is designed to illustrate this effect:

Estimating Experiment 2

Estimate how many seconds it will take you to do this simple computation: Calculate to one percent tolerance the total number of days between noon on January 1, 1900, and noon today. Write your estimate on paper. Do the calculation and write the answer on paper. Observe the elapsed time on the clock at the finish and write down how long it actually took you.

In a sample of one thousand managers, one might expect that approximately equal numbers would underestimate and overestimate their performance. But not at all — the normalized results look like this:

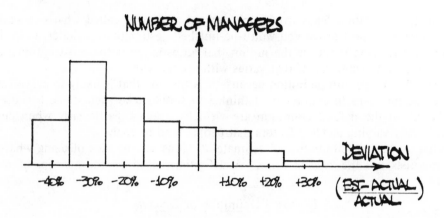

Figure 2-2. Experiment: Estimate your own performance.

The bias is a strong tendency to underestimate the time required. But, if we change the experiment so that you estimate the performance of a second party (the person beside you), then most of the bias disappears.

When your ego is involved in performance of a task, your ability to make a reasonable assessment of how long that task will take you is impaired. It takes very little ego involvement to affect your estimating ability. (The average adult probably doesn't have a lot of self-esteem wrapped up in the speed of arithmetic calculation.) When you care *a lot* about the result, the quality of your estimate approaches zero.

There is an obvious way to avoid this particular bias, an approach that is one of the fundamentals of the method proposed in this book. Let me give you a preview: Whoever does the estimating for a project must be someone whose entire ego involvement is in the quality of the estimate, rather than in the project itself (more on this idea in Chapter 3).

2.3 Poor understanding of what estimate means

An *estimate* is a prediction based on probabilistic assessment. Even people with little understanding of probability seem to accept the probabilistic nature of estimating, but there is no consensus about which explicit probabilistic assessment ought to govern an estimate.

Next time you solicit an estimate from one of your staff, follow up with this question, "What's the probability of our finishing fifteen percent later than your estimate?" You should get some kind of reasonable number, something that shows your estimator is a real-world thinker, acquainted with human fallibility and the sad facts of life pertaining to overruns and under-performance. Now ask this question, "What's the probability of our finishing fifteen percent earlier than your estimate?" Chances are, your estimator will look at you quizzically as though you might have recently arrived from some other planet. You have just learned something essential about the thought process that went into the estimate, an unstated definition of "estimate" that is more or less this:

Default Definition of *Estimate*

An *estimate* is the most optimistic prediction that has a non-zero probability of coming true.

Accepting this definition leads irrevocably toward a method called what's-the-earliest-date-by-which-you-can't-prove-you-won't-be-finished estimating [Kidder, 1981]. A variation on the same theme is the notion that an estimate is the most optimistic prediction padded with some factor that varies with the individual.

I call this the default definition because it is the one that is likely to prevail unless you take specific steps to counter it. I think you should take such steps, because estimates based on the default definition are virtually useless, particularly when coupled with the widely varying padding factors that people tend to apply.

What's a better definition for "estimate"? Consider the idea of using what probability theorists call the *median value.** A definition based on the concept of median value is

Proposed Definition of *Estimate*

An *estimate* is a prediction that is equally likely to be above or below the actual result.

In soliciting such an estimate, you would have to ask your estimator to consider the probability of finishing the project in N months, and to do that for a wide range of Ns. Rather than a single number, you would get back a curve showing how the probability of finishing in N months varies with N (see Figure 2-3). This is actually a probability density curve, and it has the characteristic that the area under the curve is always equal to one. Since the concept of probability density is sometimes difficult to digest, I consider approaching the curve as an exercise in establishing relative probabilities — we set any point on the curve and then make sure that all the others are correct relative to the first. If we then establish the scale along the up-axis so that the area under the curve equals one, we have constructed a probability density curve without ever going through all the theory underlying the concept.

The estimate described by our proposed definition is the vertical line that divides the area under the curve into two equal areas. Although the example of Figure 2-3 shows an estimate for elapsed time in months, the same approach would serve to estimate cost or manpower or elapsed time in any other unit.

One doesn't need to be terribly quick to see that nothing written here so far has solved the estimating problem. In fact, you might conclude that I've just made things

---

*The median, Xm, of a distribution is that value assumed by X for which probability $(X \leq Xm) \leq \frac{1}{2}$ and also $P(X \geq Xm) \leq \frac{1}{2}$ [Feller, 1957].

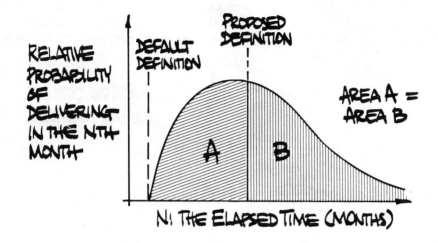

Figure 2-3. A curve submitted in lieu of an estimate.

worse; instead of having one estimate to make, you now have *N*, where *N* is as large as the whole range of months for which each month has a finite probability that completion will occur in that month. Obviously, we need to know much more about where the component estimates come from before judging the usefulness of this approach. But the proposed definition will stand us in good stead as we proceed to examine the measures suggested in subsequent sections.

2.4 Poor handling of political problems

As we've seen from the common non-estimating techniques listed in Section 2.1, most of our estimating problems are at least somewhat political in nature. Politics is usually just a reflection of underlying policy, written or unwritten (usually unwritten). What are the policies that have led us into our chronic estimating dilemma? As I see it, there is one chief villain:

Policy: Estimates shall be used to create incentives.

When such a policy is allowed to prevail, the estimating process is nothing more than a charade. Whenever estimates are required, the person requiring them is not truly interested in the estimator's probabilistic assessment of when the work will be done or at what cost. Rather, the "estimator" is being asked to *establish goals for performance*. In many cases, it's even worse: The "estimator" is being asked to accept previously established goals. And what shall the characteristics of those goals be? If they're going to serve as real prods for the development process, they have to be *totally unachievable*.

In many organizations, the estimating charade is viewed as the *ultimate* motivational tool. Managers regularly succeed in getting their incurably optimistic workers to produce so-called estimates that are blatantly unachievable. The workers then strive valiantly to meet their targets, striving really to justify their own self-esteem. While estimating quality admittedly suffers, the motivation is excellent, . . . or is it? For every dollar we spend building a system (see Figure 2-4), we spend two or more dollars fixing it. That statement is an utter indictment of the quality of delivered software. The incentives we've used to date have only served to make people apply all their efforts toward early completion, quality be damned. But most of the money we spend on software goes to pay for poor quality. Any strong incentive for early completion can only make the problem worse.

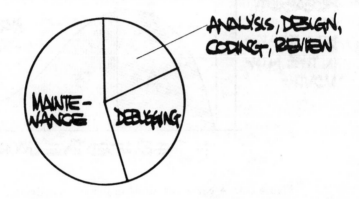

Figure 2-4. Cost by category over the life of a system.

Figure 2-5. Quality of the output depends on quality of the input.

When estimates have to serve as incentives, they will never be good estimates. And as incentives, they may not be worth much either. In order to put this situation to rights, we'll need to restructure the development process slightly in order to create

- *motivation-free estimates:* estimates whose entire purpose is to predict future costs and dates

- *estimate-free motivations:* motivations that encourage developers to maximize function delivered per dollar of net lifetime cost

2.5 Lack of useful input to the estimating process

We cannot approach the problem of garbage-in-garbage-out estimating by concentrating exclusively on the output. In order to produce usable planning estimates, we'll need some better input to the estimating process. But what shall that better input be? As you must certainly have guessed by now, I am going to argue for a set of metrics — quantifiable indications of scope, quality, complexity, and performance — to fill this role. Most of the rest of this book will be dedicated to presenting a scheme for identifying and using such metrics.

3

A NEW APPROACH TO CONTROL

If the first two chapters have been totally successful, they've still done little more than knock down the fragile house of cards that constituted our traditional attempts to control the software development process. What remains to be done is a careful reassembly of the elements into a more solid structure: a new approach to control. In this chapter, I shall lay out that new approach as a series of six proposals. Subsequent chapters will fill in the details and prescribe the methods.

Virtually all of the difficulties cited so far have been at least partly political in nature. Even when it was our methods that failed us in the past, the methods were not completely to blame — there was always a complicating political factor. In considering the morass of related political and technical considerations that arise in any real-world software project, I have come to depend on one basic survival rule: *political solutions for political problems; technical solutions for technical problems.* Following the dictates of this rule, I have included some political and some technical measures in this book. This chapter is entirely political; the rest of the book is mostly technical.

My six political proposals are presented in the headings of Sections 3.1 through 3.6: Separate the estimating function from the rest of development. Create separate incentives for estimators. Specialize the role of estimator. Make the estimator responsible for measurement. Insist that development methods be quantifiable. And, separate development from validation and verification.

3.1 Separate the estimating function from the rest of development

If you're worth your salt as a manager, you're going to motivate development personnel so that they care enormously about their work. In so doing, you will ruin their ability to estimate. So you need someone else to estimate. My suggestion is that you set up an Estimating Group and separate it entirely from the rest of development. The Estimating Group is responsible for all planning projections related to the project, but not for the work itself.

This is not a new idea, but relatively new in its application to software. In fields like printing, construction engineering, heavy equipment manufacturing, and mining, estimators are routinely separated from actual performance of the tasks they estimate. If you queried people in these fields as to why the estimators don't get involved in doing the work that they estimate (after all, they must have an excellent understanding of the work in order to estimate it — why not put all that expertise right on the critical path?), they'd think you were daft. They would point out that the dispassionate judgment required to make reasonable estimates would be compromised by ego involvement in performance.

> *Rule:* If you let one of the litigants be judge, you won't have to waste much time explaining the facts of the case. . . . But the judgment might suffer.

How separate does the Estimating Group have to be? It is essential that group members have no responsibility for development on the projects that they estimate. Better still, they should have no development responsibility whatsoever; otherwise, they tend to have a vicarious involvement in performance.

Just as it is necessary that estimators be separate from development, it is equally necessary that they be sheltered from the influence of anyone who has a stake in development. That means you, as manager. If you want the estimators to fulfill their charter and give you meaningful assessments of your projects, you have to take steps to assure that they cannot feel any pressure from you. Estimators should not report to project management or to any level of management that is responsible for carrying out the work they estimate. Figure 3-1 on the next page shows two possible ways to fit the Estimating Group into an organization. The relationship between project manager and estimator calls for *no communication with the estimator* about how happy or unhappy anyone is about the estimate. If you cannot resist telling your estimator what you think about the numbers, let's at least give the process an honest name: bullying the estimator. If the incentives are set up properly (see Section 3.2), such bullying will be virtually impossible.

Earlier in this section, I used a courtroom analogy in discussing the estimator's role. The analogy seems apt, because the kind of adversary system I advocate is similar to the one that prevails in court. Success of the estimator and the developer cannot be linked in any way. It must be possible for the estimators to succeed on a project that is an utter debacle (in that the estimators have predicted the debacle). It must be equally possible for the project to succeed while the estimators cover themselves with disgrace.

3.2 Create separate incentives for estimators

If the estimator has no stake in success or failure of the project, what is left as his/her motivation? What constitutes success for the estimator? Before you read my answer to these questions, consider one bad example of estimator's motivation:

Example: "Your estimates predicted delivery in June and they didn't deliver until the following May. What have you got to say for yourself?"

"The estimates were correct. I could have done the job in that time. Anyone could have done the job in that time. The development people blew it."

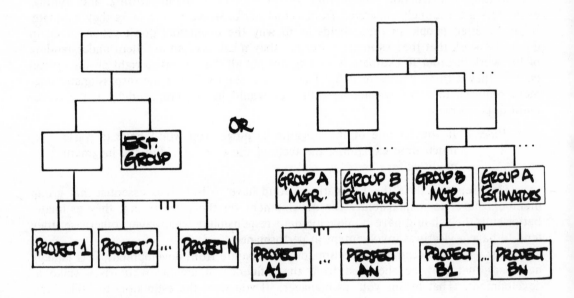

Figure 3-1. Estimating Group in an organizational context.

Right from the beginning, we must dispense with the idea that an estimate can be "correct" even though the actual result may vary widely. If the result is far from the estimated value, it was a poor estimate. The estimator's charter is not to provide targets for developers to strive toward, not to state what they *should* do, but rather to provide a reasonable planning projection of what they *will* do.

The quality of an estimate is a function only of how it stacks up against (how quickly it converges to) the actual result. Imagine a project for which the estimating record has been

01/01/80: Estimator predicts delivery cost at $2.3 million.
02/15/80: Estimator changes prediction to $3.1 million.
06/15/80: Estimator changes prediction to $3.9 million.
08/30/80: Estimator changes prediction to $3.4 million.
12/12/80: Project delivers system at an actual cost of $3.5 million.

Plotted against time, the pattern looks like that shown in Figure 3-2. The quality of the estimate is inversely related to the area lying between the estimate and the actual result, the shaded zone of Figure 3-2.

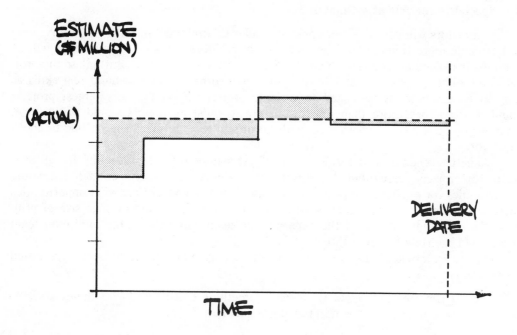

Figure 3-2. Estimating pattern as a function of time.

A useful definition of estimate quality is the reciprocal of the average discrepancy. I call this the *Estimating Quality Factor* (EQF). You calculate it by dividing the shaded area into the area under the actual result. That gives you a unitless number between zero and infinity. High numbers characterize good estimates. In the example above, EQF is 8.7 — not too bad. Chapter 15 provides some guidelines on interpretation of EQF numbers and a set of realistic EQF goals.

EQF can only be calculated when the actual result is known. From this perspective, it is a simple matter to decide when EQF measurement ought to begin: EQF is calculated from the point at which ten percent of the actual has been expended.

Once the parties have agreed on a formula for estimate quality — say, EQF as defined above — then the estimator's motivation can be tied directly to that formula. In any case, the essential rule about motivation is this one:

> *Rule:* Success for the estimator must be defined as a function of convergence of the estimate to the actual, *and of nothing else*.

With such incentives, the estimator has no inclination to dodge opportunities for estimation and re-estimation. There is no tendency to stick with a bad estimate over time, while the estimator waits for a politically appropriate moment to change it. Any change in the right direction will improve the final judgment of estimate quality, and the earlier that change is made, the better. Most of all, the estimator is unaffected by what is written in any little black book, the Catalog of Devoutly to Be Desired Results. No amount of pressure you bring to bear is likely to affect the estimate as long as you don't tinker with the estimator's independence. (If you do use coercion to obtain estimates that conform with your wishes, then you get what you deserve: lousy estimates.)

3.3 Specialize the role of estimator

Estimators will get a lot more practice under the modified incentives, because they will estimate more frequently. The practice will be more valuable, because they will be continually collecting feedback about the quality of their estimates. But unless the project is enormous, there will still be too little estimating practice to build real skills as long as an estimator is restricted to a single project. Even the very largest projects could hardly afford more than one estimator, so most estimators would work alone. They would be working in a vacuum with no one to react to ideas and no one to check their work.

A better scheme is to form a team of estimators with responsibility for all estimates for projects throughout the organization. (Since there aren't enough estimating opportunities for everyone to gain expertise, we need to concentrate what opportunities there are.) The size of the team is a function of the number and average size of projects. To guard against loss of the expertise the team will acquire, the minimum team size should probably be set at three.

In my experience with estimating teams set up along these lines, I have noted these results:

- Team members *learn to estimate,* something that never had a chance to happen in the more traditional arrangement.

- There is no subjective judgment needed to gauge their progress — the mean EQF gets better and better.

- Techniques for estimating are developed and refined by the team itself.

Because software engineering is still in its infancy, the last of these points seems the most important to me. The technology of estimating software projects is currently so crude that it is essential for estimators to rely on their own experience and expand whatever bag of tricks they start with for projecting results. Parts II through IV of this book will help to equip estimating teams with a workable set of tools, but I must admit that many of the techniques described here are not so much things that I have taught teams in the past, as things I have learned from them.

3.4 Make the estimator responsible for measurement

You can't control what you can't measure. Whoever is responsible for estimating must have responsibility as well for all measurement. Now instead of estimators, we have estimator/measurers, and the group they belong to might fairly be called the Metrics Group. The breakdown of function between this group and the development team(s) is illustrated in Figure 3-3.

3.5 Insist that development methods be quantifiable

Selection of development methods must be the responsibility of those whose incentives are tied to the project itself — the developers. Clearly, the estimator cannot dictate methods. But some kinds of methods can make the estimator's function unworkable:

"I've been assigned to be the estimator for this project. Can you tell me something about the way you'll be proceeding?"

"We plan to start right off with coding and do the design on the fly. We'll have only a single module no matter how big it gets (saves having to worry about the interfaces). Any user-related problems we'll work out during acceptance testing."

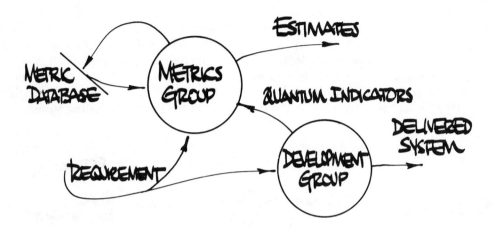

Figure 3-3. Metrics Group in a functional context.

Methods chosen have to be quantifiable. The Metrics Group must be allowed to impose this restriction on the project. Quantifiability derives from two related aspects of any method: its *granularity,* a measure of the extent of partitioning used; and its *interconnectedness,* a measure of the complexity of interfaces in the partitioning. So far, I have been vague about just what it is that's being partitioned, because the concepts of fine granularity and reduced interconnectedness apply across a wide range of project partitioning activities. The following table defines granularity and interconnectedness for three key elements of any project:

Table 3-1
Granularity and Interconnectedness in Project Activities

Activity	What's being partitioned?	Into what?	Granularity is a function of	Interconnectedness applies to
1. Project Planning	work	activities (tasks)	task size	PERT inter-task dependencies
2. Specification (Analysis)	required function	subordinate functions	size of lowest-level functions	inter-function data flow [DeMarco, 1978]
3. Design	a proposed solution	modules	module size	inter-module coupling [Yourdon-Constantine, 1979]

While the Metrics Group cannot *dictate* methods, it should be allowed to establish certain rules that constrain the developers' choices. These rules will include bounds for fineness of partitioning and an insistence that the resultant interconnectedness be fully evaluated. The Metrics Group should have no say about how much interconnectedness is *too much* — that's a development parameter — only about the required thoroughness of interconnection analysis.

3.6 Separate development from validation and verification

One final change to the organization of the software development process will leave us with Figure 3-4. This separation of the development function from system testing also follows from the dictum, political solutions for political problems. The political problem in this case is a conflict of goals imposed on the developer/tester. As tester, he or she wants sincerely to find flaws in the system. But the motivation of the same person as developer is just the opposite: to prove that the system has no flaws. Invariably, the second motivation is the stronger, and the quality of testing suffers.

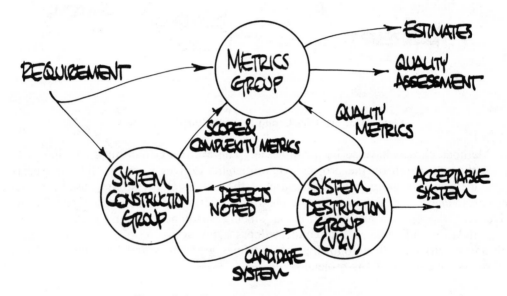

Figure 3-4. Final partitioning of responsibility.

The idea of a separate test team is not new, though it is all too seldom applied in practice. If you intend to consider seriously the first five proposals stated in this chapter, you will also be obliged to consider this, the sixth, because it is your principal tool to assure the quality of delivered work. The more successful you are in controlling performance, the more essential that you figure quality into the performance equation; otherwise, product quality will suffer intolerably as your developers optimize their methods in terms of the other parameters. Quality measurement and assurance, together with the workings of the separated Validation and Verification Team, are described in Part IV.

3.7 Summary

The proposed political restructuring of the systems development process is extensive, but not terribly expensive. It should not interfere particularly with the way systems are built, but only with the way the building effort is estimated and controlled.

Each of the proposals has been adapted from some other discipline where it is used routinely, and each has been tried successfully in the software field.

There are two problems that may surface when the proposals are first implemented:

1. Some managers don't want good estimators: They want sheep. They want to take cost forecasts directly from the Wishful Thinking Department and force them upon the hapless builders. They expect the builders (under duress of bullying) to regurgitate these numbers and then strive valiantly to meet them. Such managers, deprived of wishful thinking and bullying, will have no skills remaining to do the job of management.

2. When estimates are the responsibility of independent estimators, they have little or no significance as a goal to the builders. The result is that the development team is left temporarily without goals.

The first of these problems is unsolvable. If your organization has enough of such managers, they will scuttle any attempt you make to institute rational estimating procedures.

The problem of setting reasonable goals for development is more tractable. A proper goal for development is to maximize the quality and quantity of usable function delivered. If a team delivers work that is at or above the established quality target and does so at a cost per "weight of function" that is equal to or better than the performance target, then the team is a success. If it happens to have missed some delivery dates along the way, then those dates were improperly set, and there is no reflection on the team. Setting this kind of goal will require some meaningful and consistent way to measure two things: weight of function (discussed in Part II); and quality (discussed in Part IV).

4

PROJECTING
SOFTWARE COSTS

Imagine yourself to be an estimator in some technical field that has already developed the kind of bluebook, or estimator's handbook, that I mentioned in Chapter 1. Let's say the field is aluminum extrusion. You are required to come up with an estimate for a job that one of your company's clients has just called in. How do you proceed? Your bluebook would give you this kind of guidance:

Typical Bluebook Procedure

1. Calculate the cross-sectional area of the extruded shape. (See algorithm 4.)

2. Multiply by extruded length and add in a wastage factor from table 17 to determine metal quantity.

3. Determine what size billet or blank you will have to use by indexing table 84 in your handbook by the maximum dimension of the cross section. Look up in table 89 the average weight of these billets.

4. Express the required metal quantity as number of billets, rounding upward.

5.   Go to the Comptroller's Inventory File for the billet size selected and deduct as many billets as you will need from that table. Pick out the inventory price (last in, first out) associated with each of the billets you will be using. Use this to calculate total metal cost.

.
.
.

n_1.   Select an extrusion press, based on cross-sectional area and required speed (tables 104 and 105), and pick out the cost factor for that machine from table 163. Multiply the cost factor times the extrusion time to determine press cost.

A typical order could involve twenty to thirty steps to cost out, and you might end up using dozens of tables. When you were done, you would write the total estimated cost on a form, along with the calculations that led to it, and give the form back to the salesman. The salesman would then call the customer to quote a firm price based on your estimate.

The charming thing about this "estimating" process is that *there was no estimating involved in it at all*. You have replaced traditional wet-finger-in-the-wind estimating with something far better, something that I call *projecting*.

The point of this chapter is that whenever estimates are called for in the software process, we ought to be looking for the possibility of using projections instead. If that turns out to be at all possible for a given problem, then that problem is outside what we might think of as the *domain of estimating*.

4.1 The domain of estimating

In order to understand the concept of domain of estimating, consider the following thought or gedanken experiment.

Gedanken Experiment 1

I will throw 7 dice 100 times and write down for each trial the arithmetic sum of the 7 faces. Estimate how many of the 100 trials will result in a sum of 23.

If you're a good sport, you might accept this challenge and come up with some number that seems reasonable to you. You'd call the number an estimate. But if anybody seemed to care strongly about the quality of this estimate, you would begin to have some misgivings about the idea of estimating at all in this context. After all, you reason, this isn't really an estimating problem — it's a probability problem. Someone who remembered the probability theory involved would be able to crank through the calculation of mean expected value and come up with an answer. This answer would have a legitimacy that no estimate could ever have for such a problem.

Gedanken experiment 1 is entirely outside the domain of estimating, since the question asked by the experiment is more legitimately answered by recourse to projection based on probability theory and the known statistical characteristics of dice. The domain of estimating, the set of problems for which estimating is legitimate and should be allowed, is limited to those problems or portions of problems for which there is no recourse to more exact science.

Parts II, III, and IV of this book will try to put software development entirely outside the domain of estimating by giving you a more exact science, a combination of probability and statistics, to depend upon. Since nothing succeeds entirely in living up to its goals, I suspect we will never manage to keep *all* of the software process outside the domain of estimating. How do you deal with a problem that is partly inside and partly outside?

Gedanken Experiment 2

I will throw a *handful* of dice 100 times and write down for each trial the arithmetic sum of the faces for however many dice are thrown. Estimate the number of trials for which the sum will be equal to 23.

There is now one unknown (number of dice in a handful) for which we have no science or statistics available to help us project. In this case, it makes reasonable sense to estimate *that unknown*. It still does not make sense, however, to estimate the number of trials with a sum of 23. That is outside the proper domain of estimating. We ought to project it from our estimate of the first unknown.

> *The Moral:* Estimate only when you have no recourse to projection. Don't make a package deal: Even when there are unknowns that require true estimating, other portions of the problem might be susceptible to projection.

Our goal is to estimate the smallest possible element of any unknown and project everything else.

4.2 Empirical cost projection

The idea of predicting costs from historical data and observed statistical relationships is known as *empirical cost projection*. In most mature technical fields, empirical projection is the prevalent technique for predicting future results. In some fields (extrusion, transmission repair, masonry, and others), empirical projection methods are so refined that they form the basis of a hard quotation system, and overruns are rare enough that the quoter can usually afford to swallow them.

By the year 2000, empirical projection will be *de rigueur* for software. In 1950, that thought would have been ludicrous. Sometime in between, there must be a transition from unworkable to workable. I suggest that that transition time is now.

"But wait a minute," I can hear you muttering under your breath. "Software is different. Empirical projection won't work for software. . . ." Let me try to refute some of the objections that are leaping to mind.

4.3 Five objections to empirical projection for software

1. *"We don't have the data. Without that vaunted bluebook, the metal extrusion estimator would be nowhere. That's where we are."*

Of course, it is partly true today that we lack the numbers and formulas required. Further, it doesn't seem likely that numbers collected in different environments will soon be broadly applicable; there is just too little industry-wide convergence in software development methods. So we must set out now to collect data locally to make empirical projection work for us on a local level. A reasonable approach to this is to set up the projection machinery with built-in evaluative and corrective facilities. That way, we can begin to project almost immediately (though the early error ranges will be wide), and refine the process gradually as the data come in.

This book will provide you with a sort of blank bluebook, a template for the empirical projection handbook that you will be building over time. It will define all the tables and indicators and formulas, but provide few actual values. So where should the values come from for your initial projections? Let me suggest that you *estimate* them. The result of this approach is that your very first projections will be at least as good as the estimates that you might otherwise have had to make. They will be derived from the same empirical base you would have used in making a traditional estimate. The only difference is that you will be obliged to write down that empirical base (when you estimate the various values) and then calculate implications of those values. Traditional estimating is virtually the same process as projection, *but it's done intuitively.* Since combinatorial and probabilistic problems are notoriously counterintuitive, you probably never did justice to the purely computational part of estimating. When you take an empirical projection approach, that portion of your predictions must necessarily improve. I conclude that, even on your first try, an empirical projection will give you a higher-quality answer than a traditional estimate.

Having said that, I'll also point out that the initial projections still won't be great. The greatest strength of the empirical projection technique is that it can be improved progressively over time in a totally mechanical fashion. As you'll see, this improvement will be fairly rapid.

2.   *"Even if we have the data, we haven't got anything to correlate it with. What can we use as the early measurable indication of size? (If you say lines of code, I'll scream.)"*

A handy tool for projecting software effort would be some kind of Magical ScopiMetric Analyzer that you could wave over any requirement to get a firm reading of scope, measured, for example, in ergels (megaergels for large projects). It would then be a simple matter to organize your empirical database so that each table could be entered by number of ergels, and to organize your formulas so that they correlated ergels to whatever resultant quantities you needed to project. Number of ergels would be the *quantum indication of scope* that is a necessary input to the projection process (see Figure 4-1).

There are no Magical ScopiMetric Analyzers, and there are no ergels. So what can we use as an early quantum indicator for software? What quantifiable aspects of a requirement could serve the purpose that cross-sectional area and extruded length served for the example at the beginning of this chapter? Clearly not lines of code. The lines of code metric has been repeatedly proposed as a quantum indicator, and continually rejected. It suffers from a host of problems: It isn't available early enough in the project; it isn't a consistent indicator (some lines or groups of lines are *much* more expensive than others); and no meaningful standard has emerged for counting lines of code and probably none ever will. Finally, the whole idea has taken on a certain emotional flavor so that otherwise well-behaved people tend to scream whenever you mention lines of code.

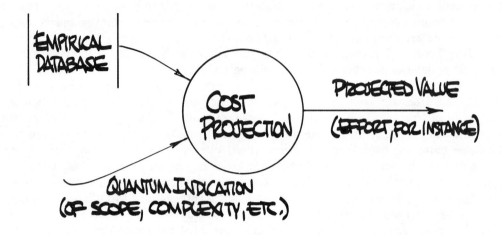

Figure 4-1. Empirical projection for software.

The kind of quantum indicator required has all of the following qualities:

- available very early in the project, probably no later than early analysis
- highly consistent in correlation to resultant cost and effort
- standardizable
- palatable to project personnel

There is no rule that says that a single indicator of scope will suffice. In fact, the idea that there might be some single factor that we could measure early and correlate strongly to results is hopelessly simplistic; if there were, we would certainly have stumbled on it long ago. It is reasonable to hope for a limited set of early indicators to serve our initial projection needs. We should then count on collecting more and more precise indicators as the project proceeds, and using these to provide the basis for continued refinement of projections.

A fruitful source of early quantum indicators is anything that constitutes a *model* of the system to be developed. A model, after all, is a miniature representation of some complex reality that shares many of the characteristics of whatever it represents. If we contrive to build models so that some of the quantitative characteristics of the modeled system are accurately represented, then these characteristics will be our quantum indicators. A model with such measurable qualities can legitimately be called a scale model. Building scale models of software systems is the subject of Part II of this book. As you will see there, a whole series of progressively more accurate models can be constructed at rather small cost as the project moves toward delivery. These models will provide the major input to our empirical projection technique.

3.   *"Each software system is different. You can't use data about developing small on-line systems in PL/I with experienced people to project results for a development of large batch systems in assembler by novices."*

It's true that no projection technique will work well when the development to be projected varies widely from the available empirical base. (It's also true that no technique of any sort will be of much help to people who develop large batch systems in assembler.) But the contention that each software system is intrinsically different is highly suspect. Take the issue of language — projection schemes in the past have been terribly bogged down trying to cope with the effects of varying language. Yet, the overwhelming majority of programming organizations in the United States are monolingual. If we were trying to build a common empirical base of cost statistics to be applied across the whole industry, we'd have to worry about language; in a local empirical base for projecting development within a single organization, we probably do not.

The kinds of variations that could strain our empirical projection scheme do pop up, but not with startling regularity. In fact, the much-talked-about dynamism of the EDP industry doesn't have much effect on most practitioners. They proceed to build the same kinds of systems of about the same size on the same machines in the same languages using the same techniques year in and year out.

Our control and cost prediction difficulties are not limited to those projects that differ significantly from other projects developed in the organization. The typical out-of-control project is likely to be one that *doesn't differ in any major way from the norm.* Even if empirical projection helps only with our bread-and-butter projects, it will lead to enormous improvement.

But an empirical projection approach can also be expected to work well on projects that deviate widely from the norm of past projects measured and included in the empirical base. (At least, the approach will be better than the kind of traditional estimating that is its only alternative.) The reason for this optimism is that, while the project may differ qualitatively from the norm, *many or most component pieces of the project will not.* Projection techniques will work well on these pieces, and you will be left with a bare minimum of necessary estimating to cope with the rest.

4.   *"The data don't converge. The tolerances will be so wide that no one will accept the results."*

In order to have a graphic example of this non-trivial problem, I have reproduced below a chart of productivity data collected as part of the Yourdon 1977 Productivity Survey [DeMarco, 1977]. As you can see in Figure 4-2, the quantum indicator used in this survey is lines of code, and the non-convergent character of the result (wide scatter) is one of the reasons that lines of code can't serve as an acceptable quantum indicator. Suppose you nonetheless tried to work this curve into your empirical projection technique. You'd have to use a combined estimating/projecting approach that would work this way: 1) Estimate minimum and maximum lines of code; 2) pick off minimum and maximum cost figures from the graph as a function of these two numbers; 3) express the result as a range. If you estimate 50,000 to 80,000 lines, the resultant range is 2.3 to 104 man-years! Picking a most likely mid-value, you still have to project tolerances of −86% and +525%. You don't have to tell me anything particular about your boss for me to understand that he or she would have apoplexy over such tolerances.

How shall we deal with the problem of non-converging results? Just for starters, we can present the non-convergence in a way that makes it easier to digest and live with (see Figure 4-3). Faced with such a curve, a typical manager will exclude small portions of the extremes (say, 10% of the area on either end), and then ascribe a corresponding confidence factor to the result: "I can have 80% confidence that the project will finish in 15 man-years, −45% and +900%." That's better, but still a long way from acceptable.

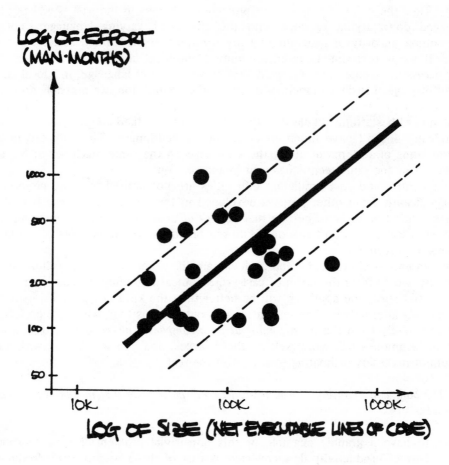

Figure 4-2. Yourdon 1977 Productivity Survey data.

The real answer to problems of non-convergence is that we have to do away with it. We have to face up squarely to each of the reasons that our data have failed to converge in the past:

- widely divergent methods used on the various projects (some had no methods at all)
- no consensus about what data to collect
- no single standard for data collection
- poorly chosen quantum indicator(s)

And we have to find a way to correct each one. Correcting them is not an easy task, but neither is it one that requires enormous inspiration and insight. It demands mostly hard work. The Walston-Felix experiments at IBM prove the value of such hard work — the data they collected did converge acceptably.*

---

*I discuss these experiments [Walston-Felix, 1977] in more detail in Chapter 16.

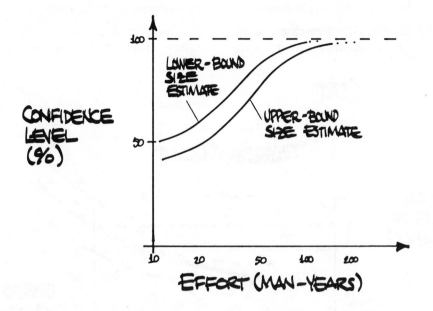

Figure 4-3. Probabilistic presentation of an estimate/projection.

Suppose you do all the hard work to rationalize your data collection process, and the data collected in your organization are still not as well behaved as you might have liked. The tolerances on your projections might be too wide to suit everyone's tastes, your own included. At that point, I suggest that it is the tastes that have to be changed. If you develop your best possible quantum indicator of scope (probably a weighted composite of several indicators) and correlate your empirical data to it in the fashion shown in Figure 4-4, then the tolerances T+ and T− that you project for a value of Q have too much legitimacy to be dismissed. If anyone doesn't like the results, that's too bad — when empirical evidence indicates a 5% likelihood of 500% overrun, all the tantrums on earth won't make the fact go away. The best managers will take note of the possibility and make contingency plans weighted by the associated likelihood of that possibility actually coming to pass.

5. *"Upper managers won't accept the projected numbers because the figures will be too high. The worker bees won't work as hard without unreasonable numbers to strive toward. Everybody's ego will be offended by the idea that the work is predictably doable and that people's efforts are interchangeable."*

The scheme of projection using empirical projection methods is an attempt to put a kind of crystal ball to work for you. Its purpose is not to solve any of the problems of actually getting a system built, but rather to make sure you encounter the fewest number of surprises as you undertake that work. The most perfect crystal ball makes no guarantee that its users will be happy when they see into the future, only that what they see will be accurate. As your crystal ball, your set of projection techniques, becomes more and more refined, you can expect these results to occur:

- Some projects will be canceled early, projects that might otherwise have run through to completion (with unacceptable overruns).

- People who desperately want to hear lower numbers will attack the projection process or attack the estimators* or ignore the projections.

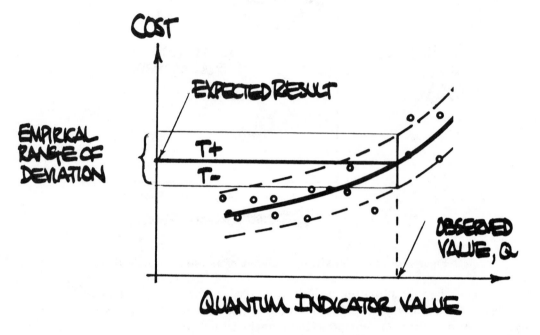

Figure 4-4. Correlated empirical data.

The notion that workers perform at their best only when under schedule pressure has always been wrong. Putting people under time pressure makes them work faster, not better. Any set of methods for measuring and projecting development parameters cannot be limited to examining only the performance side of the performance versus quality tradeoff. You have to measure both, and then determine how total lifetime system cost varies with the two. When you know that, you can reorient your staff toward some weighted composite of maximum useful function delivered per unit time and maximum quality of delivered products. (Function measurement is the subject of Part II of this book, and quality measurement the subject of Part IV.)

Software developers may indeed resent the idea that an empirical projection approach could be meaningfully applied to their work. It implies that yet another area of anarchy has begun to succumb to order. Human beings love anarchy, in limited doses, and regret its passing. The more order a manager introduces into the development process, the more he or she ought to consider ways to reintroduce small amounts of "creative disorder" (brainstorming sessions, war games,† new methods, new tools, new languages) as a means of keeping bright minds involved.

---

*If the estimators are sufficiently accurate in their projections, and insist on projecting things that are just too awful to consider, it may be necessary to fire them. This is known as the Archibald Cox Maneuver. It is best carried out over a weekend.
†I discuss Coding War Games in Chapter 21.

4.4 Making projection techniques work

No new technique will work all by itself; it has to be *made* to work. Making empirical cost projection work for software won't be any more difficult for us than it was for printers and construction engineers to make the concept work in their areas. Identification and collection of metrics to drive the projection process are treated in Part II. Formal projection techniques are presented in Part III.

5

THE COST
OF MEASUREMENT

Metrics Group activities ought to cost from five to ten percent of the manpower cost of the effort monitored. At the beginning, the cost will be at the high end of that range, since proportionately more time will be spent learning, setting up new procedures, reconstructing past history, and working by trial and error.

Measuring the development effort and not the productive use of the system might lead to an unfavorable tradeoff between development cost and quality. So measurement has to continue over the full life of the system. That means when the project ends the Metrics Group carries on measuring the maintenance process and the quality of the delivered system. The costs carry on, too, at five to ten percent of the people cost of maintenance.

5.1 The original investment

When you set up a Metrics Group, your original investment is the valuable people you assign to the group. It is essential that Metrics Group members have a reasonable command of all the principal methods used in the efforts they monitor. Since models produced by the project are a major source of quantitative evidence, Metrics Group personnel need to have virtual mastery of modeling techniques. In short, the people you should be inclined to put into the group are the very ones you'd rather put to work on the projects.

To make matters worse, the requirement that metrics people stay independent of everyone with an interest in the result means that they have to be independent of you. So, some of your best people will pass out of your domain entirely as a result of being assigned to the group. The more it hurts to see a valued senior analyst or chief programmer go into the Metrics Group, the more it will be worth to you later. Once you have come to depend on the input generated by the group, you won't be inclined to put any of them back to work at the project level.

Count on supporting the group for at least a year before it begins to produce results of much higher quality than those produced without it. Note that the group will not be entirely unproductive during this time, since it will do estimating and measurement work that otherwise would (at least in part) have been done within the projects.

If you have training dollars available to spend on group members, you should consider training in the area of statistics. Expect to invest some money as well in attendance at users groups where metrics data may be shared (for example, GUIDE or SHARE).

5.2 Setting up a pilot effort in metrics

Most people who are persuaded that they need a Metrics Group and that it will pay for itself are nonetheless disinclined to trust to mere persuasion for very long. How can you try out these measurement and control ideas at minimal cost and how soon can you expect to see results? I offer you this procedure for getting started:

1. Assign three people half-time to the Metric Function. Three is the minimum-size group for the kind of interaction required to make the learning process work best.

2. Make sure that the other half of members' time is spent on something entirely separate from the projects they will be measuring (for example, standards, training, planning, procurement, or systems support). It must be separate in both a functional and organizational sense.

3. Set up the group so that it reports to someone outside the area to be measured.

4. Select two or more projects that have a total staff of approximately fifteen. Select projects that are at or near the beginning (say, in early requirements analysis), and that are likely to be completed within six to nine months.

5. Expect the group to thrash a bit at the beginning and to be continually delayed by the projects, unable to work without data that the projects are slow to generate. During this period, the group should have a secondary charter to collect global information about the organization (how much development, how much maintenance, how much training, how many defects, how much testing, and so on).

6. As initial pilot projects near completion, add more of similar size. (This second set of projects is your real test, since most of the effort of the first cycle must be considered a cost of getting started.)

7. Insist that the group members construct a working bluebook as they proceed and that they continually monitor the quality of their own projections (see Chapter 20).

8. Evaluate the pilot effort at the end of the second cycle of projects.

5.3 Once more with feeling

You can't control what you can't measure. Measurement costs money. For years, we've expected control to be a virtually free by-product of good management. But managers are too busy managing to do the kind of careful, painstaking measurement required for control. Managers are in the wrong position to measure anyway, since they have a vested interest in the result. The politically independent professional Metrics Group fills the need. A Metrics Group is not going to be free; it will cost you at least three good people, right at the start. The running cost of a full-blown Metric Function will be about five percent of the people cost of your organization, more at the beginning. If you think that cost is high, consider the cost of being out of control.

PART II
System Models and System Metrics

Metrics derived from the code are just too late arriving to be of much use to the estimator. They may form the basis for a mid-project schedule correction, but clearly can't be a lot of help in establishing the original estimates. At the time that original estimates are called for, there is no code to measure. There is probably no design. There is only the requirement itself. The very first metrics collected about a new system have to be derived directly from the requirement.

The requirement might be considered a *model* of the system to be delivered. System modeling techniques for requirement specification have recently gained wide acceptance. The purpose of a specification model is to answer the question, What function must be delivered by the project? As such, it is a qualitative tool. But it can be made quantitative as well, becoming effectively a *scale* model of the requirement. Specification models built to scale are the source of the earliest quantitative indications of system size and complexity. Part II provides a set of methods for building system scale models and measuring their metric properties.

The model of the requirement is only one of the system models that may be constructed during the course of the project. As the developers' perception of the system becomes more concrete, they may choose to build more and more precise models of the emerging product. These models, too, can be built to scale and serve as the source of later metrics. Mid-project scale models and their associated metrics are also treated here.

In sum, Part II describes the metrics that can be collected during the course of a project. Part III then describes techniques for utilizing these metrics in the production of accurate cost and schedule projections.

6

THE CONSTRUCTION
AND USE
OF SYSTEM MODELS

Most of what has been written about system modeling is plagued by jargon. I must share some of the blame for this, since in my wayward youth I introduced some of the obfuscating terminology. In this section, I will attempt to present the concept of system modeling in jargon-free text, with never a mention of structured this or third-normal-form that. I'm going to try to make the entire idea seem like just so much common sense, which is exactly what it is.

6.1 The system model: A representation in miniature

A system model is a miniature representation of a complex reality. A model reflects certain selected characteristics of the system it stands for. A model is useful to the extent that it portrays accurately those characteristics that happen to be of interest at the moment. If there is a need to examine different characteristics at different times, it may be necessary to build several models of the same system.

Since it is a representation in miniature, a system model can typically be constructed for a modest fraction of the cost of building the system. Modeling therefore gives us an inexpensive way to study *essential aspects* of a system long before that system itself is built. I list these as the essential aspects we would most like to study early in each development project: system behavior (embodied in a specification), system internal organization (embodied in a design), and project organization (embodied in a

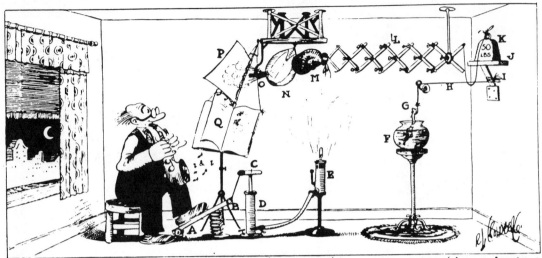

AT LAST! THE GREAT BRAIN OF THE DISTINGUISHED MAN OF SCIENCE GIVES THE WORLD THE SIMPLE AUTOMATIC SHEET MUSIC TURNER!

PRESS LEFT FOOT(A) ON PEDAL (B) WHICH PULLS DOWN HANDLE(C) ON TIRE PUMP (D). PRESSURE OF AIR BLOWS WHISTLE(E). GOLDFISH(F) BELIEVES THIS IS DINNER SIGNAL AND STARTS FEEDING ON WORM (G). THE PULL ON STRING (H) RELEASES BRACE(I), DROPPING SHELF (J). LEAVING WEIGHT (K) WITHOUT SUPPORT. NATURALLY, HATRACK (L) IS SUDDENLY EXTENDED AND BOXING GLOVE(M) HITS PUNCHING BAG(N) WHICH, IN TURN, IS PUNCTURED BY SPIKE (O).

ESCAPING AIR BLOWS AGAINST SAIL (P) WHICH IS ATTACHED TO PAGE OF MUSIC (Q), WHICH TURNS GENTLY AND MAKES WAY FOR THE NEXT OUTBURST OF SWEET OR SOUR MELODY.

Figure 6-1. A system model as a representation, perhaps an annotated drawing.

project plan). Specification, design, and project planning (since they all need to study characteristics of not-yet-built systems) are activities that can naturally benefit from use of modeling methods. Model-oriented techniques for each of these activities began to gain broad acceptance during the mid-seventies. Thus, there is a discipline for conducting the requirements analysis process in such a way that the specification that emerges is a meaningful model of the requirement; and there is a discipline for design that builds an internal model of a software system; there is a discipline for project planning that produces a project model. In the coming chapters, I'll describe these disciplines, and provide a prescription for deriving quantitative information from each of the models produced. Before getting into the details of any one of the special system models that might be built during a project, consider some fundamentals that will apply to *all* of the models.

6.2 Some fundamentals of system modeling

Modeling is a tool for coping with problems of largeness. You don't need a miniature representation of something that is already small. Trivially small systems are successfully constructed with a traditional method: Specify − design − code − unit test − integrate, working at each stage with the system as a whole (specify the whole requirement, design the whole solution, and so forth). Unfortunately, this method does not extrapolate well to larger systems. Each of the activities is still necessary for large-system construction, but can no longer be applied to the whole without causing a kind of "working buffer overload" in the brain.

The human brain seems to make use of a number of different working buffers, each with limited capacity. Some applications fit well into the brain without overloading any one of its limits. I shall characterize such applications as *tiny*. Anything other than a tiny system requires a qualitatively different approach. Long before my time, engineers had discovered the essence of this different approach:

> *First Modeling Guideline:* When a system is larger than tiny, partition it into pieces so that each of the pieces is tiny. Then apply traditional methods to the pieces.

For moderate-size systems, all that is required is to divide the whole into subsystems. Since the partitioning is a useful representation in miniature of the whole system, people refer to it as a *system model.*

Each time you partition, there are interfaces to be considered, interfaces between the various pieces of the partitioning. There may be a choice of ways to divide a whole into pieces, as in Figure 6-2.

Figure 6-2. Two partitionings of the same subject matter.

When this is true, the complexity of the resultant interfaces is a clue to which way is better. A partitioning with few and simple interfaces is preferable to one with many and complex interfaces:

> *Second Modeling Guideline:* Partition to minimize interfaces.

Of course, this implies that you do have to keep track of the interfaces that result from each candidate partitioning, and you have to do this in some fairly formal way in order to evaluate complexity. Formal interface descriptions will also lend rigor to the partitioning. What is not so obvious is the empirical observation that only *data* interfaces are worth formal tracking — controls and switches can usually be safely ignored, at least at the beginning.

> *Third Modeling Guideline:* Compile a formal census of data interfaces associated with each partitioning. Give each interface a meaningful name and define it rigorously in terms of its components. Save these definitions in the census. The census of interface definitions is an integral part of the model.

How shall we describe our partitionings? Textual description won't be adequate for any but the most trivial partitionings ("shin bone connected to the ankle bone, ankle bone connected to the foot bone, . . ."). The problem is that text is inherently one-dimensional and most partitionings are multidimensional, since a given piece may have interfaces to any number of other pieces. So we need a multidimensional representation, some sort of a picture, to describe our partitioning decisions. There are numerous graphic partitioning conventions in common use today. I offer Figure 6-3 as an example:

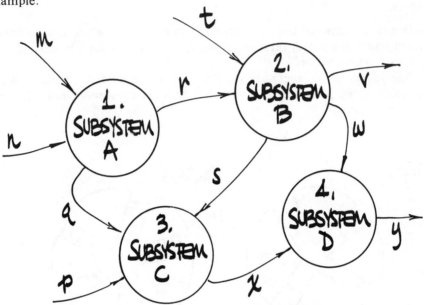

Figure 6-3. Graphic representation of the partitioning component of a model.

While the partitioning is multidimensional, the interface component is almost always one-dimensional in nature; most data that moves around a system is one-dimensional, since it consists of a simple string of component data items.* So a one-dimensional (linguistic) tool should suffice for interface definition. Each definition is presented in terms of the smaller data items that make up the interface and the relationships that bind them together. Subsequent definitions of the components may be required until everything is defined down to the elemental level. Every interface *declared* in the partitioning must be *defined* in the definition set.

> *Fourth Modeling Guideline:* Use graphics to describe partitioning by portraying the whole in terms of its component parts and interfaces between those parts. Use a linguistic tool to describe the interfaces in terms of their component data items.

As we undertake larger and larger systems, the direct partitioning into tiny subsystems becomes unwieldy — though each of the component pieces is tiny, the partition-

---

*Data on the move is almost always one-dimensional, but data at rest (say, a database) is not. More about this later.

ing itself is not (doesn't fit comfortably into the brain). The solution to this problem seems obvious:

> *Fifth Modeling Guideline:* Partition the system into a comfortably small number of pieces. If any piece is still too large to deal with as a whole, partition it further into a small number of pieces. Continue until the resultant pieces are tiny.

This constitutes a partitioning in levels: First, you divide the system into subsystems, then divide each of the subsystems into sub-subsystems, and so on. You end up with a model of the whole (your initial partitioning), a model of each subsystem (the set of second-level partitionings), and successive lower- and lower-level models. The components of the lowest-level partitioning have the quality of *tininess,* and are thus susceptible to solution all in one swoop (whatever a swoop is).

If you think of the partitioning of Figure 6-3 as a first level, then one of the second-level partitionings might look like this:

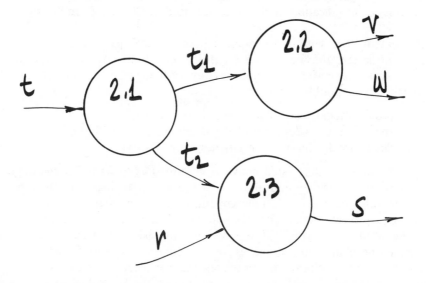

Figure 6-4. A second-level partitioning.

The relationship between the two levels is this: The lower-level (child) partitioning shows the details of one component piece of the upper-level (parent) partitioning. Interfaces at the associated component on the parent diagram are reflected as the net inputs and outputs of the child. So, the arriving and departing flows of Figure 6-4 are the same as the interfaces of one component (subsystem B) of Figure 6-3. There may be any number of levels in a leveled set. The parent-child relationship applies throughout the set, between each pair of vertically adjacent levels.

6.3 What models to build

In any reasonably complicated development, there are at least two systems worth modeling: the system to be developed (the target) and the system for developing that system (the project).

Building a model of the project along the lines described above means dividing the whole into pieces, the *tasks,* and defining the interfaces between those tasks, the *deliverables.* That sounds like project planning, and it is. I'm suggesting that project planning be undertaken as an explicit modeling activity, and that the project model be a deliverable of one of the very first project tasks. Of course, the main reason for advocating project modeling here is that it provides quantitative indicators for later cost projection. But project modeling is a disciplined and elegant way to go about project planning, and ought to be considered for that use on its own merits. Project models are discussed in detail in Chapter 13.

At the beginning of a project, the target system is just a gleam in some user's eye. At the end, it is hard code. At various stages in between, modeling can be useful to portray successively more finished perceptions of the system. So there may be more than one target system model to be built. I cite these two as almost always worthwhile: a model of the requirement and a model of a proposed solution. A model of the requirement, a miniature representation of what has to be delivered, is effectively a *specification* of the target system. And a model of the innards of a proposed solution is essentially a *design.* Specification models are discussed in Chapter 8, and design models in Chapter 10.

To the extent that you make modeling an integral part of project planning, specification, and design, the metrics we require from the models will be a largely free by-product of work that has to be done anyway. All in all, there are at least three models that can serve a double purpose:

- the project model (part of the overall project plan)
- the specification model (part of the target system specification)
- the design model (part of the target system design)

Each of the three models listed above is described as "part of" something. You might wonder what else is required along with the model to make up the whole. In each case, it is some statement of rules governing the elemental (tiny) pieces of the partitioning. The project model, for example, is complemented by a declaration of methods to be used in carrying out the component tasks. The specification model breaks a complex problem into tiny pieces, but we still need to specify those pieces. A set of tiny component specifications completes the specification of the whole. In the case of the design model (a partitioning into modules), the individual module descriptions complete the whole.

Expect some variation in appearance and technique among the various kinds of models. For instance, a tree-like hierarchy will be used as a partitioning graphic for some models, instead of a network (as shown in Figure 6-3).

Appendix A contains the project record of a simple development effort. There, you will find an example of each of the models built at successive stages of the project. The project record also contains an analysis of project and system metrics.

The sample project developed a simple Metric Support Package (MSP) to assist the functions of the Metrics Group. I chose this example because it is germane to the subject matter considered here, and because it illustrates the full range of system modeling techniques discussed in the chapters ahead. Early generations of the MSP are presented as illustrations in the body of the text.

6.4 Uses of system models

Of course, you could do specification, design, and project planning without ever building a single model, but except for truly tiny systems, such an approach would deprive you of some important benefits. System models are surprisingly useful tools throughout the development process. I list below some of the chief uses of these models (with the affected parties in parentheses):

- establish a common view of the current environment prior to automation (user and analyst)
- negotiate future system possibilities (user and analyst)
- specify selected future system requirement with minimal redundancy, thereby enabling easy updating (user and analyst)
- provide input to acceptance test generation (analyst and quality assurance staff)
- represent, evaluate, and refine design concepts (designer)
- break project into tasks with well-defined products and minimal inter-task dependencies (manager)
- deal with complexity a little at a time by progressing from the most abstract view of a system down to progressively more detailed views (all)
- provide quantitative indications of project scope and complexity (manager and Metrics Group) [see Figure 6-5]

This last use is the principal concern of this book. Models of the system and of the project can be built in such a way that their quantitative characteristics are consistent indicators of future effort. These indicators are the *metrics* upon which the discipline of quantitative analysis is constructed.

Robert Press, architect

Figure 6-5. A scale model providing quantitative as well as qualitative information.

6.5 Selected references

For useful insight on the properties of system models, I recommend

Alexander, C. *Notes on the Synthesis of Form.* Cambridge, Mass.: Harvard University Press, 1977.

Since Alexander is an architect, the systems of concern to him are communities and cities, but most of his observations are applicable to the models built in support of the software development process.

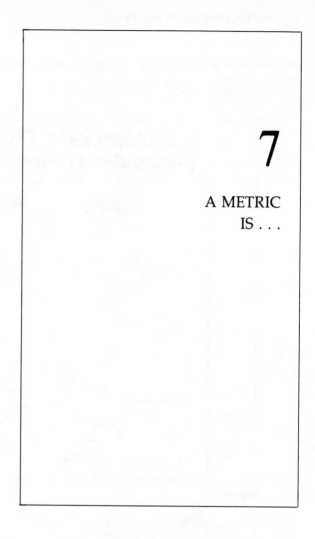

7

A METRIC
IS . . .

There is a rule of sorts in government, or ought to be, that you never do anything about a problem until you learn to measure it. Paul F. Lazarsfeld, the great Columbia University professor who developed the art of polling, used to tell his classes that the moment you attach a number to an idea you have learned something. You know more than you knew before. The number seems too large, too small, about right. You are already thinking in a more precise way.

— Senator Daniel Patrick Moynihan
Newsletter of Sept. 4, 1981

A metric is the number you attach to an idea. More precisely, a metric is a *measurable* indication of some quantitative aspect of a system. For a typical software endeavor, the quantitative aspects for which we most require metrics include scope, size, cost, risk, and elapsed time.

Metrics, as I shall use the term, always pertain to systems. And, for our purposes, the systems they pertain to are the software system under development and the system for building it (the project). If the network of Figure 7-1 represents a project, then the metrics shown might be quantitative indications of the state of completeness of the project activities. If the network represents the functions of the target system, then the metrics shown might be quantitative indications of the likely effort involved in implementation of each function.

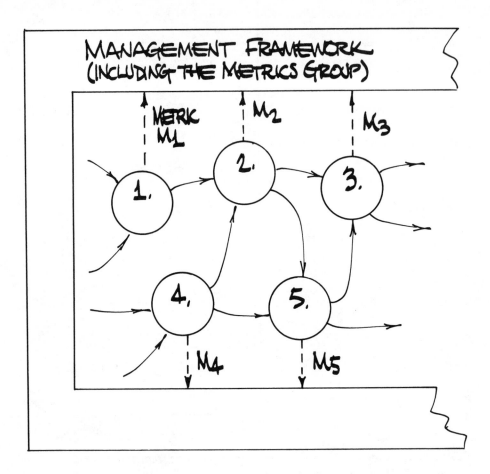

Figure 7-1. Metrics derived from a partitioned system (or project).

Just as important as what a metric is, is what it is not. A metric is not merely an observation expressed in numeric terms: "Ninety-five percent of the programmers feel that we are more than fifty percent done." In order for such an observation to qualify as a metric, there must be some measurement involved. Asking folks how they feel about a piece of work is hardly measurement. I stress this point because I know from experience that managers are all too likely to use up their measurement dollars simply by polling opinions of their workers. Such polling may be worthwhile for worker morale, or as a ploy to get workers to strive to make their own projections look good. But it is of little value in assessing any meaningful characteristic of a system or of a project.

7.1 Characteristics of a useful metric

A useful metric is distinguished by four characteristics: It is measurable, independent, accountable, and precise. These qualities are discussed below.

7.1.1 Measurability and the "unquantum"

An indicator must be measurable in order to qualify as a metric at all. If there is no measurable indication of a phenomenon (the salvation of souls, for instance), then there is no way to apply the methods described here to aid in controlling that phenomenon. Sorry.

There are many seemingly unmeasurable qualities of system projects that nonetheless have a strong effect on performance. Consider the factor that one productivity study labeled "customer interface complexity."* Of all the factors investigated, this one was correlated most strongly to relatively low productivity. In lieu of measuring the factor, project personnel were asked to rate customer interface complexity for their projects as normal, greater than normal, or less than normal. They apparently applied this judgment after their projects were over, at least in some cases. The result was, I believe, that they created something of a self-fulfilling prophecy: Project members who sensed they had not performed up to snuff were inclined to give a high rating to what they felt to be the factor with the strongest likely negative impact. The study concluded that the factors had about the same relative effect as had been expected. (Studies that prove what they expected to prove are always rather suspect.)

A factor that is unmeasured but felt to be important is what I call an *unquantum*. The principal use for unquanta is in rationalization: "The user was a disaster, so of course it took us forever to deliver the system." Beyond that, unquanta aren't good for much of anything. Any exercise that tries to give a numeric value to an unquantum without doing any real measurement along the way is a bit of a fraud.

I defined the unquantum as a relevant factor that is *unmeasured*, not unmeasurable. There is an important difference. If an unquantum is measurable and you measure it, it ceases to be an unquantum and becomes a metric. Most of the familiar unquanta that populate software projects are measurable. Take the example of customer interface complexity. That nebulous unquantum could be replaced with these true metrics:

- Change Rate: customer-introduced changes per unit time (measured, for instance, as changed lines per thousand lines of code per year while in maintenance mode, or as a percentage of the function model components of each class changed per year while in development mode)

- Change Impact: unit cost of average change (dollars per change)

- Customer Dissatisfaction: cost of change during a fixed period beginning with system delivery (changes expressed as a percentage of the delivered system)

If you observe these metrics for a small sample of projects, you will have a usable quantification of customer interface complexity, something far better than an unquantum. In all but the most informal organizations, such metrics can be collected inexpensively as a by-product of normal user interface and maintenance procedures.

Once you have defined a metric, it is a defensible activity to estimate its value during the period before that value can be observed. It makes perfect sense to estimate

---

*The study refers to the user's interface with the developers, rather than the interface with the machine [Walston-Felix, 1977].

the three metrics described above for a new project and assume that they will have an effect on the project similar to that observed on past projects. The difference between such an *as yet* unmeasured metric and an unquantum is that the metric is scaled uniformly, is subject to better and better estimates as time goes on, and is eventually resolvable with observed fact.

7.1.2 Independence

Useful metrics have to be independent of the conscious influence of project personnel. There should be no way to change the value measured other than by changing the underlying quality that the value purports to reflect. An independent metric of completeness, for example, would be one that the project team could affect in no way other than by making the project more (or less) complete.

Traditional project control schemes involve the use of *documentary deliverables* as metric indicators of project state. You plan on some standard set of written deliverables and then interpret the completion of each one according to a fixed table of the form

Delivery of	Implies project is
Functional specification	12.4% complete
Design document	26.9% complete
Program specification	41.3% complete
⋮	

WRONG

Documentary deliverables are not independent. They are controlled directly by the project team, the very people who most have a stake in management's assessment of the project. When it becomes incumbent on the team to prove that the project is on schedule, it's all too easy to wrap up whichever document is on the line and call it done.

You may think that there are no such things as truly independent metrics and, indeed, they are rare. The reason you seldom encounter independent metrics has to do with

Heisenberg's Uncertainty Principle (slightly revised)

Measuring any project parameter and attaching evident significance to it will affect the usefulness of that parameter.

The key word here is *evident*. If project members know that you count the number of smiles on Monday mornings and use that as an indication of project morale, then when they want you to believe that morale is high, they will all start smiling on Monday mornings. If, on the other hand, you keep to yourself the metrics you're using and the significance you attach to them, their usefulness (if any) will not degrade over time.

The Uncertainty Principle is the main reason for insisting that measurement be separated in a political sense from actual performance of the project. The Metrics Group members can hope to develop independent metrics. In practice, they don't even have to keep their metrics entirely secret to accomplish this. If they relied on a single observed parameter, secrecy would be their only hope of guarding its independence; but with literally hundreds of metrics being collected and applied, those who would modify their behavior to affect the metrics would be simply overwhelmed.

Figure 7-2 shows an example of two useful metrics of completion that can, with a little effort, be kept reasonably independent of conscious control by the project team. In a given development environment, the time to reach peak points of the compilation rate and of the defect detection rate, respectively, are strongly correlated to delivery time. You can arrange to measure these rates without calling great attention to that fact, since the needed data is probably generated anyway by CPU accounting or by normal record keeping during debugging. Even if project members catch on that you are measuring these rates, there is little they can do to affect them directly.

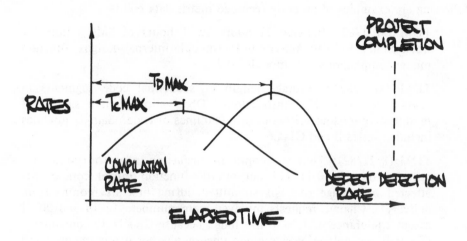

Figure 7-2. Sample metrics of completion.

7.1.3 Accountability

Metric data collection and analysis are error-prone activities. If you look at the data, draw your conclusions, and throw the data away, you will invariably lose faith in the conclusions later on. This will be particularly true if the conclusions are politically unpopular. In order to make a believable case for any metric analysis (believable even in the eyes of the person who does the analysis), it is necessary to save the raw data as well as a methodical audit trail of the analysis process. If the conclusions are reconstructible from the data, they will be easier to defend and interpret. In addition, the retained raw data will keep open the possibility of re-analysis at a later date in the light of new theories or new cost forecasting procedures.

Metric data should be collected along with sufficient control data items to assure integrity. These include, at a minimum, the date of observation, identity of the observer, and identity of the person(s) performing the work being measured. In some cases, it may be possible to validate metric data by checking the data against payroll records or expenditure reports.

I know from my own experience in running project surveys that there is an inclination to put off digesting the data. It's very tempting to stack each week's collection in a corner to be analyzed at the end of the project. The problem is that when gaps are then found in the data it's too late to reconstruct. Regular, timely analysis of the metrics collected is necessary to assure their integrity.

7.1.4 Precision

The key point about precision of metrics is not that it be maximized, but rather that it be *explicitly noted* and recorded as part of each datum collected. Useful precision is a function of accuracy. It doesn't make much sense to charge 30.125 work hours against a particular component of the system if you judge that the data are only accurate to within ten percent. But it does make sense to write down your evaluation of accuracy at the time of data collection. This will help avoid later use of the data in ways that are inconsistent with their accuracy. Precision can be indicated with a range, an explicit tolerance, or in some cases by stating the rationale or method for collecting. The following are examples of properly recorded metric data points:

> TDM (8/21/82): Charge 21 hours ($\pm$ 1 hour) of SMC's time for week ending 8/20 to Activity 6-16 (module internal design), function model component 4.3.1, module A92.

> TDM (8/21/82): Average length of sequential code segments in PPRINT system is 12.5 instructions. Observation from a sample of modules comprising 1,500 out of 6,000 lines of code. Sample modules included series B and C1-C6.

> TDM (8/21/82): User six-month dissatisfaction index for ONLAC system is noted as 0.11 (12 out of 106 function model components affected by change requests submitted during first six months from delivery). Change requests involved were numbers 16-18 and 20. I assign a tolerance of 15% to this index because CR#18 (2 components affected) was soft — user seemed unsure whether it was required and assigned a very low priority to it. Also, user still seems unhappy about CR#19 (1 component), which she has temporarily withdrawn.

In each case, the indication of precision is retained as part of the enduring record.

7.2 Results and predictors

Every metric falls into one of two categories: either a "result" or a "predictor."

> A *result* is a metric of observed cost, scope, or complexity of a *completed* system. Examples include total cost, total manpower, elapsed time, or cost or manpower or time by category. Result metrics are treated in Chapter 14.

> A *predictor* is an early-noted metric that has a strong correlation to some later result. Chapters 9, 11, and 12 present examples, as well as techniques for defining and measuring predictors.

7.2.1 Exploiting the result-predictor relationship

The relationship between a predictor and some later result is just speculation until a sample of data points has been collected to support the theory. Figure 7-3 shows such a sample. The metric qualifies as a predictor if the standard error of estimate around the prediction line is tight enough to warrant its use. "Tight enough," in this case, means that the tolerance obtained from using the predictor is less than the tolerance of the best alternative. (If the best alternative is a traditional gut-feel guesstimate, then the tolerance that the predictor has to improve upon is probably on the order of −15%, +1000%. Sorry. That was a low blow.)

I'll have more to say in Part III about techniques for a disciplined exploitation of result-predictor relationships. Figure 7-3 is a simplistic preview of these techniques.

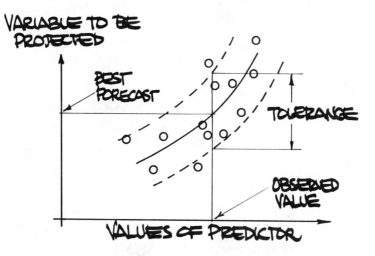

Figure 7-3. Use of predictors to forecast results.

7.2.2 Deriving metrics

Result metrics come from exhaustive, methodical data collection on projects that are under way. The data collected is about costs, particularly costs of manpower expended. These costs are correlated with components of the project model.

Predictors, in most cases, come from the system models. The richest and earliest source of predictors is the specification model (see next chapter). The design model and the version plan (the subject of Chapter 10) provide predictors that are useful in producing converging forecasts of activities near the end of the life cycle, and, in some cases, predictors of system quality and maintainability.

The following table shows at what approximate point in the project life cycle the various models are complete enough to allow observation of their predictors:

Table 7-1
Observation Point of Predictors in the Life Cycle

Specification model	20% point
Design model	50% point
Version plan	60% point

7.2.3 Using predictors: An observation

Figure 7-4 represents the process of cost projection using an empirical database and predictors derived from system models. Making this process work to your benefit is one of the major goals of this book. What reason is there to believe that such an approach will work, in particular that it will work better than traditional estimating? My purpose in this section is to give you an intuitive answer to this question. The answer is based on the observation that traditional estimating works in very much the same way as the process shown in Figure 7-4. The gut-feel estimator also works with a model and an empirical database, but the difference is that his model and database are both *intuitive*. His model is a series of vaguely quantitative hunches about the scope and complexity of the requirement, and his empirical database is a "feel" for costs and schedules based on experience.

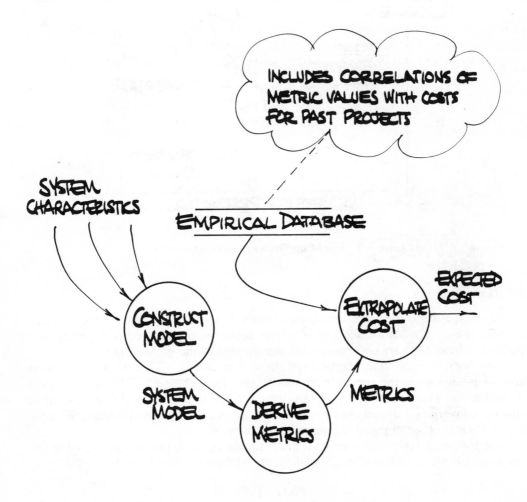

Figure 7-4. The cost projection process.

The simple acts of moving the model and the database out of the estimator's head and committing them to paper bring all of the following compelling advantages:

- The model can be made public. People other than the estimator can help to refine and complete it.

- The quantitative characteristics of the public model can be extracted with a consistency of manner that is impossible with an intuitive model.

- The empirical sample can be enlarged. All project participants can contribute data correlating costs and values of the predictors. Data can also be collected from people outside the project team.

- The purely computational part of cost projection can be done with a calculator. (When both the model and the database are intuitive, the estimator must perform his computations intuitively; no matter how good his intuition may be, it is a lousy arithmetic processor.)

However accurate traditional estimating methods are, estimating from a tangible model and database has got to be better. That doesn't prove the method will be good enough, of course, but it's bound to be an improvement on your next best alternative.

7.2.4 Using predictors to maximize EQF

Stronger and stronger predictors become available as the project proceeds. Collection of each new predictor provides an opportunity for producing tighter and tighter forecasts. Figure 7-5 portrays a typical project and its forecasting opportunities.

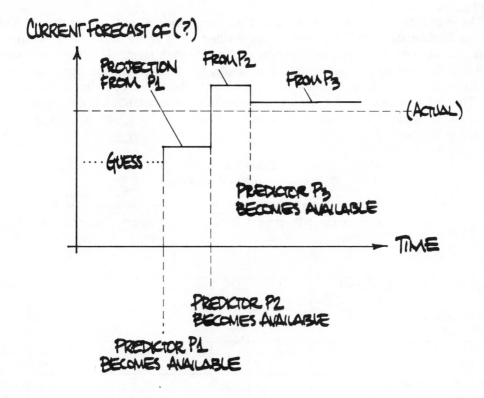

Figure 7-5. Use of successively stronger predictors to maximize EQF.

Prior to the time when a predictor can be *observed,* it can be estimated. Using this approach, you might estimate the value of a predictor ten percent of the way through a project and use a sample like that of Figure 7-3 to derive a likely value of the associated result. The tolerance for this prediction is a function not only of the spread in the data points, but also of the unknown in the estimated predictor. At some later point in the project, the predictor can be observed, the derived value of the future result corrected, and the tolerance tightened up. Figure 7-6 shows the successive use of stronger predictors — some estimated and some measured — as the project proceeds.

7.3 The Metric Premise

So far, I have stated the underlying concept of this book in its most negative form: You can't control what you can't measure. Before looking at the various metrics to be collected and the techniques for collecting them, I want you to have a more encouraging perspective on that concept, an idea that I think of as

<u>The Metric Premise</u>

Rational, competent men and women can work effectively to maximize *any single observed* indication of success.

If you publish some clear quantitative definition of project success, and if you measure and track progress toward that success, project members will align themselves with your stated goals.

In the early seventies, Weinberg and Schulman carried out an experiment that tends to confirm the Metric Premise. They divided a test group into five development teams and assigned the same programming problem to each team. The five teams were given five different goals. One team, for example, was told to complete the program in the minimum elapsed time; another was told to write the tightest possible code; and so on. The performance of the teams was carefully measured, and the results are presented in Table 7-2 [Weinberg-Schulman, 1974]. As you can see, every team excelled in its assigned goal.

Table 7-2
Weinberg-Schulman Experiment

	Goal	Rating of Team's Performance in Optimizing Objective (1 = Best)				
		Completion time	Program size	Data space used	Program clarity	User-friendly output
Goal	Completion time	1	4	4	5	3
	Program size	2−3	1	2	3	5
	Data space used	5	2	1	4	4
	Program clarity	4	3	3	1−2	2
	User-friendly output	2−3	5	5	1−2	1

The Metric Premise applies only to *observed* performance. If you assign a project the goal, "Build a highly flexible product," and then don't evaluate its performance against that goal according to some objective standard, the premise just won't hold. If you assign a dozen (often conflicting) goals, and only measure the performance of one, the premise will only apply to that one.

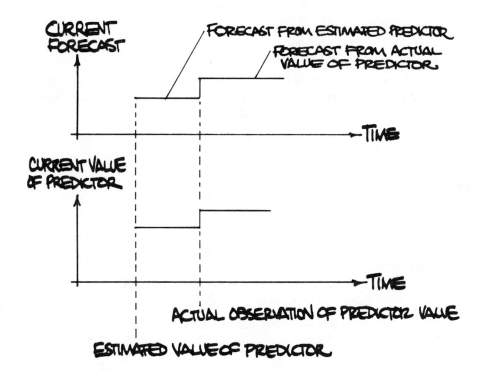

Figure 7-6. Use of estimated values of predictors.

If you don't specify *any* goal, then the default goal — the one that the rational, competent men and women of your project team will work to optimize — is whichever indicator of success is most obviously measured. Most project managers never get around to assigning a formal quantifiable goal. So what is the goal in those cases? The default goal is almost always *delivery in the shortest possible time.* Teams everywhere are working effectively to deliver products in the minimum elapsed time. There must certainly be some projects for which this is a proper goal, but as a general goal for all projects, it is a disaster. People under time pressure don't work better, they just work faster. As the example of Table 7-2 showed, they will sacrifice all other goals to optimize the one they interpret as most important (most carefully observed). The default goal, coupled with the Metric Premise, provides an explanation for this dismal state of affairs:

> In the recent struggle to deliver any software at all, the first casualty has been consideration of the quality of the software delivered. [Hoare, 1981]

By giving a disproportionate importance to delivery time, we encourage projects to make quick delivery of shabby products that are ill-matched to user requirements, unmaintainable, and unreliable. Such products, in the final analysis, cost far more than they might have if they had been more carefully constructed. Of course, we pay lip service to the very qualities that the teams do most poorly on, *but we don't measure those results.* We only measure completion time.

The Metric Premise is not quite the same as the assertion, You can control what you can measure.* But it does give you some hope of using measurement to keep a project on target and headed toward success.

7.4 Metrics to keep the project on target

Whatever the most sensible goal for a project is determined to be, we need to contrive some means to measure it and to make the results continuously apparent to team members. For most projects, the goal should be something along these lines:

Goal: Maximize amount of delivered function (weighted by years of useful system life) per dollar of total system lifetime cost.

The total lifetime cost is made up of development cost plus production cost plus maintenance cost. If you consider that to be a meaningful goal for projects in your organization, then here is a largely mechanical procedure that will help you realize it:

1.   Formulate a single weighted indicator of success against the goal. This indicator is a measure of total function delivered by the project per dollar invested from project beginning until the system is retired. My name for this most fundamental metric is "Bang Per Buck" (BPB). The formal definition of Bang is presented in Chapter 9.

2.   Collect data on a sample of projects to establish standards for BPB performance.

3.   Seek out and evaluate predictors for those parts of the BPB measure that lie in the future. Use the predictors to keep project members aware of how well they are performing during the project.

4.   Encourage project members to maximize Project BPB. Make sure they know that the actual Project BPB will be measured and published, and that their success will be a function of that weighted value, not of any one constituent part of it. Make sure they know *how* Project BPB will eventually be calculated.

5.   Publish projected BPB figures during the project and actual figures six months after delivery. (The maintenance cost characteristic during the first six months after delivery provides a strong predictor of lifetime maintenance cost — more about this extrapolation in Part IV.)

The main justification for metric data collection and analysis is not goal attainment, but goal *alignment.* Members of the Metrics Group earn their keep by helping to orient project members toward the right goals.

---

*There are many things we measure that are not controllable at all. One melancholy example is the process of human aging: I can measure very precisely that I grow 24 hours older each day, but I can hardly claim that the process is under control.

7.5 A look ahead

Maximizing the weight of function delivered per dollar of cost is the right goal for most projects. But how does one "weigh" function? That is the subject of the next two chapters: Chapter 8 will describe methods for building a scale model of the requirement, and Chapter 9 will describe the derivation of the basic function metric, Bang, from this model.

8

SPECIFICATION:
MODELING THE PROBLEM

The initial model of a target system is one that focuses on the requirement. It is an integral part of the system specification, an answer to the question, What system shall we build? Such a model excludes all consideration of the specific method to be used in constructing the system, internal organization of the software, and like concerns. As much as possible, it describes the future (the time after our project has delivered the target system and put that system into use) in terms of policies carried out inside and outside the automated component of the system without regard to how such policies are effected.

A model consists of partitioning, together with a census of interfaces between pieces of the partitioning. But a single partitioning must necessarily have a single perspective, and a single perspective might be insufficient for complete specification of a complex requirement. We might have to slice up the whole in several different ways to reveal all its essential aspects.

Before getting into the idea of multiple-perspective software system models, consider an example from another discipline (Figure 8-1). There you see a contract specification for a small figurine. The convention used among die casters, pattern makers, foundry workers, and others, for specifying solids is called three-view or orthogonal projection.

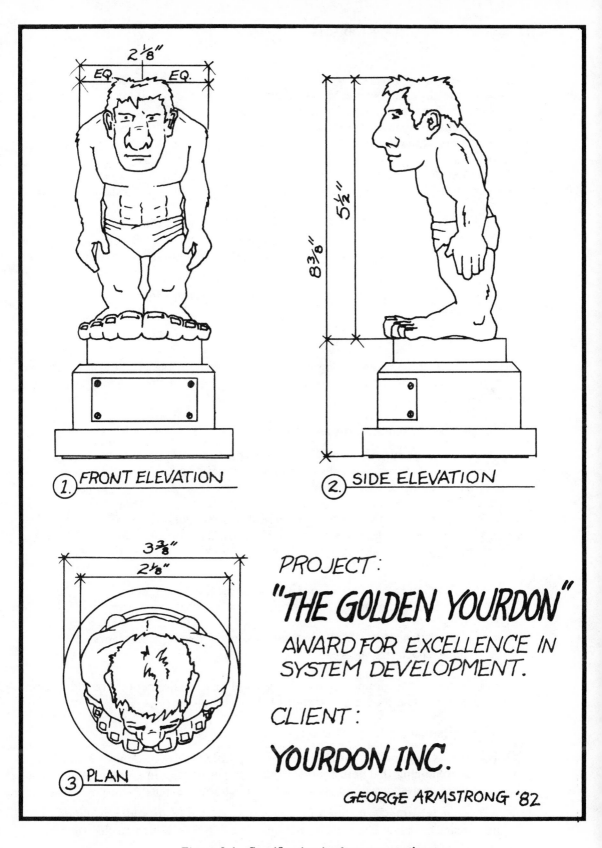

Figure 8-1. Specification in three perspectives.

As you can see, it consists of a set of three drawings, each from a different perspective. No one of the drawings would be sufficient to specify the requirement totally, since some aspects of the solid (lengths of some lines, for instance) are invisible from any given perspective. At least two drawings are required for complete specification; a convention of using three drawings has evolved for convenience. Because the perspectives are at right angles to each other, they are deemed orthogonal. The quality of orthogonality among the perspectives assures that a minimum number of drawings provide a maximum of specification, and that there will be a minimum of redundant specification over the set.

Each of the component diagrams of Figure 8-1 is a model in itself. And we need more than one model, more than one perspective, to complete the specification. The three perspectives could be considered projections (or shadows) of the solid cast onto three different spaces:

- the top view is a projection onto X-Y space (assuming the Z-axis to be vertical)
- the side view is a projection onto X-Z space
- the front view is a projection onto Y-Z space

The solid figure analogy leads one to ask, How many perspectives will be required for complete specification of a software system requirement, and which perspectives shall we choose?

8.1 Perspectives for requirement modeling

Someday, an ivory tower type (not I) will come up with a mind-boggling formula to represent any system as a pseudo-solid in an abstract N-space. From there, it will be a simple matter to prove that precisely $N - 1$ perspectives (each one a projection onto two dimensions) will be required for complete specification. Someday that will all be proved, but let's not wait. I have an empirical answer that will serve our immediate purposes: Three perspectives are all we need to specify most systems. Analyzing the requirement from those three perspectives will provide us with three component models:

- a function model (partitioned view of what the system does)
- a retained data model (partitioned view of what the system remembers)
- a state transition model (partitioned view of different behavioral states that characterize the system)

The three together constitute a *composite model* of the requirement. The three component models are described in the sections below.

8.2 The function model

The word "function" in normal use has very little precise meaning: A function is more or less something that gets done (or ought to get done). In speaking about functions performed by systems, though, we can be much more explicit:

A *function* is a transformation of an incoming stream of data into an outgoing stream of data. The transformation is governed by a set of rules (business policy).

So the transformation called "Determine Commission Amount" in Figure 8-2 is a function:

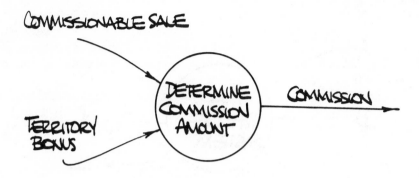

Figure 8-2. A function.

Almost all of the functions in and around data processing systems can be thought of as transformations. When I use the word "function" from here on, I shall use it in this sense. Note that the new definition of function is not incompatible with the common sense ascribed to the term. The transformations that this book calls "functions" have all the characteristics one demands of functions in general. They also have some of the characteristics of mathematical functions.

8.2.1 The partitioning portion of the function model: A network of functions

Thinking of functions as transformations leads you to take a rather topological view of a system: to consider it a network of functions.

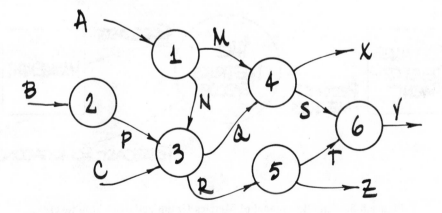

Figure 8-3. Abstract system viewed as a network of functions.

The connections in this network are data streams, each one the product of a single function and the input to one or more others. The insides of the function bubbles are the components of business policy governing the whole area. So the network of functions is essentially a partitioned view of business policy.

We could draw a circle around this whole network and think of it as a single function (Figure 8-4).

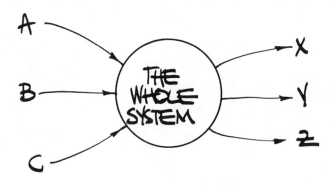

Figure 8-4. Same system viewed as a single function.

The whole system is a function, as we have defined it, since it is a transformation of inputs into outputs. The system function is made up of connected subfunctions, and the subfunctions possibly made up of sub-subfunctions, and so on. The partitioning will consist of a set of network drawings showing successively finer and finer divisions of the system into its constituent functions.

As a concrete example, consider a system for carrying out the Metrics Group activities as described in Part I. At the highest level, the entire system is viewed as a single function (Figure 8-5).

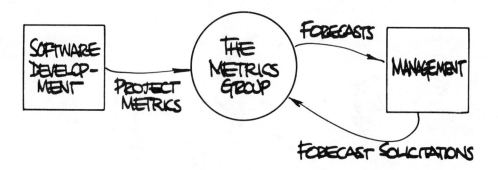

Figure 8-5. Function model of Metrics Group activities (top level).

The purpose of this high-level figure is merely to establish the context of the partitioning to follow. It portrays our system in the context of some larger whole, and shows where its net input and output data streams come from and go to.

The partitioning of the system begins with a graphic like Figure 8-6.* And there will, in general, be third- and fourth-level partitionings.

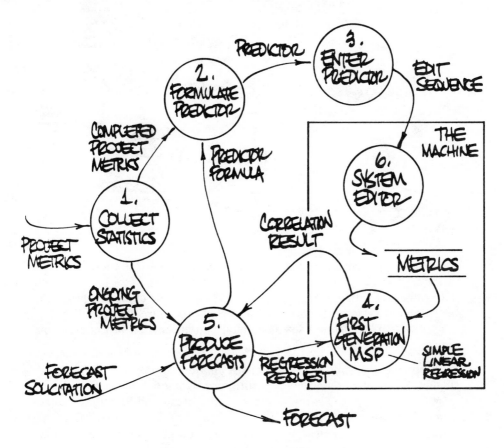

Figure 8-6. Function model of Metrics Group activities (second level).

Function 5, for instance, could be further partitioned in the fashion shown in Figure 8-7. Complete partitioning down to the level of acceptable tininess might require several further levels.

Before moving on, note these few aspects of the function model partitioning:

1.   It shows both automated and manual functions. Function models are constructed during the early phases of projects with charters to implement automated procedure. The project that produced the partitions above, for example, had a charter to produce some automated aids for the Metrics Group. Function 4, a Metric Support Package, is such an aid. The lower-level partitionings of that function break it eventually into tiny pieces, which are subsequently specified. But the partitioning

---

*I'm going to use some statistical terms (regression, standard error, and so on) and assume that they make sense to you. If you need a refresher on such concepts, please look at the Tailored Primer on Statistics, packaged as Appendix C.

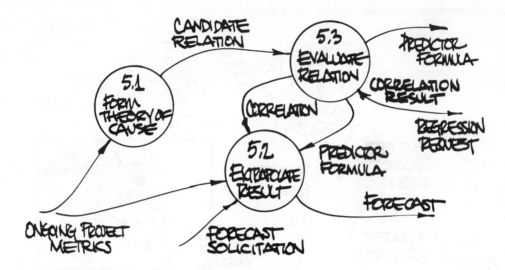

Figure 8-7. Function model of Metrics Group activities (third level).

always begins with a subject area larger than just the computer program or computer system. It portrays automated procedure embedded in the larger system (integrated set of manual and automated procedures) of which it is a part.

2. The complete partitioning will consist of one context diagram (as in Figure 8-5); one second-level partitioning (Figure 8-6); *n* third-level partitionings, where *n* is the number of non-elemental functions (functions that are larger than tiny) in the second-level partitioning; *m* fourth-level partitionings, where *m* is the number of non-elemental functions in the third level; and so forth.

3. Each lower-level figure is a detailed view of what was portrayed as a single function at the level immediately above. So, Diagram 5 is a more detailed view of that portion of the system allocated to Bubble 5 in Diagram 0. Since the lower-level figure deals with the same subject matter, it necessarily shows the same transformation with the same arriving and departing data streams.

The networks are the partitioning component of our model, showing the tiny pieces into which the system is divided. But how do we determine the relationships among pieces? The answer is through an additional model component defining the interfaces.

8.2.2 The interface portion of the function model: A dictionary of data

For each connection shown on any network, we need a definition, a formal declaration of what the name used on the network means. For instance, the network of Figure 8-6 refers to an interface named Regression-Request. A Regression-Request is an input to the automated Metric Support Package, asking for an investigation of the statistical correlation between two parameters. The data content of Regression-Request is just the names of the two parameters. More formally, we might write

Regression-Request	IS COMPOSED OF:	Dependent-Variable-Name AND Predictor-Name

This kind of formulation establishes the template into which an arriving stream of data will have to fit in order to be considered a Regression-Request. The template for Regression-Request is not quite complete, since it still hasn't defined what constitutes a valid Dependent-Variable-Name or Predictor-Name. We require a formulation for each of those items as well:

Dependent-Variable-Name	IS COMPOSED OF:	EITHER:	"TOTAL EFFORT"
		OR:	"DESIGN EFFORT"
		OR:	"IMPLEMENTATION EFFORT"
		OR:	"DEBUGGING EFFORT"
		OR:	"DEFECTS DETECTED"
		OR:	"MACHINE TIME"
		etc.	
Predictor-Name	IS COMPOSED OF:	EITHER:	"FUNCTION BANG"
		OR:	"DESIGN WEIGHT"
		OR:	"IMPLEMENTATION WEIGHT"
		etc.	

Armed with these definitions, we can determine whether a given input can legitimately be considered a Regression-Request. For instance, a request to investigate the correlation between the dependent variable DESIGN EFFORT and the independent variable (predictor) called FUNCTION ,BANG does constitute a valid instance of Regression-Request. The formulations don't give us any hint about format, just data content.

The kind of regression technique used by the first-generation Metric Support Package is a line-fitting algorithm: It finds the slope and displacement of the line that best fits the statistical data, typically by minimizing the sum of squares of deviations from the line. Then it expresses its finding by giving the equation of the line and some assessment of how good a fit the line has to the sample of data. This output is called the Correlation-Result:

Correlation-Result	IS COMPOSED OF:	Best-Fit-Equation AND Standard-Error-of-Estimate
Best-Fit-Equation	IS COMPOSED OF:	Dependent-Variable-Name AND Predictor-Name AND Slope AND Displacement

So, in answer to your Regression-Request of DESIGN EFFORT as a function of BANG, you might expect to see something of this form:

DESIGN EFFORT $= 11.3 + 8.1$ x BANG

Standard-Error-of-Estimate $= 21\%$

The interface definitions are grouped into a kind of dictionary in which each entry describes a named interface in terms of component data items and relationships among them. In order to avoid long complicated formulations, an entry can define an item in terms of non-elemental components, which must themselves be defined (described in terms of *their* components) elsewhere in the dictionary.

8.2.3 The function model: An integrated set of networks and interface definitions

The networks and interface definitions together make up the function model, a concise statement of the requirement. The function model is complete when it satisfies all of the following conditions:

- It describes the *whole* system under consideration; that is, it shows transformation of all the inputs into all the outputs.

- It partitions sufficiently so that all remaining unpartitioned (elemental) components are truly tiny, according to our special definition of that term.

- It partitions honestly so that each function is shown correctly linked to the rest of the network with no necessary data paths left out.

- It partitions usefully so that interconnections are minimized.

- It defines each data item that is declared in any partitioning network.

- It defines each data item down to the level of the data element.

8.3 The retained data model

The first perspective applied to the requirement was that of *function*. We analyzed (modeled) the requirement from the point of view of what the system was required to do. The next perspective to consider is that of the information retained as data in the system. Analyzing from this point of view will answer the questions, What information must be remembered by the system? What organization (reasonable groupings) of remembered data will serve us best? What relationships might apply among the groupings, and how shall we exploit them? In our model-oriented approach, we shall synthesize the answers to such questions into a *retained data model,* a concise representation of the system requirement from the point of view of data inside the system.

Before looking at some sample retained data models, consider this observation about systems and their relatedness to the rest of the universe:

> *Observation:* Most systems *simulate* things whose true existence lies outside system boundaries.

A computer system at your bank, for example, might simulate *you* in some limited sense. It would also simulate money stored for you, transactions involving you and that money and perhaps other simulated customers, and services performed for you by the bank. Each time you interacted with the bank, there would be two sets of activities. One would be a series of real activities — the real you receiving real money from a real teller in exchange for a real withdrawal ticket; and the second, a parallel series of activities simulated inside the system — the "you" represented by your account record on the system disk noted to have "received" some "money" from a "teller" and a "withdrawal" created to document that transaction.

Virtually all systems are simulations, usually of something that exists or is happening outside the system. Sometimes systems simulate an imaginary existence outside the system boundary (the arcade game of Asteroids® is an example). More often, as in the banking example, they simulate real people, real organizations, and real actions. When a system that is intended to simulate the real world simulates instead an imaginary world — the banking system simulates a withdrawal that you never made — we have an instance of what is called a "bug."

Systems simulate with data. Instead of setting up an actual little asteroid hurtling through space, as a mechanical pinball game would have done, the Asteroids system keeps track of certain data items that together stand for the simulated body: its mass, shape, position at a fixed moment of time, and velocity (magnitude and direction). All simulation involves retaining data about the things being simulated. That might not be a great surprise to you, but consider the inverse view of this same idea:

> *Observation:* All data retained by a system is data that describes things simulated by the system.

This statement is equally true. The typical data item stored *inside* a system is a descriptive attribute of something or someone *outside* the system whose existence is being simulated:

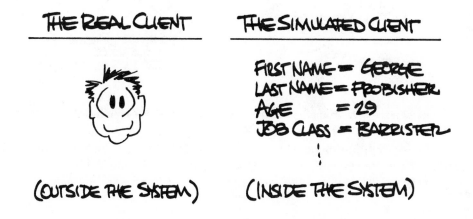

Figure 8-8. The real and the simulated clients.

This relatedness of data inside the system, and of simulated people and things outside the system, provides a kind of mapping as shown in Figure 8-9. The mapping provides a broad clue about how we ought to organize data inside the system. Following this clue will encourage us to group data items to reflect their association with the same *object of simulation*.

Most retained data items are descriptors of one and only one object of simulation. The data items FIRST NAME, LAST NAME, AGE, and JOB CLASS referred to in Figure 8-8 are descriptors of a simulated client. Thus, the object of those data items is "client."

8.3.1 The partitioning portion of the retained data model: An object diagram

In Section 8.2, you looked at some partial function models of a system for metric analysis of the software process. In order to examine this same subject area from a retained data point of view, we take a census of all stored data in the system and ask, for each data item, What object does this data item describe? For the system shown in Figure 8-6, we might conclude that each of the data items describes one of four objects:

- a *project* currently being studied by the Metrics Group
- a *task* (unit of work) serving as an accounting component of a project
- a *worker* assigned to one or more of the projects under study
- a *domain* of similar projects, having the same general characteristics for metric study purposes

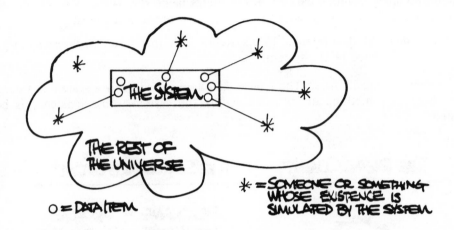

Figure 8-9. Mapping between data and the objects simulated.

All data in the system are associated with one of these objects. This kind of retained data partitioning is conveniently shown with a graphic like Figure 8-10. In this figure, the blocks represent objects, and the arrows represent *interobject relationships*.

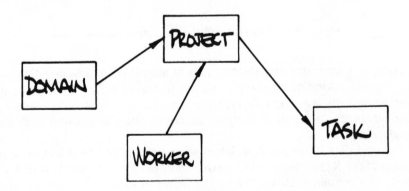

Figure 8-10. Object diagram for MSP.

8.3.2 The interface portion of the retained data model: A set of relationships

Two objects are considered related when there is an exploited association between them. For instance, the object called a domain "contains" some number of projects. This relationship — "domain contains projects" — is essential in carrying out the work of metric analysis because only similar projects, those in the same domain, can be compared to each other. So, if an organization does some batch COBOL projects and some on-line C-language projects, one would be inclined to maintain separate domains for the two kinds of work, and not mix any of the statistics across domains.

The information to retain for each relationship includes such items as the nature of the association ("contains" in our example), and multiplicity of association (one domain to many projects). All of this information could be kept in a separate set of relationship notes, or placed directly on the object diagram with a notation like this:

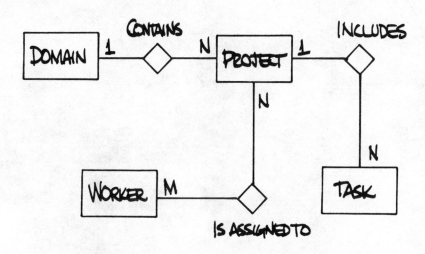

Figure 8-11. MSP object diagram (extended notation).

8.3.3 The retained data model: A database description

As the number of objects increases, we move into the world of database. With forty or more objects to automate, project members would probably be very aware of database methods, perhaps even ready to use one of the many database packages on the market, and would begin to think of the retained data model as a "schema" or "subschema." With a smaller number of objects to implement, such terms seem a little pretentious, but the retained data model is nonetheless an essential component of the whole requirement.

8.4 The state transition model

The third and final perspective needed to complete the requirement model is that of behavioral state. A typical system — particularly a data processing system — tends to go into a number of different states, each of which is characterized by its unique response to a given set of stimuli. Consider the friendly cash machine at your local bank. While it may have a large total repertoire of tricks it can do for you (give cash, check balance, transfer funds, pay bills), in a particular state it may refuse to do any but one of these. For instance, if it is in initial menu-select state, it won't do anything but accept and evaluate your function selection:

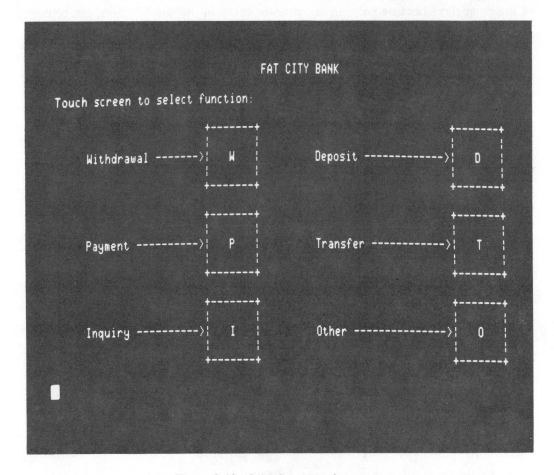

Figure 8-12. Initial menu-select state.

State analysis of the system requires enumeration of its possible states, conditions for changing state, and the characteristics of the system while in each state. This information is presented on a *state transition diagram* (see Figure 8-13).

Let's use the system for metric analysis again as an example. Consider a second generation of the Metric Support Package that first appeared in Figure 8-6. That rudimentary version was nothing more than a program to do simple linear regression on a file of metric indicators. Suppose that the second generation of the program were specified to include more and more sophisticated regression techniques to be applied as the sample size increased. Specifically,

- if the total number of samples is less than THRESHOLD1, the system should refuse to do any regression at all

- if the total number of samples lies in the range THRESHOLD1 to THRESHOLD2, the system should perform a linear regression, that is, try to fit the sample data to a curve of the form $y = Ax + B$

- if the total number of samples in the domain is greater than THRESHOLD2, the system should perform a non-linear regression, that is, try to fit the sample data to a curve of the form $y = A(x^n) + B$

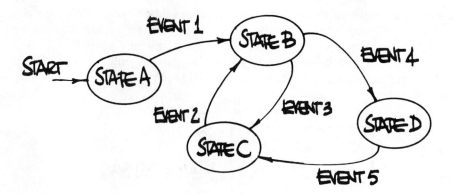

Figure 8-13. State transition diagram (abstract).

A state transition diagram to describe this varying behavior would look like Figure 8-14.

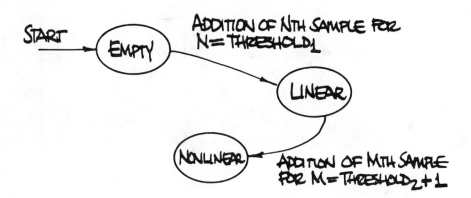

Figure 8-14. State transition diagram for second-generation Metric Support Package.

The diagram is made up of the possible states and the events that cause the system to switch from one state to another; it needs to be complemented with a set of state descriptions, one for each of the states shown.

8.5 The composite requirement model

I began this chapter with an analogy, the specification of a solid figure by three-view projection. Applying some of the terms used in the analogy, we now can consider each of the components of the requirement model a projection onto a different space. So, the function model — the partitioning into constituent functions and inter-function interfaces — can be thought of as a projection onto *function space;* the retained data model, a projection onto *information space;* and the state transition model, a projection onto *state space.*

It is reasonable to expect that one or even two of these projections may be null. The significance of there being no meaningful state model, for instance, is that the system in question does not have that dimension — it is always in the same state. Just as a two-dimensional entity might have no projection in one or two of the three views of an orthogonal projection scheme, so the system that lacks a dimension might well be described by fewer than three perspectives. Most systems, and virtually all small systems, can be adequately specified using two views, or possibly only one.

The composite requirement model (Figure 8-15) is the combined set of non-null component models.

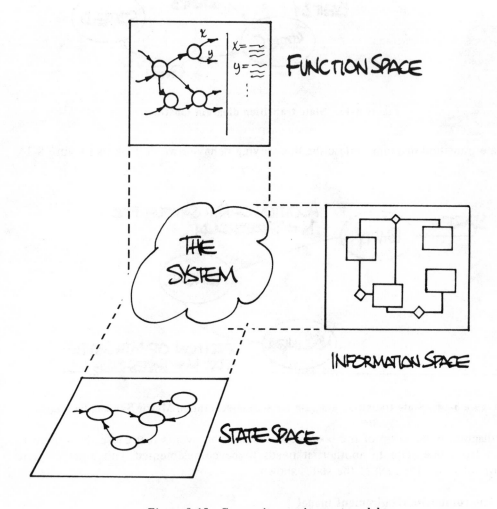

Figure 8-15. Composite requirement model.

The specification is now constructed around the skeleton formed by the composite model. The final specification consists of

- the function model (function network and dictionary of interfaces), together with one *minispecification* describing each elemental function (a minispecification is a concise statement of user policy rules governing a given elemental function)

- the retained data model (object diagram plus relationships), together with a census of all data elements allocated to each object

- the state transition diagram, together with a behavioral description of each of the states

8.6 Quantitative factors in specification modeling

Why this excursion into specification modeling? The kind of three-view modeling approach I have described in this chapter is an increasingly popular solution to the problem of building a graphic, concise, maintainable, and easily comprehensible system specification. Since the mid-1970s, system analysts have used this technique (called "structured analysis" in the jargon) to negotiate and document the user-developer contract. As such, it is principally a tool for *qualitative analysis* of the system to be developed. My reason for presenting the topic of requirement modeling in these pages is that it can also be a tool for *quantitative analysis:* Certain useful quantitative characteristics of the system can be derived directly from the requirement model.

A scheme for collecting and analyzing these *specification metrics* is the subject of the next chapter.

8.7 Selected references

The idea of using models for specification is not new. An early example is

Perrin, W.G. "Admiralty Orders of June, 1716." Royal Naval Archives, Greenwich, England.

In those orders, the high lords of the Admiralty required that before any ship be constructed, "the Master Shipwright of the yard where the same is to be performed to transmit to the Board not only a Model of such Ships as to their Dimensions, but how they propose to finish them as well within board as without so that we may inspect thereto and either dignify our approval of what shall be so proposed or order such Alteration to be made there as shall be judged necessary. . . ."

From that date onward, every capital ship, ship of the line, frigate, and brig was specified prior to construction with a precise scale model. The Admiralty models are preserved in the Greenwich Museum, and they are still today some of the finest examples I know of competent user-oriented specification.*

The basic specification modeling scheme in this chapter was adapted from

DeMarco, T. *Structured Analysis and System Specification.* New York: Yourdon Press, 1978.

The convention of modeling retained data as described in Section 8.3 was taken from

Flavin, M. *Fundamental Concepts of Information Modeling.* New York: Yourdon Press, 1981.

---

*If you are involved at all in the specification process, you owe it to yourself to visit Greenwich and see the models. Charge the whole trip to your company. Tell your boss I said it was okay.

Flavin's approach to information modeling is totally implementation independent, so it is particularly well suited to specification needs.

I know of no very good source on state transition modeling of software systems. Most of what is written on state models is oriented toward digital circuits. The notation used here for the state model is from

IEEE Standard Digital Interface for Programmable Instrumentation. New York: Institute of Electrical and Electronics Engineers, 1978.

9

SPECIFICATION
METRICS

Initial forecasts of cost and duration are called for nearly at the beginning of the project, when only the specification activity is under way. And so, the early indications of scope and complexity required as input to the forecasting process in Figure 9-1 must necessarily come from specification work. (I exclude consideration here of the pathological case in which estimates are demanded in the first microsecond of the project and must therefore be made without benefit of any input at all.)

The specification model described in Chapter 8 is an ideal source of such early indications (predictors). The estimating/forecasting process always takes for its input a miniature representation or perception of the task at hand. If you go about estimating in the traditional fashion, the miniature representation is your intuitive view of the system. If you follow the method of this book, that intuitive system model is replaced with a tangible formal specification model. Use of the formal paper model instead of the more casual intuitive version provides three benefits:

- The specification model is public; it can be refined and corrected by project members and users.
- The specification model has measurable characteristics that can be correlated to observed performance.

- The specification model is completed rather early in the project; even if forecasts are required prior to that time, completion of the model affords an early opportunity for correction of the forecasts.

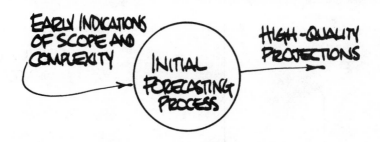

Figure 9-1. What drives early cost forecasting?

The specification model describes the requirement itself, not a particular way to meet that requirement. So, a quantitative analysis of the model will provide *a measure of true function to be delivered as perceived by the user.* This is precisely what Chapter 7 referred to as "Bang." Bang is a *function metric,* an implementation-independent indication of system size.

If your organization is already using modeling methods for specification, early predictive metrics can be derived directly from the models produced. If specification is conducted in the more loosely defined traditional method, then Metrics Group members will have to do some mechanical modeling to translate the requirement into model terms before they can observe the metrics.

9.1 Developing a quantifiable definition of Bang

Figure 9-2 portrays a development project as the creation of a complex "message to the computer," a coded system or program. The effort involved in this creation is a function of the information content of that message: The longer and more convoluted it is, the greater the effort to write it.*

The project receives as input another "message," the statement of requirement or specification. The central hypothesis of this chapter is that the information content of the output (the coded system) is a well-behaved function of the information content of the input (the specification). It follows from this that project effort, too, is a function of the information content of the specified requirement.

If you wrote specifications, even traditional specifications, in a highly uniform way from project to project, then you could do a straightforward information theory analysis of those specifications to determine the weight of content of each one. The analysis

---

*I am indebted to Lawrence Putnam for this useful abstraction [L.H. Putnam, "Software Cost Estimating," lecture sponsored by State of the Art Seminars and the DPMA Education Foundation, October 1981].

might be as simple as counting characters in the document. But traditional specifications and the procedures for building them are so lacking in structure that there is never uniformity from one specification to another. Some analysts wax loquacious in specification writing, and others are terse. Some projects have technical writers who can beef up the volume of the specification for a very low cost. Some projects have users who feel comfortable only if the specification passes a gross weight test. Some analysts include numerous examples and redundant statements of policy; others limit any specification to a single page. With so much variation in approach, the information content of the specification document is an inconsistent indicator of total information conveyed to the project.

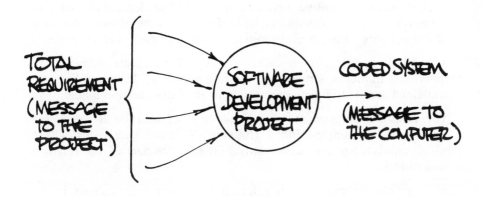

Figure 9-2. Project viewed as a message transform.

Specification models, on the other hand, are so highly structured that their information content *is* a useful quantitative indication of function to be delivered. No matter which of the prevailing standards you choose for specification modeling [DeMarco, 1978; Gane-Sarson, 1977; Ross-Brackett, 1977; Teichroew-Hershey, 1977], you can count on these characteristics:

- The completeness of the model is well defined. A given model can be demonstrated to be either complete or incomplete according to a set of unambiguous completion criteria.

- The size of the model approaches invariance with respect to arbitrary decisions of the modeler.

- The most likely effort (time, cost) to implement increases monotonically with increasing model size.

I must add a qualifier to this rosy picture: You can count on all these characteristics *only if you apply rigorous limits to redundancy.* There must be no single redundant statement in the entire set of lowest-level model components. This is a necessary precondition for the use of any metric derived from the model.

The size (information content) of the specification model is a direct measure of the quantity of usable system function to be delivered, a direct measure of Bang. The rest of this chapter is concerned with deriving a consistent and meaningful way to size models.

9.2 Counting primitive components of a model

A component of the specification model is considered *primitive* if it is not partitioned into subordinate components. Primitives are elemental by nature. Each part of the specification model (function model plus retained data model plus state transition model) is divided and subdivided and sub-subdivided down to the primitive level. Depending on what's being partitioned, you end up with one of six different types of primitive:

1. The elemental component of function is called a *functional primitive.* Functional primitives are the lowest-level pieces into which the requirement is divided using the function network (data flow diagram). Each functional primitive represents an undivided element of user policy governing transformation of input data into output data at one node of the network. Functional primitives are part of the function model.

2. The primitive data item is called a *data element.* Data elements are indivisible numbers, strings, and discrete variables. Data elements are contained in the data dictionary component of the function model.

3. The primitive component of retained data organization is the *object.* An object is a single-minded grouping of stored data items, all of which characterize the same entity. Objects are part of the retained data model.

4. The primitive component of retained data interconnectedness is the *relationship.* Relationships are part of the retained data model.

5. A primitive component of the system's required control characteristic is the *state.* States are part of the state transition model.

6. A second primitive component of the control characteristic is the *transition.* Transitions are part of the state transition model.

The six identified primitives of the specification model are summarized below:

Table 9-1
The Six Primitives of the Specification Model

Partitioning vehicle	is used to partition	to produce as primitive
1. Function network	system requirement	functional primitives
2. Data dictionary	system data	data elements
3. Object diagram	retained data	objects
4. Object diagram	retained data	relationships
5. State diagram	control characteristic	states
6. State diagram	control characteristic	transitions

Simple counts of these primitives (p-counts) provide the basic metrics from which a measure of Bang will be formulated in Section 9.4. Twelve essential p-counts are identified and defined on the next page.

FP   the count of functional primitives lying inside the man-machine boundary

FPM the count of modified manual functional primitives (functions lying outside the man-machine boundary that must be changed to accommodate installation of the new automated system)

DE   the count of all data elements existing at and inside the man-machine boundary

DEI the count of input data elements — those moving from manual primitives to automated primitives

DEO the count of output data elements — those moving from automated to manual primitives

DER the count of data elements retained (stored) in automated form

OB   the count of objects in the retained data model (automated portion only)

RE   the count of relationships in the retained data model (automated portion only)

ST   the count of states in the state transition model

TR   the count of transitions in the state transition model

TC_i the count of data tokens around the boundary of the ith functional primitive (evaluated for each primitive); a token is a data item that need not be subdivided within the primitive

RE_i the count of relationships involving the ith object of the retained data model (evaluated for each object)

As soon as the models are complete, the twelve p-counts should be recorded. (See Appendix A for an example of p-count data collection.)

9.3 Formulating a cost theory

You might reason, as I originally did, that all work in a project is work spent implementing one of the things counted by the various p-counts. This theory implies that you ought to base your function metric on *all* of the p-counts, with each one weighted by its own unique factor:

Tentative Bang =   FP × (Weighting-factor-for-FP) +
                    DE × (Weighting-factor-for-DE) +

$$\vdots$$

I have never had much success with this approach; it is statistically intractable and some of the counts overlap each other and measure redundantly.

A simpler and more productive way to characterize Bang is to choose one of the counts as a principal indicator and use the others to modify it or to indicate which of several alternate formulations will best serve. For most systems, FP ought to be the principal indicator. We'll obviously need to do something about the fact that all functional primitives are not equal — some require far more effort to implement than others. But if we can correct effectively for these variations (Section 9.4), corrected FP is almost a direct quantification of Bang.

If you feel comfortable with this last idea, you are probably most frequently involved in building what I call *function-strong* systems, systems that can be thought of almost entirely in terms of the operations they perform upon data. Some systems are not function-strong at all, but *data-strong*. A data-strong system is one that must be thought of (and specified and implemented) in terms of the data it acts upon, the data groupings, and the interrelationships, rather than the operations. Robotic applications are an extreme example of function-strong systems, and general inquiry applications an extreme example of data-strong systems. FP is an acceptable principal indicator for function-strong systems, but not for data-strong systems.

Rather than deal with a cumbersome measure that applies equally well (equally badly) to drastically different kinds of projects, I propose to divide all projects into a small number of domains and develop a different measure of Bang for each domain. The side effect of this is that you will not be able to compare projects in one domain very convincingly with projects in another. For most organizations, however, projects will all fall into only one or two domains.

The rationale for allocating projects to one domain or another can be based on two p-count ratios involving FP (count of functional primitives), RE (count of interobject relationships), and DEO (count of data elements flowing out of the automated region). The first ratio, RE/FP, is a reasonable measure of data-strength. The following interpretations of RE/FP have worked for me:

RE/FP < 0.7   implies the system is function-strong
RE/FP > 1.5   implies the system is data-strong

The middle range identifies *hybrid* systems, those whose size and complexity are strongly determined by both their function and data-relatedness.

The ratio DEO/FP is a measure of how much the system is concerned with data movement as opposed to computation. Commercial systems tend to have a high DEO/FP ratio, and scientific systems a low one. Extremely high ratios are typical of report generator applications. No actual values of the ratio are supplied to mark the transition from one domain to another, since most organizations use different languages for systems that vary along this dimension, and they allocate systems into domains based on programming language, rather than on the ratio. The DEO/FP ratio is useful, however, for identifying projects that should be classed with a different domain from the one that the language would indicate.

Allocation into domains using the two ratios is portrayed by Figure 9-3. The significance of the domains is this: New project cost forecasts should be extrapolated only from data collected on other projects from the same domain; formulation of the basic metrics may vary from one domain to another.

9.4 Formulating Bang for function-strong projects

The principal component of Bang for function-strong systems is FP. But raw FP is not an entirely satisfactory measure of effort for even the most function-strong system. The problem is that some functional primitives cost far more to implement than others. This seems quite reasonable since, clearly, some of the functions may be "larger" than others and/or substantially more complicated. The issue of largeness is treated in the next two subsections, and complexity in the third.

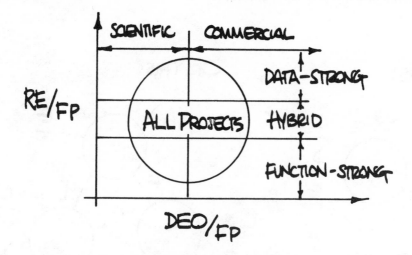

Figure 9-3. Systems allocated to domain by p-count ratios.

9.4.1 Using p-counts to achieve a uniform partitioning

During construction of the specification model, analysts will often be faced with a choice of whether to accept a given component as primitive or to partition it further (Figure 9-4). In a qualitative sense, the choice may not matter enormously; but if different projects make such decisions differently, their p-counts will be biased accordingly. The size correction of Section 9.4.2 will offset only a part of this variation.

The average token count per primitive

$$\mathrm{TCavg} = \frac{\Sigma \, TC_i}{FP}$$

can be used to control *uniformity of partitioning* over projects in each domain. Different models will be comparable as long as the modelers all respect the following rule:

> *Rule:* Leave a component as primitive only if no subsequent partitioning is possible or if subsequent partitioning will not reduce TCavg.

In order to apply this *Uniform Partitioning Rule,* you must look at the data arriving and departing at each node of the function model. Annotate each data flow arrival with the number of tokens that it carries to the node. A token might be a data element, or an amalgam of data elements that the function can treat as a whole. Annotate each departing data flow in the same fashion. Annotations for the alternative partitionings considered above are presented in Figure 9-5. The token count may be different at the opposite ends of the same data flow (this is the case of data flow J in Figure 9-5). Of course, it is exactly the same data departing from one node and arriving at the next. The reason for the different token counts is that one primitive needs to divide the data more finely than the other.

Note that you don't have to keep calculating TCavg in order to evaluate each candidate partitioning: TCavg is always reduced by a partitioning that replaces a single component with two or more, each of which has a lower TC than the original. So, for instance, in the example of Figure 9-5, the right-hand option can be selected without any knowledge of the rest of the network.

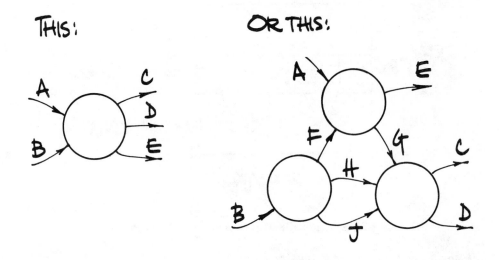

Figure 9-4. A partitioning decision.

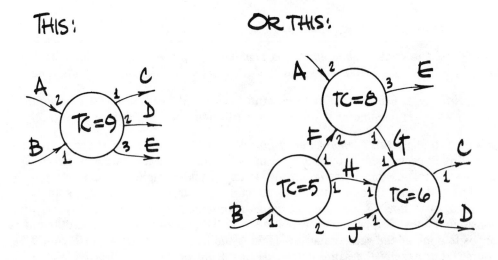

Figure 9-5. Application of the Uniform Partitioning Rule.

The Uniform Partitioning Rule may make the primitives of the specification model too small for the purposes or needs of the analysts: They might feel that such tiny minispecifications would be fragmented and unreadable. Should this happen, it seems reasonable that the model be expressed in whatever form is best for specification purposes, and that Metrics Group personnel then repartition it themselves in order to calculate Bang.

9.4.2 Correcting for variations in function size

Even with the Uniform Partitioning Rule, some primitive functions are naturally larger than others. A size correction for function-strong systems proceeds from observing that the function model has reduced the system to a series of linked primitive *transformations*. Each transformation creates output tokens from input tokens. The relative size (information content) of a transformation can be approximated as a function of TC_i, the number of tokens involved in the transformation. The problem of how size varies with TC is one that Halstead studied [Halstead, 1977]. An adaptation of the Halstead analysis leads to

SIZE (Primitive$_i$) is proportional to $TC_i \times \log_2 (TC_i)$

Table 9-2 provides weighting values calculated from this formula.

Table 9-2
Data Weighting for Size Correction of Functional Primitives

TC_i	Corrected FP Increment (CFPI)
2	1.0
3	2.4
4	4.0
5	5.8
6	7.8
7	9.8
8	12.0
9	14.3
10	16.6
11	19.0
12	21.5
13	24.1
14	26.7
15	29.3
16	32.0
17	34.7
18	37.6
19	40.4
20	43.2

Corrected FP (CFP) is now given by the expression:

$$CFP = \Sigma \ CFPI_i$$

9.4.3 Correcting for variations in complexity

While primitives do vary in complexity, they don't vary wildly or without discernible pattern. You can account for the variation adequately by assigning each primitive to a well-defined category and applying a correction factor unique to that category. I offer the following categories as relevant for most systems:

Separation: primitives that divide incoming data items

Amalgamation: primitives that combine incoming data items

Data Direction: primitives that steer data according to a control variable

Simple Update: primitives that update one or more items of stored data

Storage Management: primitives that analyze stored data, and act based on the state of that data

Edit: primitives that evaluate net input data at the man-machine boundary

Verification: primitives that check for and report on internal inconsistency

Text Manipulation: primitives that deal with text strings

Synchronization: primitives that decide when to act or prompt others to act

Output Generation: primitives that format net output data flows (other than tabular outputs)

Display: primitives that construct two-dimensional outputs (graphs, pictures, and so on)

Tabular Analysis: primitives that do formatting and simple tabular reporting

Arithmetic: primitives that do simple mathematics

Initiation: primitives that establish starting values for stored data

Computation: primitives that do complex mathematics

Device Management: primitives that control devices adjacent to the computer boundary

A beginning set of correction factors for the listed cases is presented below:

Table 9-3
Complexity Weighting Factors by Class of Function

Class	Weight	Class	Weight
Separation	0.6	Synchronization	1.5
Amalgamation	0.6	Output Generation	1.0
Data Direction	0.3	Display	1.8
Simple Update	0.5	Tabular Analysis	1.0
Storage Management	1.0	Arithmetic	0.7
Edit	0.8	Initiation	1.0
Verification	1.0	Computation	2.0
Text Manipulation	1.0	Device Management	2.5

Clearly, the last two entries in the right-hand column of this table can be accepted only with reservation; I suggest for these two cases that you correct with your own estimate based on type of computation or type of device.

Complexity weighting factors are, unfortunately, environment dependent. The relative complexity of arithmetic versus formatting functions, for example, is bound to be different in a COBOL environment from what you might expect in RPG. The values in the table should be adequate for a start, but you will need to develop your own set of weightings (and perhaps some of your own new classes).

9.5 Dealing with data-strong and hybrid systems

A data-strong system is one with a significant database, and most of the effort for this system type is allocable to tasks having to do with implementing the database itself. For such systems, the obvious p-count to base metric analysis upon is OB, the count of objects in the database. Again, some correction is required to account for the fact that some objects cost more to implement than others. The following table provides weights for each object as a function of its relatedness to other objects. You access the table by RE_i, the number of relationships at the object boundary:

Table 9-4
Relation Weighting of Objects

RE_i	Corrected OB Increment (COBI)
1	1.0
2	2.3
3	4.0
4	5.8
5	7.8
6	9.8

Bang is the sum of the corrected OB increments over all objects.

I have less experience with this table than with the table of weights for function-strong systems, but it should be an acceptable beginning. The correct weights for your environment will depend on the database management tools that you use, so some tailoring of Table 9-4 is clearly needed.

For the hybrid case, I have no better suggestion than to calculate Bang both ways ("Function Bang" and "Data Bang") and keep them separate. Project activities can be divided into those that are principally concerned with implementing (and analyzing and designing) system function, and those that are principally concerned with implementing (and analyzing and designing) the database. Now, the two Bang metrics can be used as predictors for the two different sets of activities. The net result is that the effort is treated as two projects, one function-strong and the other data-strong.

Of course, it's tempting to combine the two Bangs to form a composite predictor. The difficulty in making this work is that you need some procedure for relative scaling of Data and Function Bangs so that you can add them to form a meaningful result. You may be able to accomplish this for your own environment, but there is no way to do it for the general case.

9.6 Putting it all together

Bang is a quantitative indicator of net usable function from the user's point of view; it is implementation independent (within domain). The Bang metric has two major uses:

1. It is used as an early, strong predictor of effort. Bang is the independent variable that drives the cost model (discussed in Part III) to project development costs.

2.   It is used to calculate useful, productive effectiveness: Project Bang Per Buck. Optimization of Project BPB is the first of two quantitative goals that should be established for any development effort. (The second goal has to do with quality and is discussed in Part IV.)

Presented below are two algorithms for computation of Bang: the first for the function-strong environment, and the second for the data-strong environment.

ALGORITHM 1: Computation of Bang for Function-Strong Systems

Set initial value of FUNCTIONBANG to zero.
For each functional primitive in the function model:
    Compute Token Count around the boundary:
        For each incoming or outgoing data flow:
        1.   Determine how many separate tokens of data are visible within the primitive. This is not always the same as the count of data elements: If a group of data elements can be moved from input to output without looking inside, it constitutes only a single token.
        2.   Write Token Count at the point where the data flow meets the primitive. (Note that a data flow may involve a different number of tokens as perceived by its receiver from the number perceived by its creator.)
        Set Token Count = sum of tokens noted around the boundary.
    Use Token Count to enter Table 9-2 and record CFPI from the table.
    Allocate primitive to a Class.
    Access Table 9-3 by Class and note the associated Weight.
    Multiply CFPI by the accessed Weight.
    Add Weighted CFPI to FUNCTIONBANG.

ALGORITHM 2: Computation of Bang for Data-Strong Systems

Set initial value of DATABANG to zero.
For each object in the retained data model:
    Compute count of relationships involving that object. Use relationship count to access Table 9-4 and record COBI accessed.
    Add COBI to DATABANG.

Bang is a good predictor of some, but not all, project activities. Just as two different Bang metrics are required for database and function implementation work, so some activities require totally different metrics. It should be evident, for instance, that there is nothing in Bang that will make it a good predictor of conversion effort or retraining for new and modified manual activities. Such project tasks should be forecast from metrics based on the other p-counts.

A final caveat before moving on: The metrics derived from the specification model are only as good as the model itself. If it specifies something other than the system required, the metrics will be similarly off base. More important, if the requirement changes and the model is not revised and requantified, the metrics will be out of date and useless.

9.7 Tailoring the Bang formulation for your environment

Don't expect any of the numbers provided in this chapter to be exactly correct for your environment. I believe they will prove useful enough for you to depend on until you build your *own* versions of Tables 9-2, 9-3, and 9-4. Building these tailored sets of weighting factors is absolutely necessary to make your local formulation of Bang the strong and consistent predictor it is meant to be.

Since tailoring is an ongoing process, you must be sure to keep records of the basic p-count metrics (not just the corrected values). Otherwise, you will not be able to revise your corrections or recalculate for past projects.

Bang is meant to have important goal-significance to the project, and so it should be scaled for maximum impact on project personnel. I suggest you work into your Bang formulation a constant scaling factor so that Bang is dollar denominated and always larger than likely cost. The result will be that Project Bang Per Buck will be a unitless number larger than one, and will increase smoothly with improved project performance.

9.8 Further reading

There has been very little written so far on the subject of function metrics. The only source I know is

Albrecht, A.J. "Measuring Application Development Productivity." *Proceedings of the Joint SHARE/GUIDE/IBM Application Development Symposium.* Chicago: Guide International Corp., 1979.

The Albrecht function metrics are derived mainly from analysis of data flow across the man-machine boundary.

10

DESIGN: MODELING
THE SOLUTION

If the specification is considered a model of the requirement, the design could be considered a model of one particular way of meeting the requirement. The best designs are formal representations of the software to be implemented. When the design process goes awry, it's often because people lose sight of the representational character of a design. They come up instead with a sort of internal software organization philosophy and they call that a design. The philosophy is then viewed as a *starting point* for the implementation process, but nothing more. The meaningful decisions about software organization are improvised during implementation. And by the time the software is complete, the original philosophy statement has been totally abandoned.

If we have learned anything in three decades of building software systems, it is that this design on the fly leads to disaster. There is no substitute for thinking first and acting later, acting only when all the essential thinking is completed. Design is the thinking process that has to precede the action of implementation. A software design must therefore be thought of as a *rigorous blueprint for construction*. It must be put down on paper and kept up to date throughout the project. The design must dictate one and only one possibility for construction down to the level of the module. The roles of designer and implementor must be totally separated, even when the same person fills both roles.

The purpose of this chapter is to provide a capsule presentation of a model-oriented design approach that is consistent with the rigorous blueprint conception of design. The kind of model you build by following this approach provides certain measurable characteristics that will be useful for subsequent quantitative analysis.

10.1 The design model

I apply the word "design" to software in this very limited sense: *Design is the determination of what modules and what intermodular interfaces shall be implemented to fulfill the specified requirement.* Many people feel comfortable with this as a definition of program design, but wonder how it applies to systems design. For the purposes of this chapter, I shall treat systems very much the same as programs: Both are designed by decomposition down to the module level. The difference is that systems design will require a subsequent step, the recomposition of sets of modules into programs. The product of the decomposition into modules is what I call the *design model*.

The completed design model will consist of a *partitioning* of the whole into its component pieces (modules and sets of modules), and a *census of all interfaces* between those pieces. The design model is complemented by a set of internal module specifications describing the insides of the pieces. (This pattern should have started to look familiar by now.)

When I characterize the design as a blueprint, I mean to imply the existence of some rigid relationships between the design and the code implemented from that design. In particular,

- there is a one-to-one relationship between modules indicated in the design and modules implemented in the code

- there is a one-to-one relationship between intermodular connections indicated in the design and intermodular references (CALLS, PERFORMS, and so forth) in the code

- there is a one-to-one relationship between intermodular data interfaces indicated in the design and intermodular shared data implemented in the code

The last of these points is frequently misunderstood, so let me emphasize it: The design is not complete until each and every data item that must necessarily be shared by two modules is shown as an explicit interface between those modules. No matter how the item is shared (passed data, passed reference, or mutually accessible data in a common area), it must be shown. Any other interface convention would deprive us of important feedback about the validity of the partitioning and hence the design.

A design that ignores intermodular interfaces is grossly incomplete. It constitutes nothing more than lip service to the concept of design. Let's not mince words: Many project teams don't really design at all. They don't plan in advance of implementation; they just implement. The one-to-one relationships I've cited give you the chance to make an objective assessment of whether design was done in any meaningful sense. At the end of the project, your system should be able to pass this test:

<u>The Did-We-Really-Do-Design Test</u>

1. Put the design into a sealed envelope.
2. Give the completed software to an outside expert, someone who is not familiar with the original design.
3. Ask your expert to derive the design implied by the implementation.
4. Compare the derived design with the design in the sealed envelope.
5. If the two are not identical, you didn't really do design.

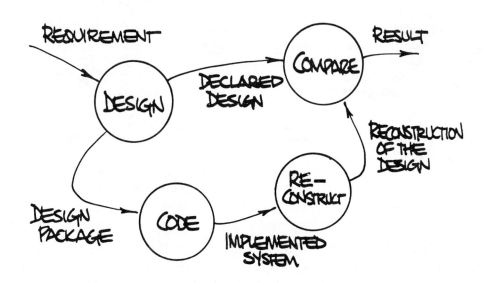

Figure 10-1. The Did-We-Really-Do-Design Test.

10.2 Synchronous and asynchronous models

The function networks presented in Chapter 8 were asynchronous: They provided no information about sequence or synchronization among the parts. The presumption of an asynchronous view is that all pieces are active at the same time and effectively self-synchronizing. This presumption is very natural for description of requirements, because it is so like the organization of a manual system in which each of the component activities is carried out by a different worker. Most people subconsciously think of computer systems as though they were made up of lots of little people, each one performing the task of a worker in simulation of the manual system that would exist if there were no computer.

You could design a system with the same asynchronous characteristic that was convenient in representation of the requirement. Such a design would allocate one task or co-routine for each elemental function of the specification model. You'd build the design model directly from the network of partitioned functions generated during analysis; you would only have to add the synchronizing flags and switches necessary for the system to control its own behavior. The resultant design would have strong one-to-one relationships to the code to be written *and* it would have similarly strong relationships to the original statement of the problem.

While an asynchronous implementation would be in many ways the most natural one (that is, most closely related to the underlying perception of the requirement), present-day technology discourages it. Most developers have such a healthy respect for the difficulty of building asynchronous systems that they would never introduce asynchronism into any application that could be built without it. I believe that this practice will change drastically during the 1980s: By the end of the decade, we'll be routinely building systems with a maximum of asynchronism, rather than a minimum. But for the present, most systems are designed to run as a single task, so the design activity entails creating a model of a *synchronous* implementation.

10.3 Design modeling notation

A common technique for synchronous design modeling is to represent a design as a hierarchy of modules:

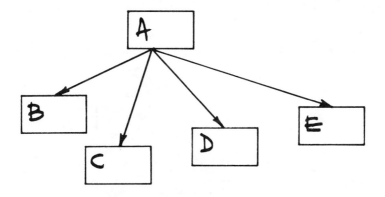

Figure 10-2. Hierarchy of modules.

The significance of one module's managing another in such a hierarchy — as module A manages modules B, C, and D — is that the manager starts the managed module by passing control to it. The managed module does its work and then returns control to its manager. At any given time, only one of the modules in the hierarchy is working. By convention, control is only passed up and down the hierarchy, never sideways.

Managed modules can themselves be managers of lower-level modules. So, a hierarchy like that of Figure 10-3 is meaningful. The modules still work one at a time. The hierarchy of Figure 10-3 is consistent with this kind of execution pattern:

     Module A does some work and then delegates control to
        Module B, which completes its task and returns to
     Module A, which then starts up
        Module C, which then starts up its subordinate
            Module E, which does its work and returns to
        Module C, which starts up
            Module F, which does its work and returns to
        Module C, which returns to
     Module A, which then starts up
        Module D . . .

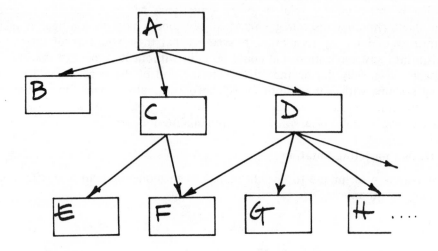

Figure 10-3. More complex hierarchy of modules.

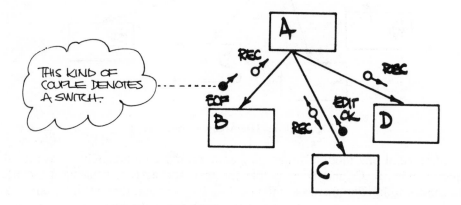

Figure 10-4. Coupling shown on the hierarchy.

The act of delegating control to a subordinate module (which will eventually return control to its manager) is called *invocation*. All the lines connecting modules on the hierarchy represent invocations, and all invocations are shown. So, the hierarchy of modules is a statement of all the possibilities for invocation of modules by other modules.

When two modules share data or control parameters, they are considered *coupled* to each other. Coupling can be shown by annotation alongside the invocation lines joining the two modules, as in Figure 10-4. In some notational conventions, coupling is shown with an interface table or matrix. The type of notation doesn't matter much — what's essential is that the coupling characteristic (the census of intermodular interfaces) be an integral part of the design.

In the two subsections below, you'll find a small sample problem. The first specifies the sample problem using a partial requirement model, and the second presents a design model, the beginning of a solution to the specified problem.

10.3.1 Example: Statement of requirement

Figure 10-5 again shows the top two levels of Metrics Group operations and establishes the context for the automated component that is our example: the second-generation Metric Support Package, or MSP-2. I've included the key data definitions along with the graphics.

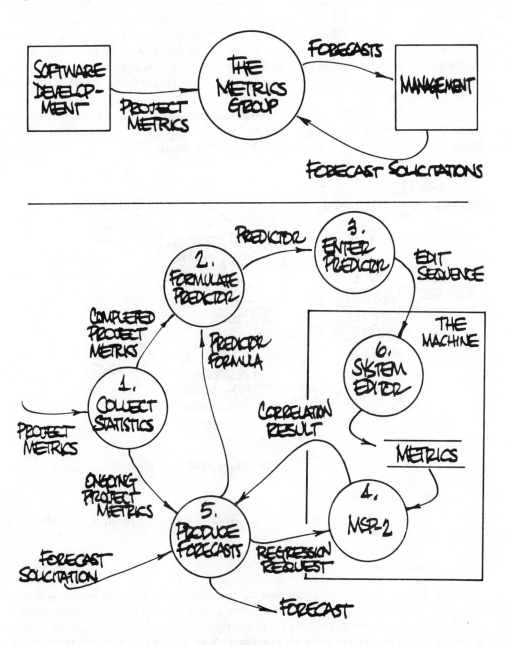

Regression-Request = Domain + Predictor-Name + Dependent-Variable-Name
Correlation-Result = Multiplier + Power + Standard-Error-of-Estimate

Figure 10-5. Top two levels of Metrics Group operations.

As you can see from Figure 10-5, a user interacts with the support package as part of his/her job of producing forecasts. The package is a set of statistical aids to help analyze data points (quantitative evidence from past projects) stored in Project-Metrics. The user solicits such analysis by submitting a Regression-Request to MSP-2. This request specifies which domain of projects (e.g., COBOL PROJECTS) should be studied. The Regression-Request also conveys to MSP-2 which particular metrics are to be studied. One of these, the dependent variable, is the one the user suspects might be strongly influenced by the other, the predictor. MSP-2 uses statistical regression to determine whether there is any correlation between the two and, if there is, how strong the correlation is. Its response is the Correlation-Result, a regression equation together with an indication of scatter (Standard-Error-of-Estimate) of the empirical points around the prediction.

Figure 10-6 is a third-level partitioning that shows the insides of MSP-2. All that's needed to complete the specification of MSP-2 is three minispecifications defining user policy for each of the three primitive functions of Figure 10-6.

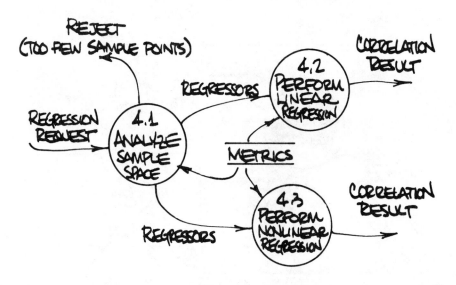

Figure 10-6. Details of MSP-2.

10.3.2 Example: The design model

Part of a design model describing a proposed implementation of MSP-2 is presented in Figure 10-7.

10.3.3 Design model granularity

Nothing in this chapter has given you even a clue about *how* you ought to design, or about what distinguishes a good design from a bad one. (The references cited in Section 10.5 do address these subjects.) My purpose in this chapter is only to indicate what a design model is, so that later observations about metrics derived from the design model will make some sense.

One procedural aspect of design is critical if we ever expect to have design metrics that are meaningful from project to project: We need to achieve a common understanding on design granularity, an answer to the question, When is the partitioning into modules complete? I propose this rule:

Rule: The design partitioning is complete when the modules are small enough to be implemented without any further partitioning. A simple test of adherence is that no implemented module shall need an internal named procedure (except for a PERFORMed loop body in COBOL).

If there is any reason to further partition a module, that partitioning should be done at design time. If the coder finds it necessary to introduce submodules, that is a signal that the design is not complete, and the design activity should be reopened.

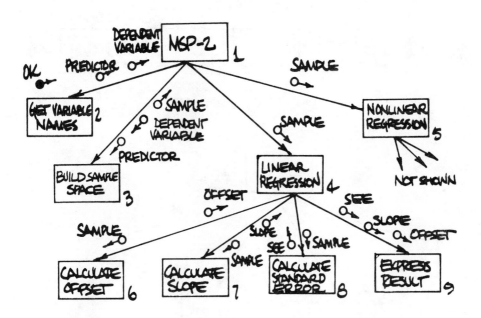

Figure 10-7. Design model for MSP-2.

10.4 The version plan: Model of a delivery strategy

Modern development practices often include a technique called *top-down implementation* or *versioned implementation*. In this scheme, subsets of the complete system are delivered as versions. Version planning is typically noted directly on the design model by drawing version boundaries, as in Figure 10-8. In this case, Version 0 will deliver two real modules (1 and 2). Any modules invoked by Version 0 modules will be replaced by *stubs,* dummy modules used only in incomplete versions.

A complete version plan of the system depicted in Figure 10-8 will consist of a set of version descriptions; each version description will consist of a marked-up design

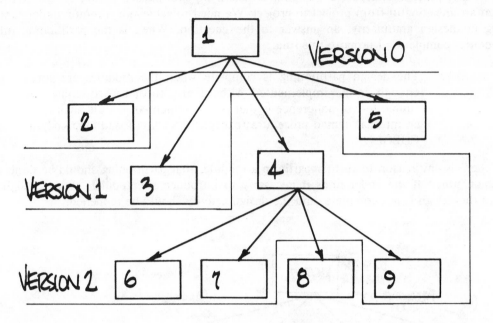

Figure 10-8. Version plan for MSP-2.

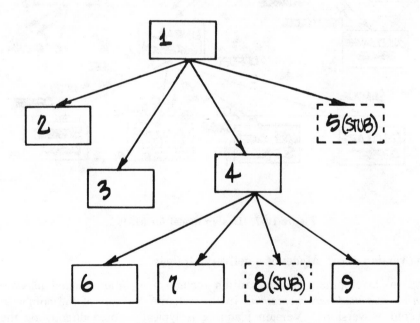

Figure 10-9. Version 2 of MSP-2.

model, together with stub descriptions and some sort of description of expected version behavior. Consider Version 2 of the MSP-2 utility shown in Figure 10-9. This version includes seven real modules (1, 2, 3, 4, 6, 7, and 9) and two stubs (5 and 8). The behavior of the version is this: Regardless of sample size, the program always does linear regression; the standard error of estimate is not calculated at all, but simply indicated as 0.

Versioned implementation has many advantages, including incremental testing, early visibility of partial products, and spreading out of machine time requirements. All of these are nice but not terribly relevant here. What *is* relevant is the quantitative information that can be extracted from the version plan, and the use of this information to deduce what the completion and acceptance of a given version suggests about the state of the whole implementation effort. Metrics derived from the version plan and from the design are described in the following chapter.

10.5 Selected references

Three valuable references on design and, in particular, on the construction of the kind of design models described here are

Myers, G.J. *Reliable Software Through Composite Design*. New York: Petrocelli/Charter, 1975.

Page-Jones, M. *The Practical Guide to Structured Systems Design*. New York: Yourdon Press, 1980.

Yourdon, E., and L.L. Constantine. *Structured Design: Fundamentals of a Discipline of Computer Program and Systems Design*. Englewood Cliffs, N.J.: Prentice-Hall, 1979.

For a discussion of versioned implementation, see Chapter 4 of

Yourdon, E. *Managing the Structured Techniques*. New York: Yourdon Press, 1979, pp. 58-85.

11

DESIGN METRICS

In order for projected time and cost to converge acceptably to the actual values, as shown in Figure 11-1, the Metrics Group must be able to generate successively more and more accurate projections as development proceeds. Cost projections made during design have to improve upon those made during the specification activity. So the design-time projections must be based on stronger metrics. This chapter is concerned with metrics derived from the design and techniques for using these metrics to come up with improved projections.

The Bang predictor described in Chapter 9 is implementation independent, a measure of function to be delivered without regard to *how delivered*. There are always options available to the design team, options that may have a substantial effect on the total effort to deliver. The trick to producing improved projections at design time is to incorporate into the projection process information about the options selected. This involves calculating the first *implementation-dependent* predictor. Since it is meant to indicate the magnitude of effort implied by the design, I call this predictor *Design Weight*. The procedure for use of such a predictor requires the steps listed on the following page.

1. observation of primitive metrics (derived, in this case, from the design model)

2. computation of the composite predictor (Design Weight) by using some sort of weighted formulation

3. collection of values of the predictor for a sample of projects, along with observed costs and times to implement each project

4. correlation of the predictor to the quantities to be projected, using the techniques of Part III (this will result in a prediction-line equation)

5. projection of new development costs from the prediction-line equation and the observed value of the predictor

The first two steps are discussed in Sections 11.1 and 11.2.* The subsequent sections of the chapter deal with some incidental design metrics and their use.

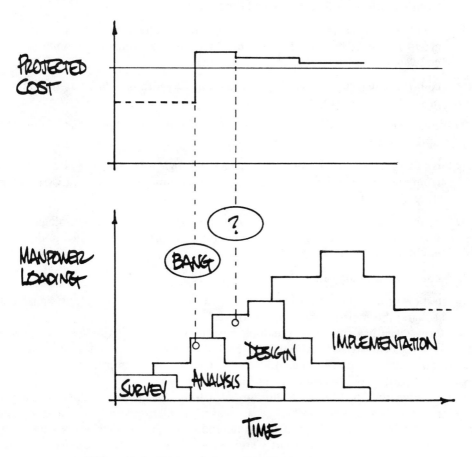

Figure 11-1. What design predictor can be used to improve on the Bang-based predictor?

---

*The subsequent steps are identical to steps in the exploitation of any metric, as described in Part III.

11.1 Primitive design metrics

The completed design model should consist of a hierarchy of modules with all connections and couples indicated, together with some sort of design data dictionary describing all data items (couples, tables, data areas, files, database(s), and structured data types). The basic metrics, observable from such a model, include these:

MO count of modules

CO count of intermodular normal connections (a normal connection is a reference from inside one module to another *whole* module, that is, a CALL or PERFORM or other subroutine invocation)

DA_i count of data tokens explicitly shared along normal connections to and from module *i* (evaluated for each module)

SW_i count of control tokens (switches) shared along normal connections to and from module *i* (evaluated for each module)

EN count of *encapsulated data groups* in the design model (an encapsulated data group is a data area made available to a limited number of modules; it is equivalent to labeled COMMON in Fortran)

EW_i count of encapsulation width of data group *i* (width is defined as the number of modules with access to the group)

ED_i count of encapsulation depth of data group *i* (depth is defined as the number of data elements contained in the group)

PA count of pathological connections (a pathological connection is a reference from inside one module to part of another module, that is, a GOTO to an internal label)

PD_i count of pathological data tokens shared by module *i* (a pathological data token is one that is obtained from a module not connected to module *i* by any normal connection)

PS_i count of pathological control tokens shared by module *i*

As an illustration of data collection for these metrics, consider the simple design model of Figure 11-2 and the metric values shown there.*

The term *token* has the same meaning here as it had in Chapter 9: a data item that is treated as an indivisible whole by the module. So, again, a data item may be counted as one token by one of the modules that uses it, and as *n* tokens by another. Such is the case of the couple called X1 in Figure 11-2.

If you find at the completion of the design activity that you cannot count each of the metrics listed above, you don't have a measurement problem; you have a *design* problem. Your developers have probably gone about design in such a way that values of DA, SW, PD, and PS are not apparent. They probably have concentrated on the control structure and ignored all data sharing. Send them back to work. The notion that design is complete even though no one has done a methodical study of the resultant data sharing among modules is simply ludicrous. Design is the organization of a

---

*See Appendix B for explanation of the notation.

selected implementation into modules and interfaces between modules. The only way to evaluate a design is by examining the volume and complexity of the interfaces, specifically of the data interfaces. If this kind of evaluation has not been performed, there is no reason for believing in the design: An unevaluated design is a bad design.

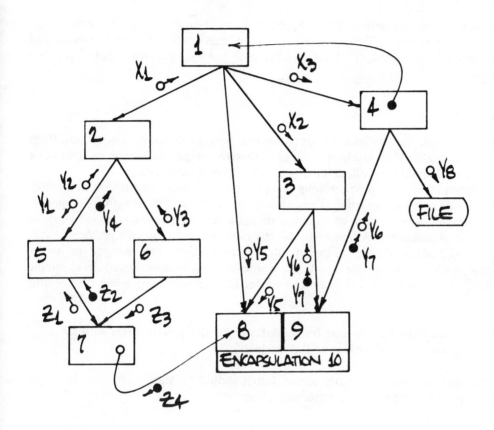

METRICS

$$MO = 9$$
$$CO = 11$$
$$PA = 1 \text{ (module 4 to 1)}$$
$$DA_1 = 4 \text{ (X1, X2, X3, Y5} - \text{one token each)}$$
$$DA_2 = 7 \text{ (X1} = 3, Y2 = 2, Y1 = 1, Y3 = 1)$$
$$SW_2 = 1 \text{ (Y4)}$$
$$DA_7 = 4 \text{ (Z1} = 2, Z3 = 2)$$
$$SW_7 = 1 \text{ (Z2)}$$
$$PS_7 = 1 \text{ (Z4, stolen from module 8)}$$

Figure 11-2. Example of design metric data collection.

From my experience conducting public surveys to collect metrics, I know that lots of organizations don't do any real design. The symptom has been in the managers' responses to my request for values of DA, SW, PD, or PS: They write "Not Applicable" in the space provided. There is a small human tragedy in that sad phrase, "Not Applicable." It means that someone has convinced the poor manager that there just wasn't time to do a complete design, to evaluate and minimize intermodular data dependencies. The manager has once again been sold the outrageous bill of goods that design is a luxury available only to those projects not under time pressure, that hurry-up projects are obliged to move immediately into coding without benefit of any meaningful design thinking.

If you find yourself writing "Not Applicable" in place of any of the basic design metrics, you're in trouble. That response has grim implications for the testability and maintainability of your product. Start looking now for excuses, scapegoats, and nice places to hide.

11.2 Design Weight

Once the basic design metrics are collected, you need some way to put them together into a single value of Design Weight. Design Weight will serve as a predictor of remaining implementation effort, chiefly effort of coding and testing.

As a result of modern programming practice, most modules in a typical domain lie in a fairly narrow range of lengths. If any two modules of the same length took approximately the same effort to write and debug, then Design Weight could be set equal to MO, the count of modules. Attempts to use the raw module count as a predictor have, however, proved disappointing. Substantially different efforts are required to implement modules whose lengths are equal, but whose internal structures vary from simple to complex. A much better predictor can be formulated by taking advantage of this observation:

>   *Rule:*   Implementation time for modules of similar length varies with the
>   number of decisions in the module.

The relationship may not be strictly linear, but it should be statistically well behaved: More decisions always imply more implementation time.

11.2.1 Predicting decision count inside a module

One way to come up with a total decision count for the design is to pseudocode each and every module. But this would be a time-consuming business, and it would delay the computation of Design Weight considerably. Worse, much of the pseudocoding might not be of great benefit to the project beyond its metric use, so the cost of the work would be exclusively chargeable to the measurement activity.

How can we derive the decision count, or at least a good estimate of it, from the design itself? One way is to assume that the internal structure of each module will be isomorphic to the data structure at its boundary. This idea was first suggested by Jean-Dominique Warnier [Warnier, 1976].

The full set of isomorphisms between data structure and process structure is presented in Figure 11-3.

This data structure: | Implies this process structure:

{ A }

[B | C]

(D)

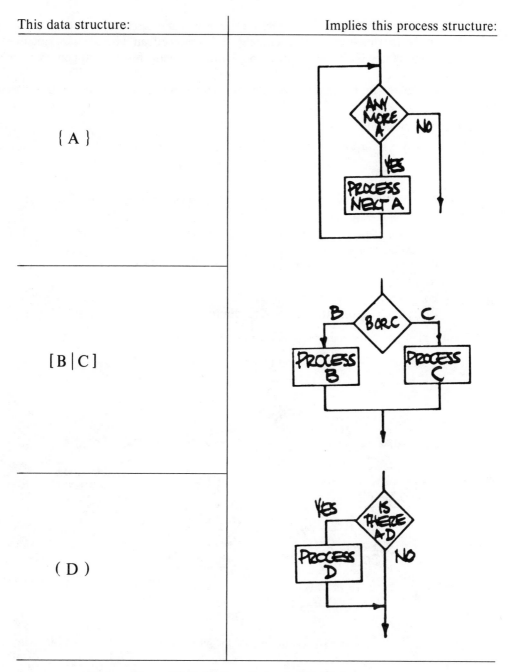

Figure 11-3. Data and process parallels.

The reasoning behind Warnier's observation is this: All decisions in the code are based on the data processed by the code; the structure of that data — that is, the associations among its component pieces — gives a strong hint as to how the code could be (should be?) written. For example, if there is a repeated substructure in the arriving data, there should be a loop in the code to deal with it. If there is an option in the data, a field that may or may not be present, then there will certainly have to be an IF-ELSE sequence to deal with the two situations, item present and item not present. In Figure 11-3, as well as in the rest of this chapter, I have used an abbreviated notation to describe data structure. If the notation is not familiar, please refer to Appendix B for its explanation.

The procedure for predicting decision counts from the data structure observed at the modular boundary is this:

Start with the decision count = 0.

1. Write down a data dictionary formulation of all data arriving at the module boundary. Express the result at the token level (from the viewpoint of the module).

2. Analyze the data structure of the result, applying the following rules:

    a) For each iteration in the data structure, add one to the decision count.
    b) For each two-way selection (EITHER-OR) in the data structure, add one to the decision count.
    c) For each n-way selection in the data structure, add $n - 1$ to the decision count.
    d) For each option (data item that may or may not be present) in the data structure, add one to the decision count.

Figure 11-4 presents a simple design model segment.

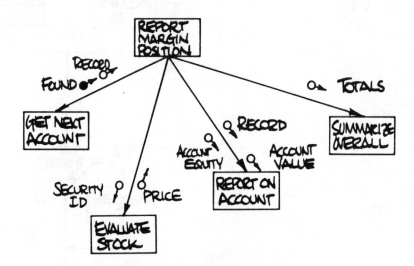

Figure 11-4. Design model segment.

The formulation of all data arriving at the boundary of the top module is

Boundary Data of Module Report-Margin-Position = Record + (Found) + Price
where   Record =   Acct# + Customer-Name + Customer-Address +
                Account-Type + {Stock-Position} + Margin-Advance
and   Stock-Position = Security-ID + Shares-Held
and   Account-Type = [REGULAR | PREMIUM | THIRTYDAY]

The predicted decision count for this case is 4. A possible pseudocoding of this module is shown below. The actual count of decisions there is indeed 4.

```
clear all Totals
GETNEXTACCT [ : Record, Found]
while Found:

        start with Account-Value and Account-Equity  = 0
        for each Stock-Position in Record

                EVALUATESTOCK [Security-ID of Stock-Position : Price]
                add (Price × Shares-Held of Stock-Position) to Account-Value

        Account-Equity = Account-Value − Margin-Advance
        REPORTONACCT [Record, Account-Value, Account-Equity]
        depending on Account-Type:

                REGULAR:        Add Account-Equity to Total-Regular
                PREMIUM:        Add Account-Equity to Total-Premium
                THIRTYDAY:    Add Account-Equity to Total-Thirty-Day
SUMMARIZEOVERALL [Totals]
```

In the notation of Appendix B, the predicted decision count is always equal to the count of left curly braces, selection separators ($|$), and left parentheses. Regardless of notation,

Predicted-Decision-Count is equal to:

the count of ITERATIONS OF operators +
the count of OR operators +
the count of OPTIONAL operators

The procedure for predicting decision counts assumes that a module will be coded to respect the isomorphism suggested by Warnier. If it's coded differently, the decision count is likely to be higher. Since the effort to implement is a monotonically increasing function of decision count, the implementor will almost certainly strive to minimize the number of decisions, and will be led, consciously or unconsciously, to the Warnier structure.

There are cases in which the estimated decision count will be wrong. Consider, for example, the module called Store-Larger-Value in Figure 11-5. Here the boundary data has no iteration, selection, or option, so the expected decision count should be 0. But the actual decision count must be at least 1, since there is a two-way decision based on a comparison of the two values. The module Report-Margin-Position in Figure 11-4 might have ignored the value of Account-Type, or been interested in only one of the possible values, in which case the actual count of decisions would have been less than the predicted number. These situations arise seldom enough to be ignored, *provided that modules are kept small.* As module size increases, both the probability and the effect of such exceptions will rise unacceptably.

11.2.2 Computing the composite predictor

Design Weight is a simple sum of the Module Weights over the set of all modules in the design:

Design Weight $= \Sigma$ Module Weight$_i$

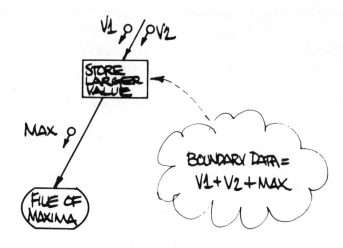

Figure 11-5. Counterexample.

The weight (cost predictor) of each module is now a function of the token count at its boundary, and the predicted decision count inside. The following table can be used, at least initially, to approximate this function:

Table 11-1
Module Weights

Decision Count →		0	1	2	3	4	5	6	7
Token Count →	1	1.0	1.1	1.2	1.4				
	2	2.4	2.6	2.9	3.3	3.7			
	3	4.0	4.4	4.9	5.4	6.2	7.2		
	4	5.8	6.3	7.1	7.9	9.0	10.5	12.5	
	5	7.8	8.5	9.5	10.7	12.2	14.1	16.8	21.5
	6	9.8	10.7	12.0	13.4	15.3	17.8	21.2	27.0
	7	12.0	13.0	14.6	16.4	18.7	21.8	26.0	33.1
	8	14.3	15.6	17.4	19.6	22.3	26.0	31.0	39.6
	9	16.6	18.1	20.3	22.7	25.9	30.2	36.0	46.0
	10	19.0	20.7	23.2	26.0	29.6	34.6	41.2	52.6
	11	21.5	23.4	26.2	29.5	33.5	39.1	46.7	59.6
	12	24.1	26.3	29.4	33.0	37.6	43.9	52.3	66.8
	13	26.7	29.1	32.6	36.6	41.7	48.6	58.0	74.0
	14	29.3	31.9	35.7	40.1	45.7	53.3	63.6	81.2
	15	32.0	34.9	39.0	43.8	49.9	58.2	69.4	88.6

All the information necessary to compute Design Weight is available as soon as the design is complete. Evaluating the formulation for boundary data for each module is a mechanical task, and can be routinely added to the designer's responsibilities. Since minimizing decision counts and Design Weight should be one of the designer's goals anyway, the cost of computing the Design Weight is correctly allocable to the project, not to the Metric Function.

11.3 A tailored Design Weight formulation

As a refinement to the simple measure of Design Weight, you might consider grouping modules into classes and applying a correction factor for each class (just as we did in correcting FP Increment in Chapter 9). Whether you take this tack or not, you ought to apply a correction factor at least to library modules (reused code or software tools). In Chapter 12, you'll find some starting values for discounting reused code. Obviously, the right discounting value for your environment will depend on the quality of the library modules you use, their size, and their portability (capability of being used without change).

The decision-weighted values in Table 11-1 will have to be tailored to each language. Module implementation cost always increases as the number of decisions increases, but the *rate* at which cost increases is language dependent: Some languages provide drastically simpler decision constructs than others. Near the end of Chapter 12, I'll describe a scheme for evaluating decision cost in a given domain from a study of the code itself and of the effort required to implement it. Once the decision cost graph is drawn, it should be used to rescale the values of Table 11-1. In rescaling, retain the values in the first column, and recompute each successive column (multiply the first column times the penalty value of the associated number of decisions).

11.4 Metrics of design compliance

The major risk in using design metrics is not that the metrics will prove to be unreliable predictors, but rather that the design itself will prove to be an unreliable indication of the shape of the eventual system. Clearly, any metric derived from the design is invalid in predicting characteristics of a project that ignores that design. Ignoring design is not a rare occurrence: Most software projects seem to implement with little or no regard for the design. Here are some of the reasons most frequently cited:

> "The design wasn't meant to *constrain* the implementors, only to give them a push in the right direction."

> "The design seemed okay *at design time,* but when we actually set out to implement it, we had to abandon some of its ivory tower concepts."

> "We did implement the module structure suggested by the design; it was only the data interfaces we ignored."

> "The design was only a political statement, something to satisfy management that we'd done all our thinking before coding. The last thing we ever intended was to implement according to the simple-minded scheme presented to management. Anything management could understand was bound not to be real world."

The one excuse I've never encountered was that the design could have been enforced, but wasn't. Good designs don't need to be enforced, and bad designs can't be.

The entire problem of noncompliance stems from a defeatist attitude toward design, the idea that nobody can honestly expect to make design decisions in advance — only the coder really sees how the system ought to fit together. It shouldn't matter that your implementors have such an attitude, because a single good design will convert them. The problem arises when *the designers* have that attitude. They will hurry through design with their brains turned to OFF and produce something for sake of appearances only. The design process is a total waste of time in such cases, and you'd be better off to skip it altogether and go directly into coding, just as your designers would really prefer to do anyway. By "better off" I mean you would waste less time and effort in arriving at the debacle that is likely to be the result of your project.

Noncompliance is always the result of bad design. But bad design itself is a management problem, a direct result of allowing the design-as-fiction-only attitude to survive. You can kill that attitude utterly by enforcing a single rule in your projects:

Rule: No deviation from the design shall be made unilaterally by the implementor. Any change in modular structure or data interface must be approved by the designer, and must result in a complete update of the design product.

With such a rule in force, there is no option but to comply. The design remains, throughout the project, a correct statement of how the system is expected to be built. More important, interface decisions are made by the designer, who has a view of the whole picture, not the coder, who has a highly local view. Where the coder might have been perfectly willing to add dozens of new data items to an interface, the designer is inclined to go back to the drawing board and revise the modular structure to avoid over-coupling. The system that emerges is of far higher quality.

As a side effect, the highly visible design revision process affords a controllable mechanism for re-evaluating the design metrics. The number of changes to the design is itself a design metric, a clear indicator of how realistic the design was in the first place.

It's all very well to talk about rules, but how can you be sure that the rules are followed? Since you can't control what you can't measure, your ability to control design compliance depends upon having a valid metric of compliance. An obvious indication of noncompliance is the production of coded portions of the system that deviate from the basic design metrics. To detect this, you will need to count the basic indicators on the design model and compare them to the same indicators collected from the code itself. Gross variations mean that the design is being ignored.

The most subtle and insidious form of noncompliance is in the data interface. The designer might have decided, for instance, that a given module needed to share only three data items with other modules (DA = 3; SW = 0; PD = 0; PS = 0). If the coder violates this assumption by modifying these or adding other data elements without informing anyone, the true coupling may be far worse. We need some simple metric to alert us to this situation. An easily obtainable metric of this abuse is the simple count of decisions in the coded module. Almost any addition to the boundary data flow will cause the number of decisions coded to exceed the number expected from the design. There are cases in which the actual count will exceed the expected count without noncompliance, and there are limited kinds of noncompliance that won't be detected by this measure. But for most cases, we can assume with small loss of accuracy that

$$\text{Design Compliance} = \frac{\text{Expected Decision Count}}{\text{Actual Decision Count}}$$

This metric can be calculated on a module-by-module basis, ensuring that noncompliance is detected at the earliest possible moment. Observing decision counts ought to be a normal metric activity during coding anyway (see Chapter 12), so the measure of design compliance is largely free of cost.

11.5 Selected references

An excellent reference on design metrics is one that I mentioned earlier as a source of design methods:

Myers, G.J. *Reliable Software Through Composite Design.* New York: Petrocelli/Charter, 1975.

In the final chapter, Myers introduces a metric of design quality, one that he implies is a strong predictor of maintenance cost. When his book first came out, many organizations enthusiastically adopted the design quality metric. But it suffers from an absolutely fatal flaw: *Its use requires a little bit of common sense.* (There are some perfectly nonsensical things you can do to your design that the metric doesn't take proper account of.) For this reason, Myers's design quality metric has not become a generally accepted design tool.

Two additional works on quantification of design quality are

Yin, B., and J. Winchester. "The Establishment and Use of Measures to Evaluate the Quality of Software Designs." *Proceedings of the Software Quality and Assurance Workshop.* New York: Association for Computing Machinery, 1978.

Henry, S., and D. Kafura. "Software Metrics Based on Information Flow." *IEEE Transactions on Software Engineering,* Vol. SE-7, No. 5 (September 1981), pp. 510-18.

The Henry and Kafura paper reports on a quality metric that proved to be an acceptable predictor of the maintenance cost of modules in the UNIX[†] operating system.

For a complete discussion of isomorphism between data and process structures, look at Chapters 3 through 6 of

Warnier, J.D. *Logical Construction of Programs,* 3rd ed., trans. B.M. Flanagan. New York: Van Nostrand Reinhold, 1976, pp. 22-82.

[†]UNIX is a registered trademark of Bell Laboratories.

12

IMPLEMENTATION METRICS

Twelve chapters into a discussion of the metric properties of systems, we come at last to the issue of metrics derived from code, specifically to the issue of counting lines of code. If you had hoped never to have your nose rubbed again in that tired old idea, I'm sorry to disappoint you. I concur with most of the objections to using lines of code as a fundamental measure of system size. But you must still count lines of code (and other measurable properties of the code) in order to maintain a continuing metric grip on projects. Part of this is due to an effect that I have modestly named

DeMarco's Theory of Cost Migration

Costs will migrate out of any activity that is measured more carefully than its neighboring activities.

If you measure exactly the work of design, for instance, and then don't measure the coding at all, people will soon catch on. Their conscious or unconscious reaction will be to push as much of the work as possible into the unmeasured activity.

Since we counted all the products and costs of the analysis and design, we must carry on evenhandedly and continue to count the products and costs of each successive activity. We will have to keep measuring even after the initial system has been delivered. Indeed, the most obvious example of cost migration is one that moves out of the project entirely and into the maintenance process: Since project development is monitored much more exactly than maintenance (which is often considered uncontrollable anyway), project members rush to deliver products that may contain known failings, failings that must then be corrected during maintenance.

In addition to keeping costs from wandering, the implementation metrics provide information for a mid-project schedule correction. A strong correction at this point is essential if we are ever to meet the required EQF goals.

12.1 The Chump metric

The first implementation metric is observable from the very beginning of coding. As soon as the first lines are being written, you can stop by the programmer area and note the value of

Chump: a binary metric whose value is set to TRUE if the code is written in assembly language and FALSE if not

Chump is an important predictor of many project characteristics, including overall success and product maintainability. It is also a strong indicator of what your metric policy ought to be. I've stressed up to this point that measurement should be an essential ingredient of the project mix. But if Chump is true, then measurement is your enemy. Certainly any quantitative assessment of Project Bang Per Buck can only make you look bad. Stop measuring immediately.

12.2 Metrics derived from completed code

We require from the code some sort of quantitative indication of the amount of work remaining. This work consists mostly of testing, version assembly, and documentation. The scheme proposed here involves taking separate measures of the volume and complexity of code and producing from these a composite predictor. This mid-project predictor, called Implementation Weight, can then be used to forecast remaining effort and cost in the project (see Figure 12-1).

12.2.1 The concept of Code Volume

How big is a given piece of code? Among the many indications of size proposed over the years are lines of executable code, lines of executable code plus declarations, source records (including comments), and bytes of object code. At least one human being somewhere has had some success with each of these measures. Most practitioners, however, end up feeling that such measures are simplistic and misleading indicators of the effort involved.

In looking for a better indicator, I return to Lawrence Putnam's observation that *code is a message to the computer*. Information theory gives us a handle on how to size the information content of any message. Applying this theory will allow us, after fairly superficial analysis, to make statements like this one: "Module A21 carries 475 bits of information to the computer." I'm going to refer to the information content of a piece of code as its *Volume*. The rest of this chapter will proceed under the following hypothesis:

The Volume Hypothesis

Efforts required to write, test, and document a piece of code are monotonically increasing functions of the Volume of that piece of code.

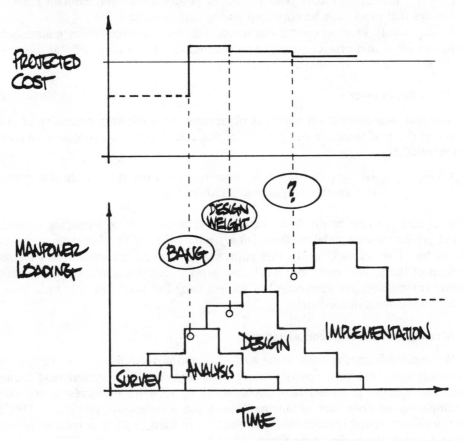

Figure 12-1. Using the composite implementation predictor.

Since all the information in the module has to be put there by the coder, digested and verified by the tester, and analyzed, justified, and regurgitated by the documenter, the hypothesis has a good intuitive basis. (It also has an empirical basis, as you will see below.) Note that the Volume Hypothesis does not say that effort is directly proportional to Volume, only that effort increases smoothly with increasing Volume. That is all that is required to make use of Volume as a predictor. We can study past projects to derive the correlation between Volume and cost, and use that correlation to extrapolate cost of future projects, as described in Part III.

Subsection 12.2.3 will add a correction factor based on code complexity. Until we apply that correction, please bear with me by assuming (marvelous what you can do with a little abstract thinking) that all the projects under study in a given domain are of absolutely equal complexity. The Volume Hypothesis clearly breaks down if you try to apply it across domains: No fair comparing development of multiple-site real-time software with development of single-user quick-and-dirty reporting programs.

12.2.2 Code Volume quantified

The Volume, or information content, of a message is quite different from the number of bits that the computer happens to use to store the message. The computer's storage scheme is, after all, a function of the representations chosen for data items and instructions. The computer might elect to store each text character in eight bits of memory, but if the characters stored were taken out of a Morse Code sequence, for instance, each one would convey much less than eight bits. The information content of a message is some function of the number of pieces in the message and of the information space over which each piece may vary. In Morse Code, the information space has three possibilities (dot, dash, or space).

In the mid-seventies, Maurice Halstead published the results of his lengthy effort to size programs using information theory as a basis and empirical verification as proof [Halstead, 1977]. Since then, numerous independent researchers [Curtis et al., 1979; Feuer-Fowlkes, 1979; Christensen et al., 1981; Shen et al., 1982; among others] have succeeded in applying the Halstead metrics as well-behaved indicators of effort.

Halstead described the information content of a module or program in terms of its Length and its Vocabulary:

$$\text{Volume} = \text{Length} \times \log_2 (\text{Vocabulary})$$

where

$$\text{Length} = \text{count of all instances of all used operators} +$$
$$\text{count of all instances of all used operands}$$

and

$$\text{Vocabulary} = \text{count of unique operators used} +$$
$$\text{count of unique operands used}$$

The process of computing the Volume of a module is relatively trivial because it doesn't require any *semantic* analysis of the code: Since the counts of operators and operands are always added, you never have to decide which is which. Once the comments and punctuation have been stripped from the code, the Length is nothing more than a simple count of "words" (strings of consecutive alphanumeric characters separated by spaces or line control), and Vocabulary is the count of unique words. For the sample module of Figure 12-2, the total word count is 31. Of these, 24 are unique. The Volume of the module is therefore 142 bits $(31 \times \log_2(24))$.

```
function unique (newword: shortstring; wordlist: list): boolean;
        {module to determine if a given word has ever been encountered before}

    var    index: integer;
    begin
    unique := TRUE;
    for index := 1 to wordlist.count do
            if newword = wordlist.word [index] then
                    unique := FALSE;
    end;
```

Figure 12-2. Code segment with Volume of 142 bits.

Your compiler won't compute Volume for you. Many code counters represented in the literature seem to have felt that metrics not provided directly by the compiler ought to be considered out of bounds. (If God wanted us to know Volume, He would have had the COBOL compiler compute it for us.) But if your dedication to measurement qualifies you as anything beyond metric dilettante, computing Volume for each module shouldn't be too much of a burden. Of course, you'll need some sort of automated aid. Appendix D provides a Volume evaluator (written in UCSD Pascal), which you should be able to adapt without great effort.

One caveat on using Volume as an indication of size: The Halstead formulation is not totally associative. So, in general,

Volume (A+B) IS NOT PRECISELY EQUAL TO Volume (A) + Volume (B)

This means that your partitioning decisions (shall A+B be a single module or separated into two?) can have an effect on the assessment of Volume and hence of effort. But the error introduced is minor. For instance, if two small modules of the Volume evaluator are merged, the total volume of the program increases by only a few percent. Larger modules tend to result in *inflated* measures of Volume; perhaps the amount of the inflation is indeed commensurate with the increased effort of dealing with larger modules. I have always ignored the small error introduced by imperfect association of the Volume function, and have not obviously suffered from it. Gross partitioning pathologies, however, may introduce substantial error: The evaluator in Appendix D has a total Volume of 2,815 bits; if the whole program is recoded as a single module, the measured Volume grows to 3,532 bits.

12.2.3 Metrics of Code Complexity

The two code segments of Figure 12-3 have equal Volumes, 53 bits each. Yet the effort required to validate the first is clearly much greater than that required for the second: The first is more complex than the second.

```
FIRST SEGMENT:       if indicator1 then
                         if indicator2 then
                             if indicator3 then
                                   indicator4 := TRUE;
                         else
                             indicator4 := FALSE;


SECOND SEGMENT:      indicator1 := TRUE;
                     indicator2 := TRUE;
                     indicator3 := TRUE;
                     move (xvalue, yvalue);
                     clearscreen;
                     indicator4 := indicator3;
```

Figure 12-3. Variations in complexity.

What is this thing called "complexity," and how does it affect software development? The nature and effects of complexity have been studied for years by systems people, but our industry has not even been able to settle on a definition. In a charming essay on complexity, Bill Curtis was driven to this one [Curtis, 1979]:

Complexity is a not-so-warm feeling in the tummy.

Perhaps, when you first began the business of software development, you were exhorted, as I was, to "Keep it simple, Stupid." The flattering implication of this saying is that we software people are all too intelligent for our own good, and that is the root cause of complexity; if we were dumber, we could write simpler software. But simple software, we now know, is never produced by the simple-minded. Taking something that is inherently complex and making it simple, or even a bit simpler, is a great intellectual achievement. The causes of complexity are so profound, and the pursuit of simplicity so difficult, that Niklaus Wirth, the man whose very name is synonymous with elegant simplicity, was led to this wistful remark:

> You vow to make it simple at all cost. You accept complexity as your enemy. Then you build it, doing your best to control complexity . . . and it comes out complex anyway [Wirth, 1981].

We may never have a firm enough intellectual grasp of complexity to eliminate it from our work. But the estimator's requirements are considerably less ambitious than that. The estimator needs only an answer to the question, Given that a given module came out as complex as it did, how much should I expect it to cost to complete its implementation?

A workable approach to answering this question was developed by McCabe, and extended and empirically validated by Chen [McCabe, 1976; Chen, 1978]. The approach is best described by representing a piece of code in terms of its connected segments in flow-graph fashion (Figure 12-4).

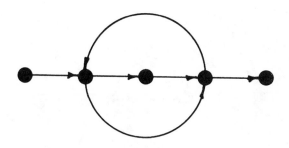

Figure 12-4. Flow graph representing module UNIQUE of Figure 12-2.

Here the nodes stand for sections of code that must be executed serially (there are no branch points within the nodes), and the lines stand for control paths that join these sections (Figure 12-5). McCabe investigated the notion that complexity is a function of the number of decisions in the code. So, modules A and B in Figure 12-5 are of equal complexity. C is more complex than B, and D is more complex than C. All we require further is some uniform algorithm for measuring the complexity of even the most convoluted graph, and then a trick for doing the measurement without having to draw the graph.

Chen defines complexity as a unitless number equal to the number of intersections between the graph and a line that connects the outside of the graph with all of the domains described by the graph. In order to evaluate Chen's Number, you join the start and end of the graph and then draw the line that passes from the domain outside the graph into each of the graph domains with the fewest intersections. Chen's Number for the graph of Figure 12-6, for example, is 5. McCabe's indicator, called the *Cyclomatic Measure,* is even simpler:

Cyclomatic Measure = Count of Connections − Count of Nodes + 2

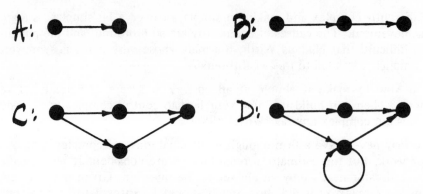

Figure 12-5. Modules of varying complexity.

I've presented these complexity metrics in the form of graphs as they were originally presented by their authors, because the graphs give some intuitive justification for
them. But you can dispense entirely with the graphs. Both the McCabe and Chen
metrics are direct functions of the count of decision points in the code. For instance,
the Cyclomatic Measure is always one more than the number of decisions.

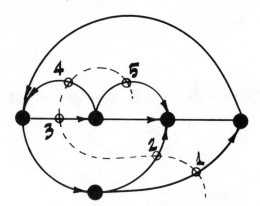

Figure 12-6. Example of Chen's Number.

Chen's Number is a slightly more esoteric function. Precisely what the function is
hardly matters; if you accept that complexity is a function of the count of decisions
alone, then you can collect empirical data directly correlating variations of cost (per unit
of Volume) with the count of decisions. Gaffney did precisely this and came up with
the relationship of Figure 12-7. Gaffney's data indicate that productivity decreases in a
nonlinear fashion as the density of decision points increases. This is undoubtedly true
for large modules and monolithic programs, but the complexity of small modules can
better be described in terms of the *absolute* number of decision points. By collecting the
implementation cost for each module and expressing it as a function of decision points
in the module, you can build a graph like the one in Figure 12-8. This graph was
developed from a small sample of COBOL projects. I offer it to you as a beginning,
something to use until you have collected data for your own difficulty relationship,
tailored to your environment. Note that data to derive this relationship are quickly
acquired, since every module gives at least one data point, and there are typically many
modules per project.

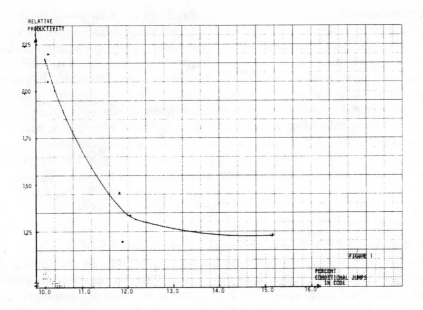

Figure 12-7. Variations in cost per unit.*

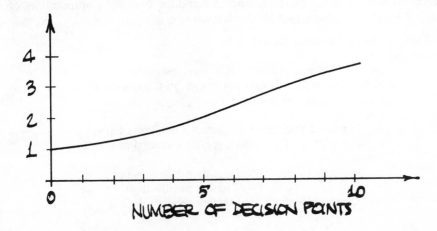

Figure 12-8. Difficulty of implementation as a function of module decision points.

It is trivial to build a software tool to count decisions in a coded module. All the tool has to do is add up the number of IFS, WHILES, UNTILS . . . (whatever two-way deci-

---

*J.E. Gaffney, "Program Control Complexity and Productivity," *Workshop on Quantitative Software Models for Reliability, Complexity, and Cost: An Assessment of the State of the Art,* IEEE Cat. No. TH0067-9 (New York: Institute of Electrical and Electronics Engineers, 1979), p. 142. Copyright © 1979. Reprinted by permission.

sions your language provides), and add to this total $n - 1$ for each n-way decision (such as a CASE construct). I haven't provided such a tool because I have never found it useful. Long before the code is actually written, the coder should know this number. He or she can easily pick off the decision count from the pseudocode, Nassi-Shneiderman Diagram, or some other tool used to sketch out module internals. Modules with high complexities (with large numbers of decisions) should be reconsidered. If there is no way to modify internal structure to reduce the number of decisions, then it may be necessary to return to the design activity, and further divide the module. McCabe suggests that modules whose Cyclomatic Measure exceeds ten are candidates for repartitioning. I encourage you to make an exception to this rule only for very wide CASE constructs (perhaps count each CASE as one decision for this purpose, regardless of its width).

12.2.4 Allowances for adapted code

Code that is adapted from previous work, from module libraries, or from toolkits like the Programmer's Workbench [Dolotta-Mashey, 1976] must be discounted. Whatever a module's computed volume turns out to be, it should be scaled downward for purposes of projecting future work. The scaling factor is obviously dependent on how solid and easily adapted the code is. At the University of Maryland's Software Engineering Laboratory, adapted code is discounted to 21 or 22% of its computed value.* I suggest you use that number until you come up with a tailored Adaptation Factor of your own.

12.2.5 The composite implementation predictor

The composite implementation predictor, Implementation Weight, is now defined as Volume corrected for Complexity and Adaptation Factor. Computation of Implementation Weight is accomplished by the following procedure:

> Start with Implementation Weight = 0
> For each module:
>> Evaluate Volume in bits using Volume evaluator
>> Note decision count and use it to pick off Complexity Factor
>> from Figure 12-8 or equivalent
>> Compute
>>> Corrected Volume = Volume × Complexity Factor
>> If the module is adapted from previous development or from a
>> standard library of reusable modules,
>>> Discount Corrected Volume by Adaptation Factor in use
>>> (reduce to about 21% of its computed value)
>> Add Corrected Volume into Implementation Weight

12.3 Metrics of compliance

So much for sizing the code. This and the following sections will describe some additional implementation metrics that can be used to advantage by the manager and the estimator.

---

*V.R. Basili, private communication, 1981.

Almost everyone acknowledges the value of structured coding, but acknowledgment sometimes amounts to nothing more than lip service. Some of the people who endorse the concept most strongly are a bit vague about just what it means. I know of one company that considers its code sufficiently "structured" if there is at least one comment for every line of code. Now here is the bad news: You don't get the benefits of structured code (benefits that have been so universally observed) unless you actually do structure your code. Just waving your hand over it and calling it structured won't suffice.

In order to control the quality of code, you need to measure compliance to coding guidelines. That doesn't mean that you publish a guideline saying that all code should be structured and then "measure" by asking the coders, "You folks *are* writing structured code, aren't you?" The only safe way to lock in the benefits of modern coding practice is to measure all code as a matter of course using the following quantitative indication of compliance:

> Code Compliance = percent of all decision points implemented as
> single-entry, single-exit IF-ELSE,
> DO-WHILE, REPEAT-UNTIL, and CASE style constructs

There are cases in which a coder should be allowed to insert an emergency break in the middle of a tight loop or make use of some other nonstandard construct. But if code compliance comes in below ninety-five percent, something almost certainly is wrong: Your coders don't understand the concept or they need to be convinced that it's worth obeying.

Code should also be analyzed for design compliance as indicated in the previous chapter. This analysis involves verifying that the one-to-one relationships between the design and code have been respected:

- Modules on the structure chart correspond to modules in the code (no modules in the code that weren't on the structure chart).
- Connections on the structure chart correspond to invocations in the code (no additional intermodular connections; no pathological connections).
- Couples on the structure chart correspond to shared data tokens in the code (no additional shared data).
- The decision count predicted at design time (based on module coupling analysis) corresponds closely to the code's actual decision count.

It may seem obvious, but here is an observation that's important enough to be stated in its baldest form: If the implementation deviates substantially from design, the cost and effort projected from the design predictor are meaningless. Low design compliance is a clear indication of a project that is going badly off course and heading toward debacle.

12.4 Quantification of trouble in the implementation process

It isn't enough to be able to measure things well when a project is going well. A complete metric analysis also ought to be able to detect signs of project dysfunction and impending slip. An early and inexpensive indicator of mid-project thrashing is the Compilation Rate. Figure 12-9 shows a typical compilation pattern for a healthy project and, underneath it, the pattern for a sick project. Compilation Rate will always decrease as the project proceeds toward completion. The point at which it should begin its decrease (dotted line in Figure 12-9) is fairly consistent from project to project within a domain of similar efforts. Failure to start downward at this point is a sure sign of project distress. The Compilation Rate metric is most useful if you can ensure that

- modules are separately compiled (when entire programs are compiled together, the true thrashing, the module change rate, is obscured, though the metric is still valuable)

- measurement of Compilation Rate is built directly into the compilation procedure (so that it is largely invisible to, and thus independent of, the implementors)

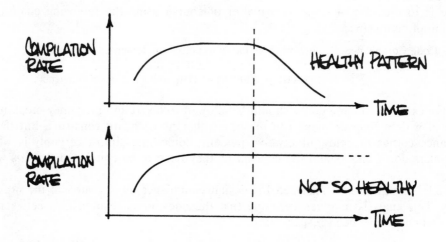

Figure 12-9. Thrashing indicated by Compilation Rate over time.

It may seem like a shabby trick to spy on implementors in this fashion. It may be a shabbier trick not to. What I've called "thrashing" in the development process could also be thought of as "anguish," since that's just what it represents to the people involved. The longer you fail to detect it, the longer before you can take steps to correct it.

12.5 Measurement of progress during testing

My friend and colleague Tim Lister makes this observation about management of the testing process:

> It's during testing that many managers cease to function as managers and become "cheerleaders" instead. They urge their troops on: "Work harder, be smarter, go faster." That may be heartening to the workers, but it just isn't management.

The difficulty in managing a testing effort is another result of poor or nonexistent measurement. Since effective measurement of testing is beyond the wildest imaginings of many managers, they can think of little more to do during this critical activity than cheer people on.

There are some obvious measurements that will help you to track the testing process. Consider, for example, the approach illustrated in Figure 12-10.

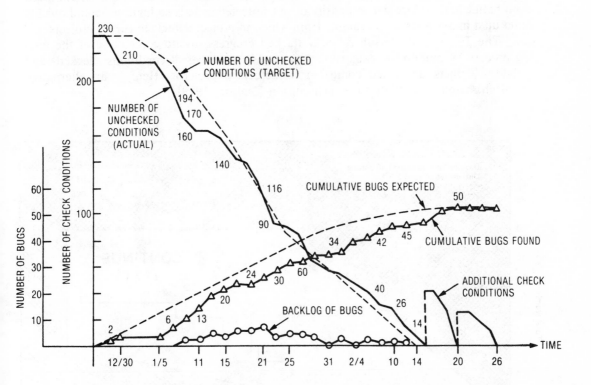

Figure 12-10.   Some testing metrics observed by Tajima and Matsubara.*

This scheme makes available at all times a measurement that indicates how far the testing has proceeded. At the heart of Tajima and Matsubara's metric of test completeness is the assumption that no piece of software can be considered validated until one or more tests have exercised each path segment of the code. All segments will have been exercised when each decision point has been followed in each of its possible directions. The graph shows that 230 unique decision point exits have been identified, and these are checked off as the tests progress.

The chart of Figure 12-10 implies some foreknowledge of the number of defects expected. Where does this come from?

To assure software quality for the users, the division's engineers practice statistical testing during the debugging stage. Using empirical data and statistical analysis, they advise the implementation group to enrich their test conditions in certain areas [Tajima-Matsubara, 1981].

By tracking and recording defects during debugging, engineers in the Tajima and Matsubara study built a profile of expected defect density as a function of Code Volume. This approach is seldom practiced in the United States, but it would work even better here: Since defect density of our untested code is so high, we could quickly build up a massive statistical sample from which to project defects in future projects.

The Tajima and Matsubara study tracked progress toward completion of the testing process by monitoring exhaustiveness of tests (number of conditions checked) and stability (defects unearthed compared to defects expected). Here is an alternative approach, based on stability alone [Thompson-Chelson, 1979]:

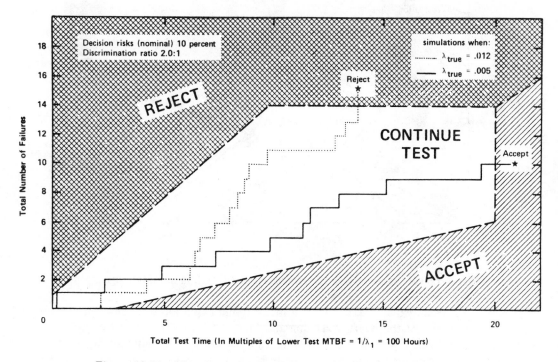

Figure 12-11. Measurement of stability by Thompson and Chelson.*

The two projects tracked in the figure show clear, *measurable* progress toward their respective results. The Thompson and Chelson approach is based on the determination *before the project begins* of just exactly how much stability is required for acceptance. This is indicated by placement of the ACCEPT and REJECT zones in the figure. The acceptance criterion implied by Figure 12-11 is a graphic statement of the stability levels required by the client (in this case, the stability requirement was specified by Military Standard 781C), and a statistical analysis of likely remaining defects as a function of defects already detected.

I refer you to Thompson and Chelson's article for a discussion of how the domains are drawn, given a textual statement of required stability. The important point for purposes of this section is that ACCEPT/REJECT zones of the diagram set out a quantitative policy for acceptance and rejection. Once you have drawn these zones, the ability to track progress is assured. But can you always draw a grid like the one in Figure 12-11? I assert that you can, *provided that there are objective acceptance standards established in advance.* If you fail to establish some standard for how much stability is required for acceptance, the whole acceptance procedure is little more than a charade. Your success or failure to win acceptance is then a matter of political skill, clout, and fancy footwork. And it's unmeasurable.

Part IV will return to the subject of tracking defects.

12.6 Quantification of delivered versions

The versioned delivery approach described in Chapter 10 affords an additional opportunity to measure progress toward completion. Each delivery implies something about the system's overall state of completeness. Consider the delivery plan shown in Figure 12-12.

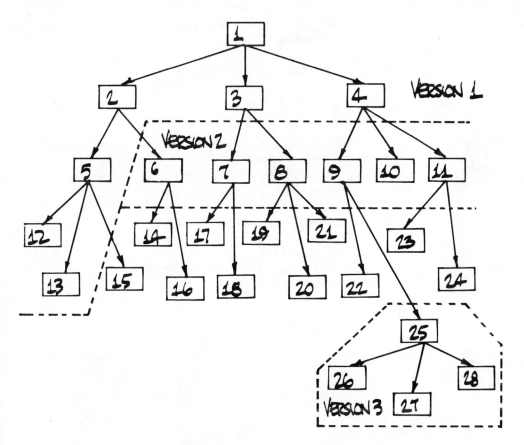

Figure 12-12. Versioned delivery plan.

Version 1 contains 7 out of 28 modules. If all modules were of equal Volume and Complexity, you might conclude that delivery of Version 1 implied that the post-design portion of the project (coding, testing, integration, documentation, and so on) was 25% done. Since Volume and Complexity do vary, you have to base your interpretation accordingly:

$$\text{Completeness implied by Version } n = \frac{\text{Implementation Weight (Version } n)}{\text{Implementation Weight (whole system)}}$$

Delivery of each new version allows the estimators to detect deviation of the project from its schedule, and to correct the schedule accordingly.

12.7 Selected references

The most important source on measurement of code is

Halstead, M.H. *Elements of Software Science.* New York: Elsevier North-Holland, 1977.

I must warn you that Halstead's book can be a bit terrifying. The author chose to place a long untranslated Russian quote on the second page of the introduction, and many readers never make it past there. But time has proved that Halstead was on the track of some very fundamental truths about the quantitative analysis of code.

Verification of Halstead's work is now widely reported. Two very readable papers on successful application of Halstead metrics are the following:

Christensen, K., G.P. Fitsos, and C.P. Smith. "A Perspective on Software Science." *IBM Systems Journal,* Vol. 20, No. 4 (October 1981), pp. 372-88.

Curtis, B., S.B. Sheppard, and P. Milliman. "Third Time Charm: Stronger Prediction of Programmer Performance by Software Complexity Metrics." *Proceedings of the 4th International Conference on Software Engineering.* New York: Institute of Electrical and Electronics Engineers, 1979, pp. 356-60.

Required reading on software complexity is the now classic essay

McCabe, T.J. "A Complexity Measure." *IEEE Transactions on Software Engineering,* Vol. SE-2 (December 1976), pp. 308-20.

13

PROJECT PLANNING: MODELING THE DEVELOPMENT PROCESS

A system is an integrated set of procedures (some automated, some manual) used to achieve a business end. A project is also a system in the sense of this definition, *a system for building a system*. Some of the system modeling techniques described in past chapters can be usefully applied to model the project. You can probably guess my reason for presenting project modeling in these pages: Like the other models I've been describing, project models provide some useful quantitative information about the development process.

13.1 The project model: A single-shot methodology

Since project models are a simple variation of the function models introduced in Chapter 8, I'm going to omit any textual description and plunge directly into an example. A partial project model for a typical small project is presented in Figure 13-1. A dictionary of interface definitions is required to complement the network of activities. The interface definitions might look something like this:

Specification Pkg IS COMPOSED OF: Function Model AND
Retained Data Model AND
Narrative Introduction AND
Table of Contents AND
Appendix (describing notation and sources)

Design Pkg IS COMPOSED OF: Structure Charts
Design Data Dictionary AND
Module Descriptions (selected ones) AND
Operational Flow Diagram AND
Design Notes

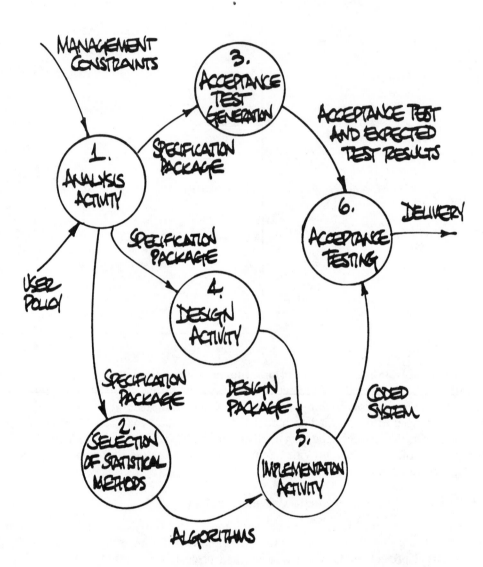

Figure 13-1. Project model for MSP-2 project (network component).

Along with the project model, we'll need a set of rules for carrying out each of the activities declared in the project model. These rules might be in the form of lower-level modeling (partitioning plus interfaces), narrative statements, or a note of reference, such as "Activity 4, DESIGN, will follow the method described in *Structured Design,* by Yourdon and Constantine (1978)."

The model, together with the rules for each of its activities, constitutes a complete project plan, carefully tailored to one particular project.

13.2 Project models versus the one-size-fits-all methodology

I finally decided my future lies,
beyond the Yellow Brick Road.
> — Elton John
> *Goodbye Yellow Brick Road,* 1973

In form, at least, the project model looks very much like a *methodology.* The key difference is that a methodology tries to be applicable to all projects, while the project model tries to be applicable to one and only one project.

As I get older and crankier, I find myself more and more exasperated with the great inflexible sets of rules that many companies try to pour into concrete and sanctify as methodologies. The idea that a single methodology should govern even two different projects is highly suspect: The differences between projects are much more important than the similarities.

I think of a project model as a *specification* of one project. A methodology, by analogy, is a specification of all projects. The notion that there could ever be a single general-purpose specification of all projects is about as credible as the idea of writing a single general-purpose specification for all systems. The differences between systems are much more important than the similarities, so the specification must concentrate on those differences. That's as true for the project as it is for the system the project delivers.

Most managers know that a methodology can't hope to prescribe one Yellow Brick Road for all projects to follow. But they're quick to defend *their* methodologies with a statement like, "The project teams know that they have to tailor the methodology for the differences in each project." The higher you go in the management hierarchy, the more prevalent is the assumption that some common-sense tailoring of the methodology is expected at the beginning of each project. But at the lower levels, exactly the opposite attitude prevails: Workers at the bottom of the hierarchy *know* that tailoring is discouraged or specifically prohibited by the methodology.

In a great fit of optimism, I once wrote my own methodology. The purpose of that effort was to establish once and for all that methodologies *must be tailored* for each and every project. Built right into the methodology was an activity that produced a customized version of the methodology; and that customized version governed the rest of the project. My incredulous client dubbed it "Tom DeMarco's Wild-card Methodology." It was tailored only one time: The client removed the tailoring activity and published the rest as a poured-in-concrete formula.

There is some evident resistance to the idea of a methodology that doesn't declare itself immutable. Since the concept seems radical, I want to present it very formally.

> *Proposal:* Let there be a specifically tailored methodology for each project. Use the prevailing methodology only as a starting point for tailoring. Present the tailored methodology in the form of a project model.

Any methodology that prevails in an organization ought to be an *input* to the project planning activity, not an *output*. If you coerce project personnel into espousing the methodology as the project plan, then no real planning takes place.

The project model is an early project deliverable, typically produced during the first month of work. I anticipate that you might have some reservations about this approach, and I'll address those in the following sections.

13.3 The political arena: Who is responsible for project modeling?

The project model establishes a tailored game plan for development, and an accounting scheme for keeping track of development effort as well. That's fine if the work of building a project model is not excessive; but if it results in putting each project into develop-THE-methodology mode at the beginning of the life cycle, the projects may not deliver anything but hot air. That would be too high a price to pay for the advantages. In order for project modeling to be a viable approach, it is essential that it be done in the very limited context of the project at hand. Modelers are allowed to address only the question, How shall *this* project proceed? not the larger question, How shall *all* projects proceed?

Custom modeling each project without paying an inordinate cost (cost to reinvent the wheel each time) depends on making a careful division of responsibility for project decisions between the project team and the standards organization. I propose this split of responsibility:

- The project team is responsible for all project *strategy*.
- The standards organization is responsible for *tactics*.

The following subsections describe these responsibilities and roles in more detail.

13.3.1 Role of the project team

The project team should be allowed to make all the major strategic decisions affecting the project, including what activities are needed, what precedence of activities, what deliverables, what method to be used for each activity. These are the very decisions that must be made in order to construct the project model. I conclude that the business of project modeling should be the sole responsibility of the project team. Whatever the standards organization does for or to the project, it ought not to dictate any of the decisions that lead to building the project model.

Many organizations are horrified at the idea of letting projects make their own strategic decisions. They would feel much more comfortable with a complete reversal of roles, with the Standards Group responsible for all the important decisions and the project team simply carrying those decisions out. In order to defend *that* concept, however, one is obliged to ignore the overwhelming failures it has caused nearly everywhere. These failures take one of two forms: Either the project teams follow the standards slavishly and blame any project failure directly on them; or they ignore standards altogether.

When project teams are made directly responsible for strategy, they build their own project methodologies, *and they obey them*. Of course, there is always someone ready to object, "But the methodology they used wasn't as good as the one we would have imposed upon them." Even if you're ready to concede that the Standards Group could put together a better approach, there is little advantage to be derived from their superior strategy if no one actually follows it. "Just a little enforcement problem," you say? Yes, but a little enforcement problem that virtually no one has solved.

13.3.2 Role of the Standards Group

In an environment in which strategy is the prerogative of the project team, a rational role for the Standards Group is to provide support for the project modeling process, to help the teams build their models with a minimum of reinvention. This implies that the Standards Group collects project models with a view toward making their components available for reuse. The group can also provide some overall guidance in project modeling: a standard for what a project model must contain in order to be complete, checklists, and examples.

Under such a scheme, all of these are legitimate Standards Group activities:

- *packaging activity templates:* redocumenting component activities from a past project model so that they have the maximum probability of being plugged unchanged into future project models
- *packaging deliverable templates:* generalizing deliverable descriptions made available to the projects for possible inclusion in their models
- *collecting sample deliverables:* gathering actual specifications, designs, test plans, and so forth, from past successful projects
- *developing prototype project models:* developing skeleton models to be customized by the project teams

The following activities should *not* be considered legitimate for the Standards Group to perform, but should be reserved for the project itself:

- selecting a method to accomplish a given activity
- selecting the deliverables and deliverable types
- project planning

Our industry has recently seen an exciting experiment at Bell Telephone Laboratories in the use of software tools: implementation of a development environment called the Programmer's Workbench [Dolotta-Mashey, 1976]. Programmers in this environment are supplied with a library of *tools,* tiny reusable modules developed and collected by the organization's toolsmith. The function of the Standards Group should be analogous: The Standards Group ought to perform the toolsmith's function for the project manager. It ought to supply him/her with a library of reusable components, a Manager's Workbench, for building project models.

In practice, the concept works this way: At the beginning of a new effort, the project manager looks over the set of prototype models (suggestions) prepared by the Standards Group. The manager chooses the one that fits most closely with his/her own concept of how the project ought to proceed. Those portions of the prototype model that are exactly like that view will be retained; the rest will have to be customized or built from scratch. The project manager then selects a method for carrying out each of the activities in the model. Before writing down the description of rules, procedures, and notations for each activity (a formal declaration of method), he or she approaches the Standards Group to see if any of that work has already been done. If so, the Manager's Workbench component can be used, possibly in modified form; otherwise, the project team will have to write its own. A copy of the completed model is delivered to the Standards Group to be packaged for potential reuse by others.

13.4 The technical arena: What approach to project modeling?

Since the project team is responsible for building the project model, it is convenient to use a modeling technique that team members have already mastered. I suggest they use whatever technique they have adopted for function modeling, as described in Chapter 8. There are natural parallels between the system to be built and the system for building it. These parallels imply that a technique for specifying the one will be viable for specifying the other. And a project model is nothing more than a *specification* of the project.

While the function modeling techniques of Chapter 8 should be useful for project specification, they may not be sufficient. The complete project specification (project plan) ought to include

- activity network (analogous to the function network)
- descriptions of deliverables (analogous to the data dictionary)
- set of detailed method descriptions, one for each primitive activity (analogous to the minispecifications)
- timing of activities
- manpower requirements for each activity
- PERT or CPM analysis of critical paths
- tentative individual assignments

13.5 The project model as a cost data collection standard

The component activities of the project model are cost generators. Any quantitative analysis of the completed project will require careful assessment of how much manpower and expense is used on each of these activities. So the project model serves as a basis for collecting this cost data during the project. That means project manpower has to be charged to specific accounting categories established by the project model.

Project task accounting is hardly new. The most common schemes for task accounting often masquerade under the grandiose name "project control system." Experience with these systems has varied over the whole range from poor to positively awful. Since I am proposing use of a similar scheme, I feel obliged to indicate why you are likely to have more success with it than you might have had with project control systems in the past.

13.5.1 Why project control systems don't control projects

There are several dozen project control systems available on the market today. They vary widely in the form and quantity of their output, attempting to outdo each other in sexiness of report layouts and in sheer volume of output. They all work more or less this way:

1. You divide your project into as many tasks as possible. The project control system may suggest likely tasks with an exhaustive checklist, and it may establish a maximum size for tasks.

2. You come up with a detailed manpower estimate for each task. The project control system is probably silent on how you do this.

3. You give each task a unique control number.

4.   Your project members charge time against the tasks by number.

5.   When all the time allocated for a given task is used up, the task is complete.

Of course, the presumption of the last point is perfect nonsense; but it is *integral* to the project control system philosophy. What's worse, it is usually accepted implicitly by team members, at least in a political sense.

The approach might hope to give you a measure of control to the extent that it causes late tasks to be signaled as they come close to exceeding original estimates. But in the real world, it doesn't work that way at all. There is such an onus associated with re-estimating a task that it just isn't done. Time is not charged against a task until everyone involved is confident that charging the time will have no adverse political effects (won't require re-estimating and thus admitting that something was wrong in the original plan). If the hours to be charged would use up the remaining allocated time and the task is still clearly incomplete, then the worker looks for someplace else to hide the time: "Why, here's a charming possibility! Task 45-6792.4, INVESTIGATE USER SECONDARY PREFERENCES, a task with 260 remaining hours." The tasks are often so wishy-washy that almost any kind of effort can be charged to them without stretching anyone's credulity.

The result of all this is that *few tasks show slip until almost all tasks have used up their time allotments,* leading to this familiar state of affairs:

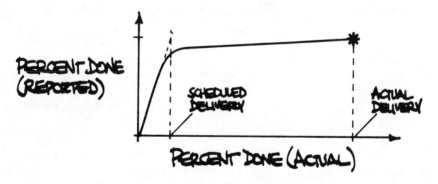

Figure 13-2. The (early) illusion of control.

The first observed failing of project control systems is that they don't give any meaningful control over projects. Perhaps just as unfortunate is the second failing: They result in an obscured record of how time was actually spent. Any attempt to profit from quantitative evidence of the past is hampered by the fiction built into the record.

I see two reasons for the difficulties in making reasonable use of project control systems:

• There is an unresolvable conflict between the two goals, task accounting and control.

• The fineness of partitioning (often down to tasks of ten man-hours or less) is ludicrous; the precision of such partitioning is far greater than its accuracy.

The primary goal of a project control system — to control the project — is never attainable through any mere accounting scheme. Measuring the *input* to a task (manpower) gives you no indication of state of completeness of the task. To judge its completeness, you have to measure the *output* of the task (the product). The secondary goal — building a meaningful record of how manpower was expended — is invariably sacrificed to the first.

13.5.2 Task accounting without illusions of control

Task accounting has to have all control significance stripped from it in order to function effectively. When a worker charges time to a given task, he or she must feel confident that there are no political ramifications whatsoever, that the accounting is for a historical record only. The obvious way to effect this attitude is to make task accounting the responsibility of people who have no stake in controlling the project: The Metrics Group should do all task accounting. Its record of which worker spent how much time on what tasks should be protected from project management.

The Metrics Group collects records on a regular basis, usually weekly. Metrics Group members meet with each project worker to find out how the intervening time has been spent, and they decide the allocation of hours to tasks. The worker has no knowledge of how time is charged, or of the original time estimated for the task, time used to date, or time remaining. The worker doesn't fill out documents and is not obliged to account for the full work period.

All parties to this discussion are aware that the record is confidential to the Metrics Group. Should other parties need information about how the individuals spent their time, those other parties will have to collect their own data. Managers are sometimes offended at the idea that potentially useful information is purposely kept from them by policy of their own company. Agents of the IRS are equally offended that the Census Bureau won't share income data with them. In both cases, the rationale is the same: The data can't be collected if it is not protected; if the data is useful, then protecting it should be considered part of the price of collecting it.

Removing the political overtones from task accounting is only half of what is required to make the collected numbers meaningful. The other half is to take measures to remove subjective judgment in deciding where time should be allocated. If there are two or three or more different ways to allocate a body of work, the project model is at fault: It has divided the work into ill-defined tasks. Consider these examples based on a popular project control system package:

> 0-1-64: Schedule, prepare, and conduct additional interviews
> 1-3-98: Review proposed systems pending development
> 2-6-67: Verify current client/user community
> 4-0-05: Review system objectives
> 4-1-19: Assemble working papers

What do you suppose "additional interviews" are? How does one "verify" a community? Most of all, how do you know when any of these tasks is done, since no one could hope to define their products? There is no way to collect meaningful task accounting data with such vague and indefinite tasks.

If you partition your project using the function modeling methods described in Chapter 8, your tasks will tend to be far more definite than those listed above. The reason is that function modeling doesn't allow you to concentrate on activities without regard to what products those activities develop. That leads us to the following rule:

Cardinal Rule of Project Modeling

A project activity is defined by its deliverable.

There is one activity per deliverable. The only work charged against that activity is work spent producing that deliverable. The activity is complete when the deliverable is delivered and accepted.

Deliverable-oriented project modeling may yield some overly large activities, at least by the arbitrary standards of common project control systems. But further dividing those activities into components that produce no discernible product is to invest precious effort in an illusion of detailed planning.

13.5.3 Concept of the binary deliverable

Your project, the whole project, has a binary deliverable. On scheduled completion day, the project has either delivered a system that is accepted by the user, or it hasn't. Everyone knows the result on that day.

The object of building a project model is to divide the project into component pieces, each of which has this same characteristic: Each activity must be defined by a deliverable *with objective completion criteria*. The deliverables are demonstrably done or not done. The associated task is judged, based on the state of the deliverable, to be 0% or 100% complete. Completeness of the overall effort is judged by a weighted ratio of components that are done to those that are not done. (A weighting is required because of the different sizes of the components.)

The more binary deliverables you can incorporate in your project, the finer you make your partitioning. This results in *meaningful* detail built into the project plan.

Insisting on binary deliverables will oblige you to consider some variation in your development methods. You might have always felt before that a task like "Investigate current user environment" was a necessary part of any project plan. But it fails the binary deliverable test. There is no way to say when the task is done. It could run forever or be closed out immediately, based entirely on subjective judgment. The function modeling approach gives you an alternative, to redefine the activity in this fashion:

> Build a function model according to the method of [whatever source you choose] to describe the current user environment. Model a domain large enough so that none of the changes proposed in the project charter has impact outside the domain. Solicit and obtain user concurrence that the model is correct.

This task achieves the same end as "Investigate current user environment," but it has objective completion criteria. The model is either complete or it isn't. It isn't complete if there are interfaces declared but not defined, or if there are demonstrable sources or sinks of data, or if there aren't proper connections with the outside world (if the view from inside is inconsistent with the view from the outside). It is either accepted as correct by the user, or it isn't.

When tasks are defined in terms of binary deliverables, task accounting can be precise and rigorous. There is seldom a question of which task to charge for time worked.

13.5.4 Binary deliverable task accounting

A project model is a leveled function model of project activities and binary deliverable interfaces. The partitioning is made as fine as possible without introducing ill-defined tasks (tasks with no deliverable or with a deliverable that has no binary completion criteria). Activities declared in the project model define the categories for task accounting. Each hour of project effort is associated with one of these categories.

The project model thus serves two distinct but related purposes: It is a formal customized work-plan for one specific project; and it is a data collection standard for costs charged to that project.

13.6 Summary

A methodology *could* be made to serve as a prefabricated project plan for all projects, but only if you're willing to accept the resulting imprecision and vagueness. When the project team is made responsible for its own planning, project-specific plans are built and followed. The specificity assures that tasks are well defined and that task accounting produces a useful project record. Because the project team follows its own plan (as opposed to ignoring the standard plan that comes down from on high), there is *more* concurrence of method throughout the organization, and so the trends in the statistical data are stronger and more evident.

The discipline of project modeling requires no additional tools or skills beyond those used for system specification. Support by a Standards Group will assure that common elements of project models are made available for reuse.

13.7 Selected references

A modern methodology that explicitly calls for project modeling is

Dickinson, B. *Developing Structured Systems: A Methodology Using Structured Techniques.* New York: Yourdon Press, 1981.

Since this methodology is meant to be modified and adapted for each project, it is really a *meta-methodology,* or a kit for the project modeler. Such a methodology encourages rather than discourages meaningful project planning. The Dickinson work is oriented to large projects, say, those that exceed one hundred man-months of effort.

For smaller projects, I suggest you look at

Yourdon, E. *Managing the System Life Cycle: A Software Development Methodology Overview.* New York: Yourdon Press, 1982.

This, too, is a usable meta-methodology, something you can cut and paste to construct a project model with a minimum of effort.

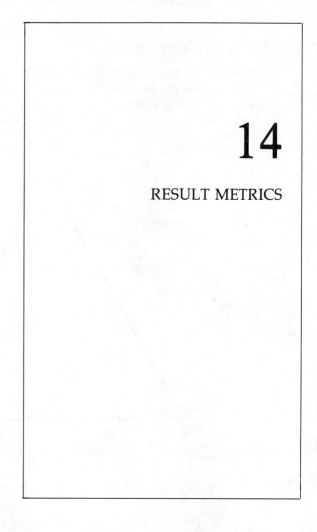

14

RESULT METRICS

Result metrics are quantitative indications of costs of completed work. These are the numbers you will be required to forecast for future projects. Forecasting future results requires that current project result metrics be methodically collected and correlated. The purpose of this chapter is to set out a list of results to record, along with some data collection standards and techniques.

All results can be thought of as costs. (Using the word "cost" in this broad sense implies that some costs may be denominated in units of time or of risk.) Results to be collected fall into four categories:

- metrics of *project* cost
- metrics of *post-project* cost
- metrics pertaining to performance of the *organization* as a whole
- metrics of the *Metric Function* itself

Each of these categories will be treated in its own section below.

14.1 Measuring project cost

Evaluation of project performance (Figure 14-1) must include consideration of all three of the cornerstone parameters: Bang delivered, cost to deliver, and quality of the delivered result. Measurement of Bang was treated in Chapter 9, and measurement of quality will be treated in Chapters 20 through 22. This section focuses on the evaluation of cost to deliver.

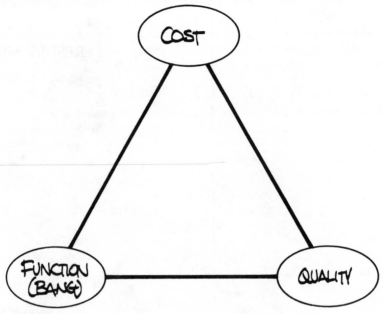

Figure 14-1. Cornerstones of project performance evaluation.

14.1.1 Collection of relevant project costs

For most projects, the key costs are manpower and elapsed time. Elements of manpower and time have to be tracked on a timely basis, probably weekly. As part of this tracking, all of the following should be noted:

- Who performed the work?
- What accounting category or categories shall the work be charged against?
- How much manpower shall be charged?
- What is the tolerance of measurement?
- Over what period did the work take place?
- Who is measuring?

A company just beginning to collect these data invariably starts by designing a questionnaire for the purpose. It presents the questions on a snazzy worksheet on colored multipart paper with the company logo prominently displayed. And then two small tactical errors send the whole project cost measurement scheme downhill:

First tactical error: Managers require that the worksheets be filled out by personnel performing the work.

Second tactical error: Managers use the worksheet for personnel accounting (how many hours did this employee work over this period?).

For cost data to be meaningful, a single standard for allocation must be applied. Entire teams and sets of teams cannot all be expected to measure by the same standard, no matter how elaborate a written definition of the standard you provide. The only way to assure uniform reporting is by *putting responsibility into the hands of professional measurers,* members of the Metrics Group. Once a week, the measurers conduct a two-minute interview with each worker in order to record his/her time. Workers will have to keep some simple private records of time spent in order to supply the information accurately, but need not grapple with the question of how such time should be allocated. The interview is an excellent opportunity for the measurer to pick up additional information about progress, perhaps gut-feel perceptions that could never be conveyed by a form. Since their incentives are totally oriented toward correct forecasting of progress, the measurers profit directly from this on-the-spot data collection. An additional advantage of having Metrics Group personnel keep the records is that project workers don't feel burdened by (what they consider to be) bureaucratic work.

Project cost recording should be separated from personnel accounting. Forcing employees to account for thirty-five or forty hours every week will only distort the record. An employee who works only twenty hours in a given week can hardly admit that to the paymaster. So, he finds some likely project activity and buries the time there. He feels no compunction about this because he may have worked eighty hours the week before; time reporting is just a formality. But the record is now spoiled for forecasting purposes. By setting up the Metrics Group as an independent organization that collects data *only for its own purposes,* you can minimize the potential for distortion. When your workers feel secure that data collected by the group is confidential, then they can report more honestly. This helps to assure that lost time is reported correctly, rather than hidden; and that time spent on unanticipated tasks is reported correctly, rather than allocated to the nearest approximately similar task.

Keeping track of unplanned activities is essential [Orr, 1981]:

It isn't the tasks you planned for that kill you (by costing more or taking longer than you expected); it's the things you never planned for at all.

Only by keeping a record of modifications required for each project model as the project proceeds can you hope to predict the likely impact of unanticipated tasks on subsequent projects. In a recent Yourdon project survey [DeMarco, 1981], unanticipated, unclassified, and miscellaneous activities constituted fully fifteen percent of manpower. For some reason, these activities were skewed toward the end of the project (Figure 14-2). Since unanticipated OTHER activities tend to take up disproportionately much time near the end of the project, their damaging political effects are magnified. Managers in the survey proved themselves to be poor-to-awful estimators, but their estimates of time spent in the OTHER category were even worse than the rest.

The OTHER category is, by its very nature, counterintuitive. So the only way to deal with it is in a mechanistic, empirical fashion: Build a profile of amount and timing of unanticipated work, and assume that future projects will repeat the pattern.

A similar approach is required to deal with lost time. No matter how good you are at wet-finger-in-the-air estimating, chances are you never provide quite enough allowance for all the time that implementors spend doing something other than implementing (see Figure 14-3). By measuring lost time carefully on current projects, you can allow for similar patterns in the future. This means that estimates and forecasts can be made assuming one-hundred percent useful time (a lot less counterintuitive, somehow) and then corrected by a uniform factor.

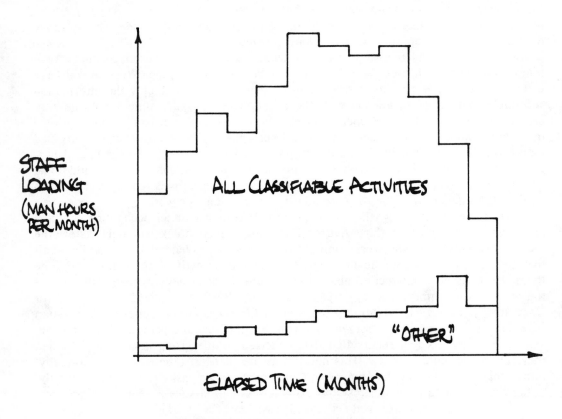

Figure 14-2. Effect of the dreaded OTHER.

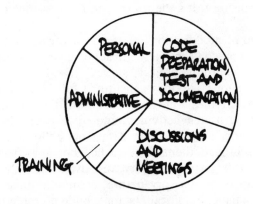

Figure 14-3. How programmers spend their time.

14.1.2 A simple project cost accounting scheme

Project cost data must be collected in such a way that all of the following cost breakdowns are possible:

- total cost for each component of the specification model from start of project through completion
- cost for each module (design, code, test, and document)
- cost for each activity of the project model
- cost for meaningful groups of activities (for example, all the design subtasks)
- costs by class of work (negotiation versus development versus review)
- certain combinations of the above

You might, for instance, want to be able to answer a question like, What were the design-code-debug percentages for modules implementing area 4.3 of the specification model?

In order to satisfy all of these requirements, every hour of work recorded must be charged against each of the following four categories:

- activity performed (component of the project model)
- function delivered (component of the specification model)
- module implemented (component of the design model)
- class of work

The resultant record looks something like this:

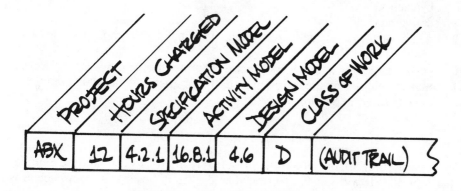

Figure 14-4. Example of a project cost accounting record.

The portion labeled "Audit Trail" contains information about the performer, date of work, date of measurement, measurer, and perhaps some notes.

There may be some work that can be allocated only to groups of model components. A side effect of the numbering scheme illustrated in Appendix A is that meaningful sets in the hierarchy (of the specification model, design model, or project model) can be described by truncating the number. So, for example, if work were spread across specification model primitives 5.2.1, 5.2.2, 5.2.3, and 5.2.4, the time should be charged to non-primitive component 5.2. Clearly, some of the early project work can't be charged against the design model, since that model won't yet exist.

A word about units of measurement: You can't collect cost data in units finer than an hour because the error of measurement makes fractions of an hour pointlessly over-precise. You can't collect cost data in units much larger than an hour either, because project members don't work whole days or weeks on single tasks. I suggest that cost data be collected in hourly units with only this wrinkle: The basic unit of cost measurement is the *uninterrupted* hour. (This idea has a sobering implication for work environments in which there is no such thing as an uninterrupted hour — so be it.) The nature of systems development work is such that restart time is long, about twenty-five minutes after each interruption. If a worker dedicates ten six-minute periods over a day to some programming task, he or she has accomplished nothing — all sixty minutes should be charged to lost time.

14.1.3 The project history record

When the project is completed, a final project history record should be assembled and preserved. The history consists of all the following items:

1. project charter and abstract description
2. specification model
3. metric analysis of specification model (p-counts plus Bang computation)
4. design model
5. metric analysis of design model (basic design metrics plus computation of Design Weight)
6. version plan
7. metric analysis of version plan (computation of percent done implied by each version)
8. delivered code
9. metric analysis of delivered code (volume and complexity of each module)
10. costs charged by activity, by function, by module, and by class of work
11. metric analysis of the maintenance characteristic of the delivered product (treated in Section 14.2)

14.1.4 Failed projects

The typical study in the literature of software metrics documents a sample of n completed projects. It will never mention that the study began with m projects, where m was larger than n (sometimes considerably larger). The difference $m - n$ represents the projects that failed to complete for some reason or other: They were canceled or postponed, or they simply failed to deliver a product. You have to be a very suspicious reader to infer that projects studied by authors of astute papers in prestigious journals *ever* fail. But *lots* of projects do fail. From my own study of project failure and from the rather sparse literature on the subject, I have concluded that *fifteen percent of all projects never deliver anything.*

When a project fails, the scurrying for cover by all participants can be awesome. No wonder there's never a systematic record of the cost of the failure; those who might have assembled the record were reassigned within microseconds of cancellation. But that record, if it could be assembled, would be invaluable. How much is spent on a canceled project prior to cancellation? Whatever the average amount is, it is a major component of the cost of system building. Suppose you knew, for your organization, that a typical failed project used up 75% of its budget prior to cancellation. If you also accepted my grim 15% figure, then you might conclude that your risk of cancellation for a $1 million project is $112,500 (that is, 15% × 75% × $1M). Or maybe you don't want to know that. . . .

14.2 Measuring post-project characteristics

The cost migration effect can have particularly unpleasant consequences for post-project costs: If you stop measuring as of delivery day, then costs will tend to migrate out of the project and into the maintenance period. You may conclude that the project was a success, but only because of ignorance of what shoddy-but-quick development procedures cost after delivery. You will never be able to answer questions like these: How successful was the design? (How easy was it to modify?) How successful was the analysis? (How much modification was required after delivery, and how much of it could have been foreseen?) How successful was the quality assurance program? (How dense were the defects in delivered code?)

The success or failure of project methods is judged by characteristics of the completed product. But given that a software product might have an eight-year life, you can hardly wait until it's retired to evaluate the methods used. You need some faster feedback than that, something that is available within six months of delivery. That leads us to

The First-Six-Months-As-Predictor Theory

Post-project characteristics collected during the first six months following delivery will be an acceptable indication of values of those same characteristics over the entire life of the system.

There is, as yet, no empirical confirmation of this idea; such confirmation would necessarily take as long as eight years to collect. What has been empirically confirmed is the observation that most of the characteristics recorded seem to settle into a stable pattern within six months.

The First-Six-Months Theory suggests a way to close out a project record, at least tentatively, within half a year of delivery. By that time, you should be able to publish maintainability, stability, and defect density figures projected over the whole system life, as well as a projection of how long that life will be.

All of the following are post-project characteristics that ought to be collected:

- user change request frequency (distinct requests per month)
- user change request average impact (Bang of average requested change)
- domain of impact per change (modules affected)
- defects detected (defects per thousand bits of volume, defects per thousand lines of code)
- cost of defect detection and removal (dollars per defect)
- persistence of defects (days between detection and removal)

- domain of each defect (modules affected)
- length of search path (number of modules traversed between symptom and defect; number of modules considered in seeking cause)
- defect clustering (number of defects in each module)
- productivity (Bang Per Buck) in implementing unanticipated additions

14.3 Measuring the organization

The first activity for a newly formed Metrics Group ought to be the measurement of global characteristics of the organization. These include costs of development, maintenance, support, overhead, space, machines, and training. Without a clear perception of how EDP funds are actually spent, your strategy for improvement will be flawed. The following paragraphs provide some real-world examples of misguided company policies.

A Connecticut insurance company currently sends an internal bill to each project manager for machine resources used. This funny-money instrument quotes charges based on depreciated book value of the machines, plus a substantial provision for profit for the computer center. The result is that developers are charged at rates that are far higher than market rates (for example, hourly use of a 64K region of memory costs nearly half of the *purchase price* of an equivalent 64K at the local computer store). A manager at that company told me he could prove, using these figures, that the investment of ten programmer-weeks to trim the size of one production program by a few percent would be cost justified.

A bank spends a stingy 3.5% of its programming payroll on space and amenities for programmers. The result is that workers are crowded together in an environment that inhibits any form of concentration. There seems to be some dunderhead in every company whose whole function in life is to figure out how to cram in more programmers per square foot, with scant regard for lost effectiveness.

More than half of all programmers in the United States have never taken a training course, do not subscribe to any professional journal, and have never purchased a book on any aspect of software development. (But look at how much a company can save by routing that single $2.50 copy of the *IBM Systems Journal* to the whole staff of 800!)

EDP people across the nation seem to believe that split between hardware cost and software cost is about 50-50, and they make their tradeoffs accordingly. The actual split is 9-91. Careful measurement of the organization is required to assure that decisions made at the project level and above are consistent with overall corporate goals.

14.4 Measuring the measurers

Metrics of the Metric Function itself will have to include cost (expected to be five to ten percent of the effort being measured), as well as forecasting efficiency (Estimating Quality Factor). The simple EQF introduced in Chapter 3 was defined as the reciprocal of the average deviation between estimate and actual, or

$$\text{Simple EQF} = \frac{\text{Actual Value of Estimated Quantity} \times \text{Duration of Unknown}}{\int |(\text{Estimated Value (t)} - \text{Actual Value})| dt}$$

That is, EQF is the crosshatched area of Figure 14-5 divided into the area under the actual result (A × D).

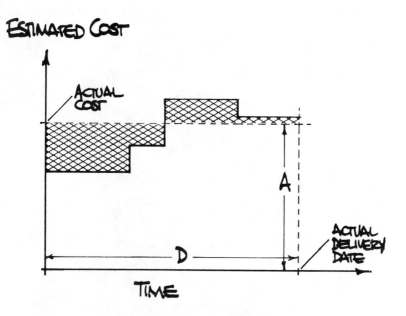

Figure 14-5. Estimating Quality Factor.

Estimating Quality Factor should be recorded for each of the (perhaps hundreds of) forecasts put out by the Metrics Group. Increase in average EQF over time is an indication that the group is improving its estimating capability.

Some managers find the simple EQF definition incompatible with the political realities of their environments. They feel obliged to stress more heavily the estimates made at the beginning, and don't care terribly much about the last ten to twenty percent convergence at the end. In such an environment, you might define an alternate or time-weighted EQF as the ratio of the moments of the two areas:

$$\text{Time-Weighted EQF} = \frac{.5 \times \text{Actual value} \times \text{Duration}^2}{\int |(\text{Estimate (t)} - \text{Actual Value}) \times (\text{Duration} - t)| \, dt}$$

Exactly which formula you choose to represent estimating quality doesn't matter much. What does matter is that such a formula exists in your organization and is consistently applied. Without a publicly stated quantitative method for assessing forecast quality, you cannot expect that quality to improve.

PART III
Cost Models

I have but one lamp by which my feet are guided and that is the
lamp of experience. I know of no way of judging of the future
but by the past.

— Patrick Henry

An experienced manager is likely to do better than a novice at predicting the costs
of a project. Experience provides data from the past that shed light on the future. The
scheme for applying the lesson of the past in predicting future cost is the manager's *cost
model*. In traditional estimating, this model is intuitive.

A *formal cost model* is a predictive tool based on statistical science, rather than on
intuition. It applies quantifiable past experience in a disciplined fashion to project the
future. It provides an explicit assessment of how trustworthy its projections are.

15

COST PROJECTION: MODELING RESOURCE USE

Most models *look like* the things they represent. The shape of the model is derived from the shape of the real thing it stands for. Pieces of the model correspond to pieces of the real object and the shapes of the pieces of the model are derived from the shapes of the pieces of the real thing. I think of this quality of visual likeness as *isomorphism* (sameness of shape). The model in Figure 15-1 is isomorphic to the system it represents, a ship.

There are useful models that do not have this quality. Consider, as an example, the family of curves in Figure 15-2. The figure represents the ship's forward velocity as a function of wind speed and wind direction. Since it is a representation in miniature, the figure does qualify as a model. But it's not isomorphic — its shape is not derived from the shape of the system it represents, but rather from one aspect of its behavior (its sailing speed as a function of angle to the wind and wind strength). I'm going to refer to non-isomorphic models as *abstract*. Abstract models are usually presented in the form of mathematical equations and sets of such equations, so they are also termed *mathematical models*. Examples include such simple predictive formulas as

$$Distance = Rate \times Time$$

as well as those complex sets of equations used to forecast the weather or the coming year's gross national product.

Figure 15-1. Isomorphic model.*

*From Edward H.H. Archibald, *Kunstgeschichte der Seefahrt,* (Oldenburg, W. Germany: Gerhard Stalling Publishers, 1966).

Most of the models used in system work are isomorphic in some sense; the models' shapes are derived from structural characteristics of the system. Flow charts and HIPO diagrams qualify as isomorphic system models, as do all of the system models discussed in Part II. The major abstract model of interest in systems development is the *cost model*.

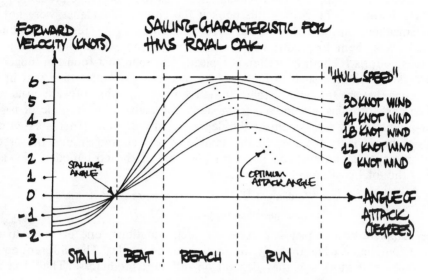

Figure 15-2. Non-isomorphic model of same ship.

15.1 The concept of a cost model

A cost model is a formula or set of formulas used to predict the costs likely to be incurred in a project. Anyone who survived Algebra I is accustomed to the idea of using formulas to predict real-life or simulated processes. Whether it's a time-speed-distance problem or one of farmers shoveling dirt at a fixed rate or of water flowing at 9.2 gallons an hour into a reservoir that is leaking 24,226 liters a week, you apply some sort of analysis to reduce the problem to a set of algebraic equations and solve those equations. The equations are deterministic: They give one and only one answer. The process under study is assumed to be similarly deterministic. So, using the equation to predict the process makes sense.

Many people are inclined to give up on any kind of formulaic prediction when they realize that the process they're trying to predict is not deterministic. They may also give up if some of the influencing factors are unknown or unmeasurable or if some factors must be disregarded to make analysis computationally tractable. Estimating the cost of a software project — and here I include all the various kinds of cost, including manpower, time, opportunity cost, and lost benefit — is certainly subject to these problems. Cost is not deterministic. Even though cost is *influenced* by a number of factors, knowing those factors exactly will still not enable you to predict cost exactly. Cost depends on far too many factors to study; even the most ambitious cost modelers have limited themselves to collecting and analyzing only a half dozen or so of the most important cost parameters and have ignored all the rest. And some cost factors are impossible to quantify: "My user is a pussycat, but his assistant is intent on scuttling our whole project."

These problems don't necessarily invalidate the idea of predicting based on mathematical formulas. They do, however, introduce imprecision into the answers such formulas provide. If the degree of imprecision is acceptable, then the formulas are still useful. Only empirical evidence can assure us that formulaic prediction is suitably precise. I wouldn't be writing this book if the empirical evidence were not favorable. Organizations around the world have had encouraging results building cost models and using them to predict future efforts acceptably. (Section 16.2 reports on some of these efforts.) The imprecision is typically less than that found in longer established forecasting sciences such as meteorology, and it is far better than that in the ad hoc predictions that are the only visible alternative for estimating software costs.

When cost formulas are derived from statistical analysis of a sample of past projects, a by-product is an assessment of the degree of imprecision. This is essentially an indication of how widely the data in the sample were scattered around the prediction line. The measure of imprecision is an integral part of the cost model. So, a given equation of the total cost model might take on this form:

$$\text{Cost}_i = K0 + K1 \times (\text{Predictor 1})^{P1} + K2 \times (\text{Predictor 2})^{P2} + \ldots$$
$$\pm \ (\text{Some statistical measure of scatter})$$

The complete cost model is a series of such equations, one or more to predict each of the component costs that together make up the whole. The different equations will have different factors and may depend on different predictors. They'll also have widely different degrees of imprecision: You can expect, for example, to be able to predict debugging time much more exactly than time spent negotiating with the user.

15.2 Transportable cost models, or "Waiting for Godot"

There was a good deal of flirtation with cost modeling in the early 1970s. Experimenters reported great success in using locally developed models to predict future work. They seemed to be achieving what Barry Boehm has called a reasonable target for estimating accuracy: eighty percent likelihood of the estimate being within twenty percent of the actual. *But,* if you tried to apply one of the models to your own projects, you would invariably fare much worse with it. It's not too difficult to figure out why this should be so:

> Many models have been proposed over the last several years, but, because of differences in the data collected, types of projects and environmental factors among software development sites, these models are not transportable and are only valid within the organization where they were developed. The result seems reasonable when one considers that a model developed at a certain environment will only be able to capture the impact of the factors which have a variable effect within that environment. Those factors which are constant at that environment, and therefore do not cause variations in the productivity among projects produced there, may have different or variable effects at another environment. [Bailey-Basili, 1981]

This should have been evident from the wide variation in form of the models that different organizations found useful. If you compared all the cost models in the litera-

ture, you might conclude that the organizations that developed them were not even trying to solve the same problem. Of course, they weren't. Each model was tailored to its
own environment. Only excessive optimism encouraged hope that any such models
might be transportable to other environments.

There are no transportable cost models. If you wait for someone elsewhere to
develop a set of formulas that you can use for cost forecasting in your own shop, you
will probably wait forever. Much of our industry concluded, upon realizing this fact,
that cost modeling was therefore irrelevant. I think that was the wrong conclusion. If
locally developed cost models can be used to improve the precision of the cost-
forecasting process, and if the improvement is worth the cost of developing the models,
then the concept is viable. If this tradeoff works in your organization, then it's reasonable for you to get into the business of constructing your own cost models. I believe
that the tradeoff does work for all but the smallest organizations.

15.3 The construction of cost models

There is nothing secret or the least bit abstruse about building cost models.
Required ingredients are time, a bit of statistical savvy, and a good deal of grubby hard
work. The process of building a cost model looks something like this:

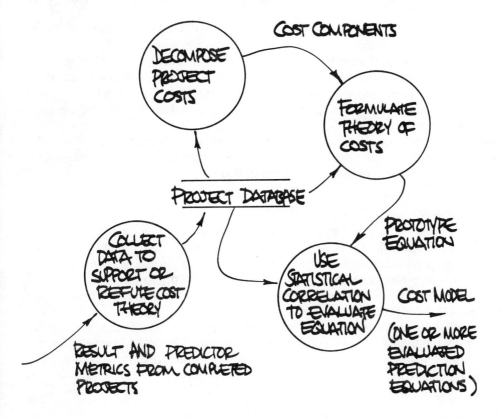

Figure 15-3. Construction of a cost model.

The four component activities are described in the following paragraphs.

Decomposition of cost: Almost any cost that you need to predict is worth decomposing first into pieces. Your prediction for the whole then becomes the sum of your predictions for the pieces. By predicting the pieces instead of the whole, you take advantage of certain "statistics of aggregation," the partial canceling of errors in predicting one of the pieces by opposite errors in predicting another of the pieces. The statistics of aggregation work for you to the extent that the pieces are independent (not all subject to increase or decrease for the same reason), and to the extent that inaccuracy introduced by the decomposition itself does not outweigh the benefits of aggregation. Independence will never be total among the elements of software cost, but even partial independence can afford some advantage. The result of all this is that you will want to break cost into its evident components (for example, Software Cost = Specification Cost + Design Cost + Implementation Cost + . . .) and then model these elements separately.

Decomposing total project cost into its components is exactly the process that I described as project modeling in Chapter 13. If all projects in a given domain could use the same project model, the cost decomposition just mentioned would be that model. Since different projects can use somewhat different project models, the cost decomposition process must involve forming a *super-model,* one that can be applied equally well to all projects in the domain.

Formulation of a cost theory: When there is a causal relationship between some result you're trying to predict and some early observable predictor, then there will surely be a strong statistical correlation between the two. However, the converse of that statement is not true. Statistical correlations do not necessarily imply cause, since there may be chance correlations between totally unrelated data items. A simple guard against chance correlations is to insist that any statistical analysis follow, not precede, formulation of a theory of cause.

Suppose, for instance, you suspect a linear relationship between one of the elements of cost, called C, and some measurable factor (candidate predictor) called P. The theory is expressed as a prototype equation in this form:

$$C = K0 + (K1 \times P)$$

More about this theory in Chapters 16 and 17.

Data Collection: Support or refutation of the theoretical relationship between C and P will require collecting C, P pairs from a sample of projects. Some of the data may be retrieved from records of past projects. My own experience in trying to reconstruct data from old project records has been dismal, due mainly to the wide practice of keeping virtually no records at all. Most data points, at least most required to support new theories, will have to be collected from new projects.

Correlation: A statistical tool is now used to fit a curve of the basic shape hypothesized by the theory into the set of points collected. The best-fit curve is defined by actual numeric values for each of the dummy factors in the prototype equation. The result might look something like this:

$$C = 1.299 + (.0355 \times P)$$

This equation implies perfect fit, but the data points used can be expected to have scattered about the prediction line defined by the equation. The amount of scatter is usually expressed as a standard error of estimate, and presented as part of the equation:

$$C = 1.299 + (.0355 \times P) \pm 14\%$$

The statistical tool used to derive an equation of this form is called *simple linear regression.* * The resultant cost model consists of a set of evaluated prediction equations, each useful for projecting a particular component of total cost with a known margin of error.

15.4 Convergence as a measure of usefulness

One measure of the probable usefulness of a cost model is the degree of convergence of sample data around the prediction line. After deriving the model, you plot the line indicated by the equation and then plot each of the data points from your database on the same grid. When there is a lot of convergence (very little scatter about the line), the model is likely to be a real boon in predicting future costs. If there is little convergence (wide scatter), the model will not be very useful (see Figure 15-4).

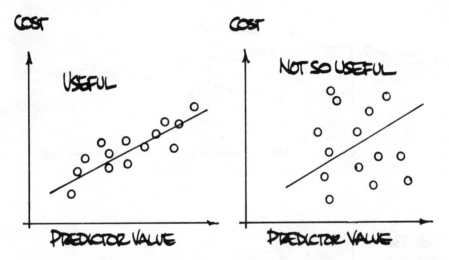

Figure 15-4. Useful and not-so-useful cost models.

There are numerous reports in the literature of cost modeling schemes that have resulted in acceptably narrow scatter. Specifically, they converged with a standard error of estimate of 25% or less. Imagine that you had such a model working for you in your own organization, a model tailored to allow you to project development cost as a function of Bang with a 25% standard error. The implication of a given standard error is that you have a 68% likelihood of estimating within the range of that error, and you have a 95% likelihood of estimating within twice that range. So, if you use your 25% model just once to project final cost, you will achieve an Estimating Quality Factor (as defined in Section 3.2) of 4 or higher in 68% of your projects.

An EQF of 4 is not much to rave about, but it is better than average.† So a reasonable cost model in its very first use ought to give you a 68% chance of producing a better-than-average estimate.

If you couple the technique of cost modeling with the political rearrangements suggested in Part I (so that the estimator has no disincentives against frequent re-estimation), then your EQF will improve appreciably. In fact, it will double as you

---

*Please look at Appendix C, "A Tailored Primer on Statistics," if you need a refresher on the use of regressions and standard errors.
†Average EQF for projects studied in [DeMarco, 1981] was 3.8.

approach the goal of treating estimation as a continuous function. Predictions from the model will continue to have a 25% standard error, but that percentage will be applied to a decreasing total. If you estimate at the project midpoint, for instance, the 25% standard error implies an absolute error of only 12.5% of the total work, only half the absolute error that the initial prediction was subject to. The absolute value of the error decreases steadily through the project. The result is that you have a better than 68% probability of attaining an EQF of 8 (see Figure 15-5). Furthermore, by the same analysis, you have a 95% probability of an EQF of 4 or more. So use of the model to forecast cost should give you a 95% probability of producing better-than-average estimates.

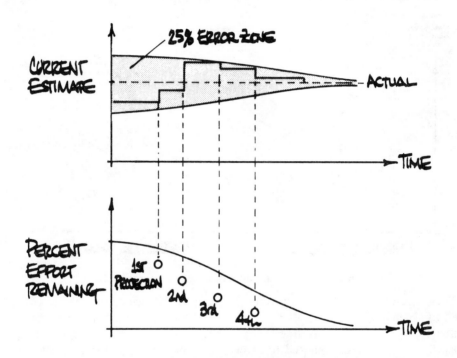

Figure 15-5. Estimating Quality Factor attained through continuous model use.

The best use of a cost model is to treat its result as input to the estimating process, not as its final output. The estimator looks at the projection produced by the model and estimates the likely deviation from that value, based on an assessment of factors that differentiate this project from those in the model's database. The final estimate is the sum of the model's projection and the estimated deviation. Whatever EQF the model can achieve by itself, the EQF for the model with a human correction is usually better.

I have set an EQF of 10 as a target for Metrics Groups to strive for in their model-oriented approach to cost forecasting. Although my sample is small, it affirms that this target is reachable.

15.5 Data requirements for constructing a useful cost model

A number of the models in the literature are based on data collected by the Rome Air Development Center. The RADC database contains information about more than five thousand projects. But please don't despair; much smaller sets of data have been used with excellent results. In my judgment, a sample as small as ten projects can be useful for cost modeling, provided that the projects are reasonably alike: same organization, same language, same class of business.

Building databases of completed projects is a time-consuming and expensive undertaking. I hope I have persuaded you in Part I that the expense of such data collection should properly be considered the cost of keeping control of each project. But even if you think of data collection as free, the *time* involved in building a reasonable local sample is substantial. I have no reassuringly glib solution to this problem. If you set out now to implement the Metric Function as I have described it, it will probably be a year or more before the benefits of model-based prediction are first realized. On the other hand, if you don't elect to incur this one-time startup cost, then your organization's estimates in the years to come will be of no better quality than those of today.

You can add data about whole projects only as quickly as you complete whole projects. But some essential data can be accumulated at a much faster rate. In the time it takes to add a single data point on total project cost to your database, you may be able to add thousands of data points on such components of total cost as defect cost, module internal design cost, walkthrough cost, test generation cost, test run cost, and cost of documenting a new user procedure.

15.6 Summary

Cost modeling is a scheme for disciplined exploitation of the cause-and-effect relationships that influence the cost of development. While these relationships are always present, they can only be exploited within domains of similar projects developed in similar ways. You can benefit from cost modeling, but only if you build the models yourself and tune them to your own environment. The cost of building cost models is part of the overall Metrics Group expense as quantified in Chapter 5.

15.7 Selected references

The IEEE has published two collections of papers on software cost modeling:

Workshop on Quantitative Software Models for Reliability, Complexity, and Cost: An Assessment of the State of the Art. IEEE Catalog No. TH0067-9. New York: Institute of Electrical and Electronics Engineers, 1979.

Basili, V. *Tutorial on Models and Metrics for Software Management and Engineering.* New York: Institute of Electrical and Electronics Engineers, 1980.

These collections describe the experience and insight of some sixty different authors reporting on their uses of cost modeling techniques. The two books together make an excellent introduction to the topic, and should be required reading for Metrics Group members. A good dozen of the papers that I have cited and will be citing here are included in one or both of the IEEE collections.

16

CORRECTED
SINGLE-FACTOR
COST MODELS

The purpose of this chapter and of the one that follows is to acquaint you with some of the more successful cost models now in the public domain. Chapter 18 will then lay out a scheme for adapting to your own environment selected techniques from the public domain models.

16.1 A class of simple models for local use

There are literally hundreds of parameters that can affect software cost. A straightforward approach to cost modeling would be to list the factors as best you could in descending order of probable effect, and then try to fit your sample data with a curve of the form

$$\text{Cost} = K + M1 \times P1 + M2 \times P2 + \ldots + Mn \times Pn$$

where Pi stands for the ith parameter and Mi is its multiplier. A little less simplistic would be a model that assumed nonlinear effects, something in this form:

$$\text{Cost} = K + M1 \times P1^{E1} + M2 \times P2^{E2} + \ldots + Mn \times Pn^{En}$$

The precision of such models is far greater than their accuracy. Noise in the development process will add a scatter of from ten to twenty percent. It's pointless to keep track of parameters whose impact is substantially less than the noise level. So the value of the equation is not reduced by truncation, that is, by removal of all factors that contribute less than, say, five percent.

That might still leave a half-dozen parameters to consider. Regression with so many parameters can be rather cumbersome. (In fact, nonlinear regression with multiple parameters is already beyond the computational capacity of most organizations.) An obvious solution is to truncate after the first parameter

$$Cost = K + M \times P$$

or

$$Cost = K + M \times P^E$$

with some expected loss of accuracy. The result is a *single-factor model,* a projection based on only one predictor.

Eliminating all but the most significant factor is not ludicrous. The most significant factor is always some measure of the volume of work (or complexity-weighted volume of work). Of course, many factors other than the volume of work can affect how much it costs to do a given job. But for exclusive use in one environment — in your organization, for instance — such a model can work rather well, because the truncated factors don't vary much from project to project *in that environment.* If the projects in your organization are fairly homogeneous, a single-factor model may be all you need. If the mix does vary, it may be necessary to collect data in separate domains (sets of projects with similar characteristics), and to build a separate model for each domain.

In most cases, one or more of the truncated factors will cause significant variations within the sample set or even within domains of the set. When this is true, the model requires empirical correction to account for the effect of the factor(s). A simple approximate correction for the half-dozen or so most important factors should be sufficient to make the model converge to within the natural noise level of software development. Empirical correction is discussed in Section 16.4.

16.2 Examples of successful single-factor models

Since it relates work to cost, a single-factor model is essentially a productivity model. There are obvious problems inherent in productivity models, but some organizations have nonetheless managed to use them profitably. The following subsections examine the problems in light of the experiences of three organizations that have succeeded in building workable single-factor models.

16.2.1 A cost model from IBM

Walston and Felix measured sixty projects at IBM and built a single-factor model based on the sample [Walston-Felix, 1977]. They found that effort (manpower) was related to volume of work by this equation:

$$E = 5.2 \times L^{0.91}$$

where E was measured in man-months, and L, units of work, was measured in thousands of (sigh) lines of code. I know all the arguments that conventional wisdom has advanced to prove that such simplistic productivity models aren't "real world." But don't dismiss this one until you look at Figure 16-1 at the kind of convergence that Walston and Felix obtained with it even before correcting for the truncated factors.

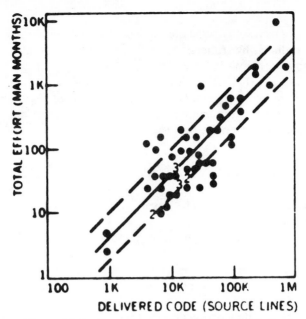

Figure 16-1. Convergence in the Walston-Felix data.*

The data points in the sample represent actual projects carried out by the IBM Federal Systems Division. The projects varied in size from 12 to 11,758 man-months.

Such respectable convergence indicates that the experimenters managed to overcome most of the problems that have given productivity modeling a bad name in the past. I have listed below the set of generally perceived problems, together with a capsule explanation of how Walston and Felix tackled each one.

Problem: Data are invariably collected differently on different projects. Walston and Felix imposed a rigid data collection standard and stuck to it. With a sample of projects that goes outside the bounds of a single organization, the problem of varying standards for collecting data can be virtually insurmountable. But within a company or within a division of a large company, it is possible to exercise sufficient control on data collection to avoid mixing apples and oranges. The problem virtually goes away when an independent Metrics Group collects the data instead of letting the project teams collect their own.

Problem: Productivity is not constant; individual differences can be enormous. Differences between individual producers are large, but they damp out quickly as the size of the project team increases. For projects of seven or more people, individual differences can be expected to cancel out. Projects with three or fewer people, however, may be dominated by exceedingly strong or weak producers.

Problem: Productivity models presume that time and people are interchangeable. They aren't. We all know that ten people working one month on a complex set of tasks can't accomplish as much as one person working ten months. But over a fairly narrow range, there is a workable tradeoff between people and time. The IBM projects were restricted to that range. Chapter 17 addresses the limitations of trading off people against time.

---

*C.E. Walston and C.P. Felix, "A Method of Programming Measurement and Estimation," *IBM Systems Journal,* Vol. 16, No. 1 (January 1977), p. 62. Reprinted by permission. Copyright © 1977 by International Business Machines Co.

Problem: Lines of code is a poor metric because some lines are more complex than others. This effect may apply in general, but is probably not a very important factor within a single environment where code complexity usually varies very little. Such seems to have been the case in the Walston-Felix experiment. The problem of varying complexity is a largely tractable one, anyway: The complexity metrics of Chapter 12 work fairly consistently in accounting for the effects of varying complexity. The real objection to lines of code is not that it is an inconsistent metric, but that it is a *late* metric. I'll have more to say about that in just a bit.

Problem: The factors ignored by such a simple model are too important to ignore. Again, this is true in general, but may not be very significant within a given environment. Walston and Felix got good convergence even while ignoring such factors as past customer experience with the application and machine time availability. They did, however, improve their single-factor model substantially by correcting for the effects of some of the truncated factors.

16.2.2 A cost model from the University of Maryland

Bailey and Basili, working with a sample of 19 projects, came up with this single-factor model [Bailey-Basili, 1981]:

$$E = 3.4 + .72 \times DL^{1.17} \pm 25\%$$

The parameter DL is a composite measure of work, based again on lines of code. Different classes of program segments were given different weights before they were summed. Bailey and Basili also improved their model (finally achieving a standard error of estimate of about 15%) using correction techniques described in Section 16.4.

Note that there is no hope of resolving the Maryland model with the one from IBM. If one model predicts reasonably in a given environment, the other will be useless in that environment. You should expect that neither will work well for you. Each model was constructed for its own limited environment and is unusable elsewhere.

16.2.3 COCOMO

The COnstructive COst MOdel (COCOMO) was developed at TRW [Boehm, 1981]. The model is based on a sample of 63 projects, which were divided into three separate domains defined by product type and by certain characteristics of the project and its team members. (For instance, embedded system projects were separated into their own domain.) Boehm calculated an effort equation for each domain:

Table 16-1
Basic COCOMO Effort and Schedule Equations*

Mode	Effort
Organic	$MM = 2.4(KDSI)^{1.05}$
Semidetached	$MM = 3.0(KDSI)^{1.12}$
Embedded	$MM = 3.6(KDSI)^{1.20}$

*Barry W. Boehm, SOFTWARE ENGINEERING ECONOMICS, © 1981, p. 75. Reprinted by permission of Prentice-Hall, Inc., Englewood Cliffs, N.J.

MM in the table stands for the nominal number of man-months, and *KDSI* is a simple count of source statements. Convergence of the model is shown below [Boehm, 1981]:

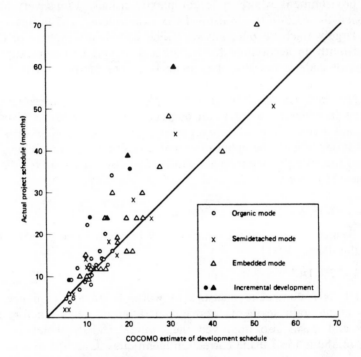

Figure 16-2. Basic COCOMO effort estimates versus actual results.*

When the data were corrected for some of the truncated factors (including ten different languages, four different classes of computer, and development methods varying with project start dates from 1964 to 1979), the convergence was more than respectable (see Figure 16-3).

16.2.4 The model from the manager's head

When you look through the convergence evidence of these and other public domain models, you're likely to find the odd point that deviates by a factor of two or more. Is an estimating technique to be rejected because it can (if only in rare instances) be off by so much? I'm afraid there is no way to reject the concept of cost modeling. If you don't use the formal modeling technique I suggest here, you'll simply have to revert to the informal model in the manager's head, because the old estimate-by-wet-finger-in-the-wind approach is a kind of cost modeling. It uses data samples and correlations and weighting factors as well as other basic modeling concepts. But in the intuitive model, the samples are tiny, the weighting factors are emotional, and the correlations are performed without recourse to statistical science.

---

*Barry W. Boehm, SOFTWARE ENGINEERING ECONOMICS, © 1981, p. 87. Reprinted by permission of Prentice-Hall, Inc., Englewood Cliffs, N.J.

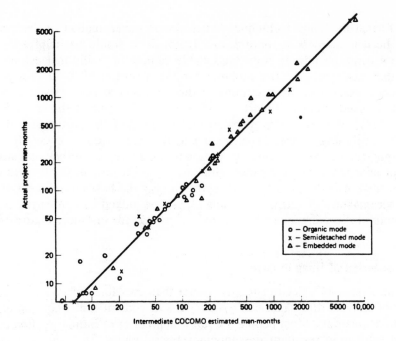

Figure 16-3. Corrected COCOMO effort estimates versus actual results.*

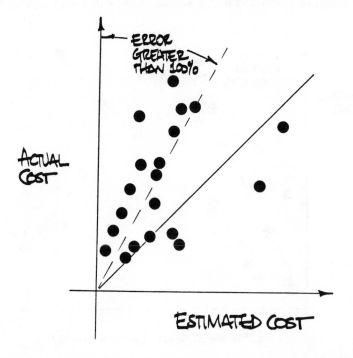

Figure 16-4. Convergence of traditional estimates in the 1978 Yourdon Survey.

*Barry W. Boehm, SOFTWARE ENGINEERING ECONOMICS, © 1981, p. 139. Reprinted by permission of Prentice-Hall, Inc., Englewood Cliffs, N.J.

One formal modeling technique that is almost never applied to the model in the manager's head is *analysis of convergence.* I thought it would be helpful if, just once, there were a careful study of some reasonable sample of traditional estimates, to see how well they converge. In the proposal for the Yourdon 1978-80 Project Survey, I asked project managers at the beginning of their projects to state expected effort. And at the end, I asked them to report actual effort. The result is shown in Figure 16-4 [DeMarco, 1981]. I should also mention that nearly half the participants dropped out between the beginning of this experiment and the end. I don't know all the reasons managers might have had for failing to complete the survey once they had started, but I suspect that poor project performance with respect to meeting estimates was one of the reasons. So Figure 16-4 may very well represent only the best fifty percent of the data.

The acceptability of formal modeling should be judged by comparing convergence with the model to convergence without, by comparing, for instance, Figure 16-3 to Figure 16-4.

16.3 The question of lines of code

The most serious objection to any model that uses lines of code as an indication of volume of work is this: You can't *count* lines of code at the beginning of a project; you have to estimate it. Most people are not much better at estimating line counts than they are at estimating resultant development costs. Figure 16-5 shows estimated and actual line counts for a sample of projects from the Yourdon 1978-80 Project Survey. The estimating error, compounded by the scatter, results in a very poor projection.

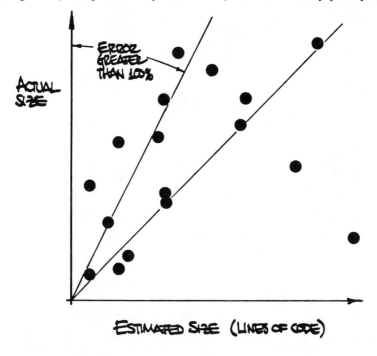

Figure 16-5. Estimated versus actual line counts in the Yourdon Survey.

The fact that a model cannot be used successfully from the beginning of a project doesn't mean that it is of no use at all. It may still be a valuable tool for tailoring forecasts while the project is in progress. Models based on lines of code can be exceedingly useful for any forecasting called for *after the point in a project at which an accurate count of lines of code can be made.* As an example, consider some of the important component costs in the latter half of the project, such as unit testing cost or integration cost. Using methods from the University of Maryland or IBM studies [Bailey-Basili, 1981; Walston-Felix, 1977], you can build an excellent single-factor model correlating such costs to some weighted composite measure of lines of code. True, you can only use this model from approximately the midway point of the project, but from that time on, it will be a valuable aid in producing estimates that converge to the actual.

A single-factor cost model can be based on any consistent metric. In particular, you can build such models to project costs from the Bang and Design Weight predictors. The methods of construction (decomposition, hypothesis, data collection, and correlation) are no different for Bang-based cost models, for instance, than for cost models based on lines of code.

16.4 Empirical correction of single-factor cost models

The convergence of uncorrected data in the examples of Section 16.2 is an impressive affirmation of the fundamentally causal nature of software development. But, frankly, it is not sufficient for the political needs of modern projects. Too many of the data points in the samples are a factor of two or more away from the prediction line. In order to produce estimates with an EQF of 8 to 10, we will require substantially better convergence. Convergence can be improved to the necessary degree by applying a simple linear correction to compensate for the effect of a small number of the most powerful of the truncated factors. This was the approach used to correct each of the three models described in Section 16.2. The basic scheme is illustrated in Figure 16-6. The key procedures of the correction scheme are these:

1. *Calculate prediction error for each project.* Compare the value predicted by the uncorrected single-factor cost model to the actual value for each project in the sample space. Express the difference as a signed percentage. This quantity is the prediction error for your uncorrected model.

2. *Quantify likely correction factors.* Study the factors truncated from the single-factor cost model, and isolate those most likely to affect performance over the domain. For each factor, establish a coding scheme to specify discrete values. The kinds of factors to consider will vary from one domain to another and from one company to another. Table 16-2, presented later in this section, provides an example of the kind of factors to consider, and the approximate degree of precision you can hope to achieve in quantifying each one. Quantify each project in the sample space according to the factors selected.

3. *Correlate correction factors to prediction error.* Use a statistical tool (multiple linear regression) to correlate the prediction error with the values of the correction factors. Express the result as an equation of this form:

    Prediction Error = W1 × Factor1 + W2 × Factor2 + . . .

4. *Apply correction and evaluate.* Apply the correction to each of the points in the sample space by subtracting the expected prediction error of the formula from the projection. Compare the result to the actual. Calculate a new standard error of estimate as an indication of convergence.

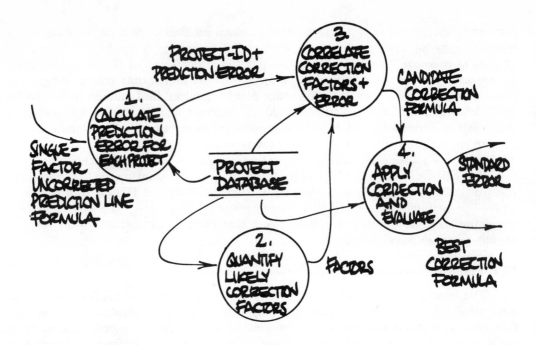

Figure 16-6. Empirical correction.

I have described the correction process as though the model were used only to predict a single result (say, total effort), instead of the component parts of that result. Clearly, the correction process must be repeated for each of the results to be predicted.

The following table lists in adapted form the factors that Walston and Felix worked with in correcting their model:*

Table 16-2
The Walston-Felix Factors

Factor	Meaningful Values
Customer (user) interface complexity	Simple, Normal, Complex
User participation in specification	None, Some, Much
Customer- (user-) originated design changes	Few, Many
Customer (user) experience with application	None, Some, Much
Overall personnel experience	Low, Average, High
Percentage of programmers participating in analysis and design	0% − 24%, 25% − 50%, 51% − 100%
Previous experience with the hardware	Minimal, Average, Extensive
Previous experience with the language	Minimal, Average, Extensive
Previous experience with application of similar or greater size and complexity	Minimal, Average, Extensive
Ratio of average staff size to duration (people/month)	0 − .49, .5 − .9, Over .9

*C.E. Walston and C.P. Felix, "A Method of Programming Measurement and Estimation," *IBM Systems Journal,* Vol. 16, No. 1, p. 64. Reprinted by permission. Copyright © 1977 by International Business Machines Co.

Factor	*Meaningful Values*
Hardware under concurrent development	No, Yes
Development computer access, open under special request	0%, 1% − 25%, Over 25%
Development computer access, closed	0% − 10%, 11% − 85%, Over 85%
Classified security environment for computer and for at least 25% of code and data	Yes, No
Use of structured programming (expressed as percentage of control constructs that are SEQUENCE, DO-UNTIL, DO-WHILE, IF-THEN-ELSE, or CASE)	0% − 33%, 34% − 66%, Over 66%
Percentage of all design and code subject to formal walkthrough	0% − 33%, 34% − 66%, Over 66%
Use of top-down development (expressed as a percent adherence to the concept of designing, coding, and testing calling modules before their called modules)	0% − 33%, 34% − 66%, Over 66%
Use of Chief Programmer Team concept	None, Partial, Rigorous
Overall complexity of delivered code	Below average, Average, Above average
Complexity of application processing	Below average, Average, Above average
Complexity of program flow	Below average, Average, Above average
Overall constraints on program design	Minimal, Average, Severe
Program design constraints on core	Minimal, Average, Severe
Code for real-time or interactive operation, or under severe timing constraint	0% − 9%, 10% − 40%, Over 40%
Percentage of code for delivery	0% − 90%, 91% − 99%, 100%
Code classified as non-mathematical applications and I/O formatting programs	0% − 33%, 34% − 66%, More than 66%
Number of classes of items in the database per 1,000 lines of code	0 − 15, 16 − 80, More than 80
Number of pages of delivered documentation per 1,000 lines of delivered code	0 − 32, 33 − 88, More than 88

In any single domain, many of these factors will be constant, and thus can be ignored. The large number of factors in the Walston-Felix study reflects the nature of the organization studied (a contractor) as well as the investigators' decision not to divide the sample into homogeneous domains. In a typical non-contracting environment, one that does divide the sample space into reasonably homogeneous sets, a dozen or so factors from the table would probably suffice. (The Bailey-Basili study began with some thirty correction factors, and eventually discarded all but two.)

Note that the Walston-Felix factors reflecting code complexity should not be included in the scheme described here, since such factors are already figured into the code metrics (discussed in Chapter 19) used to deduce weighted source line counts.

16.5 Netting it out: What a local cost model can do for you

I have described a two-part scheme for local cost modeling, involving a single-factor nonlinear model with linear correction. By collecting data on ten to twenty projects from your organization, you should be able to construct such a model that will converge to within 25% (standard error of 25% or less). To the extent that you succeed in this, you will be able to use the model to forecast costs with an EQF of 8 or better.

16.6 Reprise of the theme of the metric specialist

I know from presenting these ideas in my seminars that some managers have difficulty accepting the implied scope of the cost modeling activity. They're concerned about the sheer volume of work involved in data collection and analysis: "Who's got time for all this? Who's got time to investigate the relationships among the literally scores of components of overall cost and the still greater number of factors that influence them? We've got code to write," they complain.

When medicine was a sideline of the friendly corner barber, he might have made the same kind of objection: "Who's got time to take people's temperatures and blood pressure? We've got hair to cut." The quantum leap into modern medicine required creation of specialists, doctors whose entire concern could be medicine. A similar quantum leap into solidly based, reliable cost forecasting will require a similar specialization. The metric specialist can take the time to collect and analyze cost-relevant statistics on a broad scale, provided only that value of the improved forecasting more than offsets cost of the Metric Function. For all but the smallest and least critical projects, I predict that it will.

16.7 Selected references

The best source I know on software cost modeling is

Boehm, B. *Software Engineering Economics.* Englewood Cliffs, N.J.: Prentice-Hall, 1981.

In addition to its very specific and understandable cost modeling guidelines, this book provides helpful advice on other aspects of quantitative analysis of software, including risk analysis and decision theory.

A set of prescriptions for building your own local cost model is contained in

Bailey, J.W., and V.R. Basili. "A Meta-Model for Software Development and Resource Expenditures." *Proceedings of the 5th International Conference on Software Engineering.* New York: Institute of Electrical and Electronics Engineers, 1981, pp. 107-16.

The paper is presented in the form of a kit for cost-modelers. It suggests what data to collect, what statistical methods to use in analyzing it, and what confidence factor to attribute to the modeled result. It also provides a set of data points from projects studied by the Software Engineering Laboratory at the University of Maryland. The meta-model described by Bailey and Basili was developed to correlate lines-of-code based metrics with effort, but the methods described in the paper are equally applicable to cost models based on other metrics.

Any reading on cost modeling ought to include

Walston, C.E., and C.P. Felix. "A Method of Programming Measurement and Estimation." *IBM Systems Journal,* Vol. 16, No. 1 (January 1977), pp. 54-73. [Reprinted in *Writings of the Revolution: Selected Readings on Software Engineering.* E. Yourdon, ed. (New York: Yourdon Press, 1982), pp. 389-408.]

17

TIME-SENSITIVE
COST MODELS

Time-sensitive cost models provide a way to quantify the effects of trading off people against time. The two manpower-loading patterns of Figure 17-1 are not equivalent. Both use up fifty man-years, but only the most naive project manager would expect the two to have equally productive results. You cannot increase staff by a factor of X and achieve a reduction to $1/X$ of the time. But that does not imply there isn't some sort of well-behaved tradeoff between people and time. Figure 17-2 presents a speculative view of how the tradeoff might look. The broken line shows a simple inverse relationship, representing the unattainable proportional tradeoff. The real situation is better portrayed by the solid line to the right. For any given project, there is a limit to how much time reduction can be achieved by increasing staff (striped asymptote). Further staff increments do not reduce delivery time; they probably increase it.

An alternative way to think of this effect is that productivity is a function of team size. Individual productivity falls off somewhat as the number of people interacting increases. The productive capacity of the entire team, measured as Bang delivered per unit of time, varies as shown in Figure 17-3. In this figure, the dashed line represents the limiting case, in which the productivity increment from adding the nth person is equal to the increment from the first. The solid line represents a realistic situation. The area between the two lines is the cost of interaction.

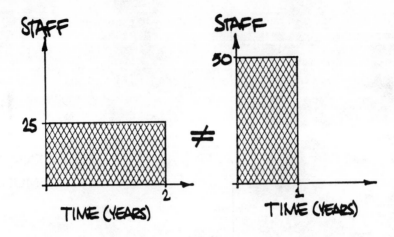

Figure 17-1. Unequal staffing patterns.

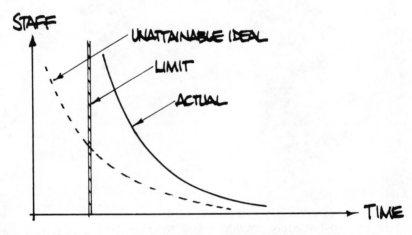

Figure 17-2. People-time tradeoff (speculative).

There may be a set of such curves, each one defining the interaction costs for a different project (see Figure 17-4). The differences are due to different technical approaches, and to differing degrees of *connectivity* among the project activities. But in all cases, the real productive capacity lies to the right of the dotted line.

Accelerating the project by increasing staff will always result in some per-person productivity loss. Rapid acceleration may also result in additional loss due to the project's inability to absorb new staff at such a rate. Trading off people against time is only feasible within certain limits.

To accompany these *qualitative* observations, we require the following pieces of *quantitative* information:

- What is the optimal scheme for adding staff to a project over time?
- What delivery date will result from an optimal staffing pattern?
- What variation of staffing will effect delivery at an earlier date?

- How does total cost vary as a function of the people-time tradeoff?
- What are the limits to the people-time tradeoff?

A time-sensitive cost model is one that attempts to answer these questions. It might be thought of as a *two-factor* model, where the second factor is time. The rest of this chapter will present the topic of time-sensitive cost models from a more or less historical perspective.

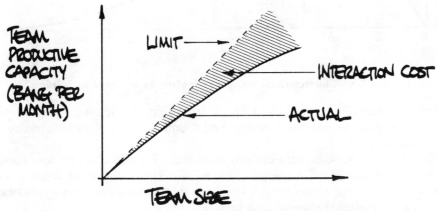

Figure 17-3. Team productive capacity as a function of team size.

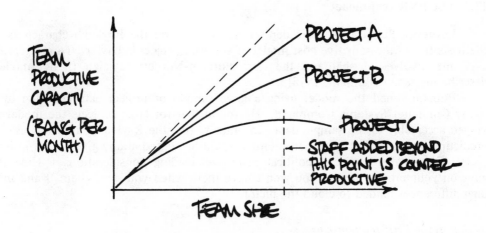

Figure 17-4. Varying cost of interaction.

17.1 The Norden observations

One of the earliest time-sensitive models was developed by P.V. Norden of IBM during the sixties [Norden, 1963]. Norden studied the rate of staff buildup and decline for engineering and development projects at IBM, and concluded that there was a strongly recurrent pattern. He plotted manpower curves for each project, showing how many staff members were assigned to the project in each project month, from start to end of development. Projects tended toward a staffing pattern of the form shown in Figure 17-5.

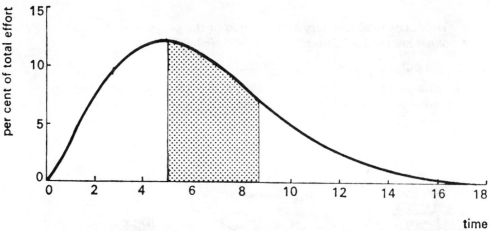

Figure 17-5. Characteristic manpower loading as observed by Norden.*

The characteristic curve looked like a probability distribution. Norden matched the curve to known distribution formulas and found one, the *Rayleigh distribution,* that fit it well [Norden, 1963].

Norden's observations were entirely empirical. There was no evident reason why manpower should exhibit a Rayleigh characteristic as a function of time; it just did. The characteristic curve seems to be a function of how people interact as they carry out the connected activities that make up a project.

17.2 The PNR cost model

Lawrence Putnam used Norden's observations and the Rayleigh characteristic as the basis for a time-sensitive cost model of software project behavior. To give credit to everyone involved, I shall use the term Putnam-Norden-Rayleigh (PNR) model to describe the result [Putnam, 1978].

Putnam tuned the model using a large sample of project data collected by the Army Computer Systems Command. He found that for large projects the model converged acceptably to the sample data. In other words, the Rayleigh curve was useful in predicting how an effort of *n* man-months would be staffed at any given point in its life cycle. For smaller projects, political manpower-loading considerations ("Hide these guys on your project now or you won't have them when you need them") and individual differences tended to cloud the picture.

17.2.1 Basic PNR relationships

The PNR model is built upon two equations, one governing total effort and the other governing manpower loading as a function of time. The mathematical complexity of the equations is a bit disconcerting, so I have elected to present them first in functional form (see next page).

---

*Peter Norden, "Useful Tools for Project Management," *Operations Research in Research and Development,* B.V. Dean, ed. (New York: John Wiley & Sons, 1963), p. 4. Reprinted by permission.

Effort (man-months) DEPENDS ON

> Volume of Work
> Difficulty Gradient (a measure of complexity)
> Project Technology Factor (a measure of staff experience)
> Delivery Time

Manpower (count of project staff at any given moment) DEPENDS ON

> Total Cumulative Manpower
> Project Acceleration Factor (a measure of how quickly
>> the project can absorb new staff members)
> Project Month

The model seems to promise a way to forecast effort *and* describe an optimal manpower-loading scheme to apply that effort, provided only that you can figure out a way to quantify each of the independent parameters, and a way to predict the value of each of the parameters early enough to suit your forecasting needs. Neither of these is a trivial requirement.

Since the PNR effort equation is based on a lines-of-code metric for volume of work, I won't advocate its use here. I suggest rather that you use a locally developed Bang-based model (as described in Chapter 16) to project man-months of effort and then apply a variant of the PNR manpower equation to the result in order to determine plausible schedules for development. Since the manpower equation is more germane to the method proposed here, I'll begin by discussing it and its significance in the next subsection. In Section 17.5, I'll return to the effort equation for the insight it can provide about the effect of varying certain project parameters.

17.2.2 Project manpower loading

The PNR manpower equation assumes that you already have a forecast of the man-months of effort required for your project, and now need only to determine how staff ought to vary over time. The equation describes manpower loading as a Rayleigh distribution of the form

$$\text{Manpower } (t) = 2K \; a \; t \exp(-at^2)$$

where a is the Acceleration Factor, a shaping parameter that establishes the initial slope of the curve, and K is the total manpower cost (man-months of effort). K is equal to the area under the manpower curve in Figure 17-6 [Shooman, 1979].

The curve and the equation represent one way to apply K units of manpower without significant waste. There is a family of such curves, one for each feasible value of a. Each curve shows a manpower-loading strategy that does not violate any natural rule about how people in projects interact. If your project is governed by a given PNR curve, then some manpower will be wasted if you load staff differently. Suppose, for instance, that the PNR curve of Figure 17-7 applies to your project [Putnam, 1980].

Suppose further that your actual staff loading is shown by the rectangular pattern superimposed upon the curve. The areas that don't lie under both the PNR curve and the actual pattern represent manpower that is likely to be wasted, at least to some degree. The manpower allocated in those areas is inconsistent with the project's ability to absorb staff or its need for additional staff when there is more work than the current staff can handle.

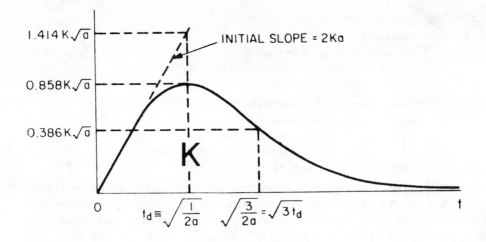

Figure 17-6. Annotated Rayleigh manpower curve.*

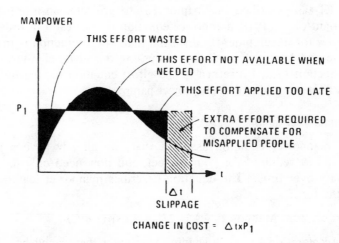

Figure 17-7. Ideal and actual manpower-loading strategies.[†]

17.2.3 Variation on a theme by Putnam

An alternative time-sensitive cost model has been proposed by F.N. Parr of the Imperial College, London [Parr, 1980]. This model predicts essentially the same behavior as the PNR model except during the early part of the project (see Figure 17-8). Just for the record, the best-fit equation that describes Parr's manpower curve is

$$\text{Manpower } (t) = 1/4 \; \text{sech}^2 \left[\frac{(at + c)}{2} \right]$$

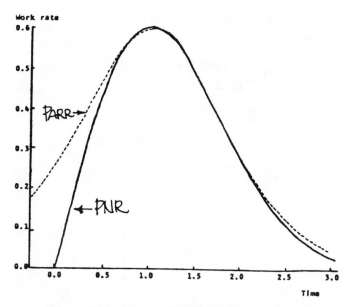

Figure 17-8. Parr and PNR models compared.*

The Parr model is intended to fit projects for which some staff is already working and up-to-speed at the beginning of the project. This would be the case if the project were a follow-up to some previous work, or in certain contracting relationships. The Parr model also seems to apply to smaller projects, those involving manpower of fifteen man-years or less. For a sample of some two dozen such projects studied in the Yourdon 1978-80 Project Survey, the Parr curve fits the composite manpower curve quite well [DeMarco, 1981]. This is shown in Figure 17-9.

My own initial reaction to the Parr model was: "Hyperbolic secants? You must be kidding!" and I don't doubt that you're feeling somewhat the same way. If the PNR manpower equation was mathematically exotic, the Parr equation is positively bizarre. But keep in mind that it is the *curves* (in both cases) that reflect observed evidence. The mathematical equations that approximate these curves are of interest only because they give you an abbreviated way to write down the shape of the curve. This is handy, for instance, if you want a way to tell your computer the shape of the curve so that it can draw one for you. Beyond that, you need have no interest in the math.

Once you have any properly shaped PNR or Parr curve, you can use graphic methods exclusively from there on: You simply rescale the horizontal axis to correspond to your delivery time, and rescale the vertical axis to correspond to your staffing. Figure 17-10 presents an unscaled PNR curve in a full-page format so that you can easily use it for your own projects. A simple approximation to the Parr curve is also shown in that figure. (The approximation uses a linear buildup during the period before the peak and the PNR curve from that point on.)

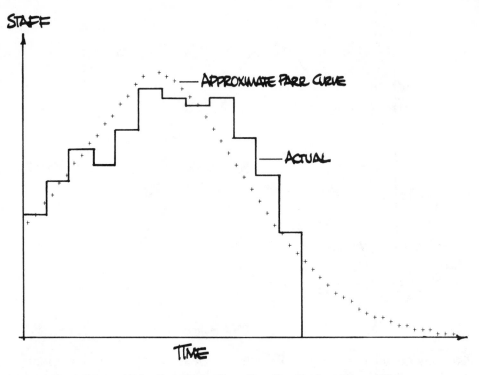

Figure 17-9. Parr curve fit to Yourdon Project Survey data.

17.3 Delivery time as a function of manpower loading

Both the PNR and Parr models treat the project as a connected set of development *and maintenance* activities associated with a given piece of software. So the curves show staff loading throughout the life of the software. Only part of this is what is typically called the development project, the part to the left of t_d on the curve (Figure 17-11) [W. Myers, 1978].

In the graph, t_d is defined as the time of first operational capacity, the initial delivery of all specified function. For large projects, Putnam found that t_d typically occurred at or near the manpower peak. The area under the curve to the left of the peak is 39% of the total. For smaller projects, t_d can be expected to occur to the right of the peak. As an example, for 24 commercial data processing projects in the range of three to five man-years, t_d on the average occurred at about 250% of time-to-peak [DeMarco, 1981].

This implies that there is a well-behaved relationship between delivery time and manpower, provided that the Acceleration Factor remains constant. Within a given domain, acceleration should not vary too much, and so there should be a reasonably constant relationship between man-months and elapsed time to deliver. For a sample of projects from TRW, IBM, and RADC, for instance, the relationship reported by Boehm was

$$t_d \text{ nominal} = 2.5 \times (MM)^{.33}$$

where t_d nominal is the most likely delivery time for a project expected to use MM man-months of effort [Boehm, 1981]. The MM used in this relationship is the effort to the left of t_d.

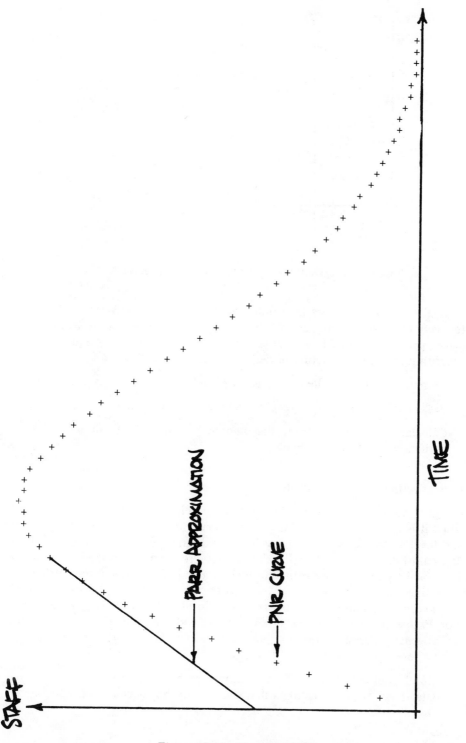

Figure 17-10. **Unscaled PNR curve.**

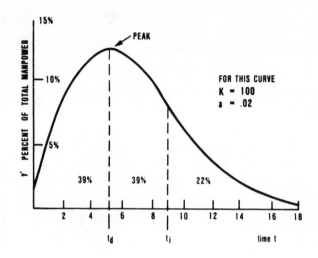

Figure 17-11. Delivery time shown on a PNR curve.*

The t_d nominal equation describes how much time it takes to use *MM* man-months of effort effectively for a typical project. While a given project may deviate from this pattern, it makes good sense to plan on delivery time consistent with the equation. So, a prudent algorithm for early prediction of delivery time is the following:

1. Compute Bang from the specification model.

2. Project effort from the corrected single-factor cost model.

3. Calculate t_d nominal from the Boehm equation or from a locally verified version of your own.

17.4 Limits affecting manpower strategy

Although t_d nominal represents the most likely delivery time for an effort of *MM* man-months, it is not the only possibility. The curves in Figure 17-12 show a succession of staff-loading strategies for applying the same manpower over shorter and shorter periods [Putnam-Fitzsimmons, 1979]. Under pressure from your management, you may decide to shift your strategy from the most gradual curve (maximum staff of 30) to the center one (maximum of 40) or even to the steepest curve (maximum of 61). You cannot continue indefinitely shifting the curve to the left. There is some maximum Acceleration Factor that applies to the mix of project and staff. The limit will be a function of the interdependence of the component project activities. There are really two effects at work here:

● natural interdependence among component pieces of the requirement (data and control connections that show up in the specification model)

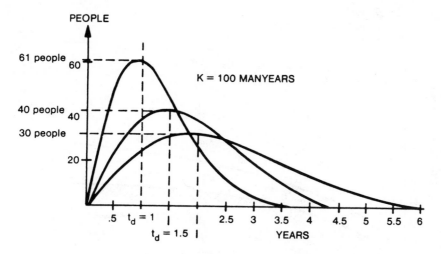

Figure 17-12. Alternative manpower-loading strategies.*

- added interdependence due to your method for tackling the requirement (data and PERT-style connections that show up in the project model)

In most organizations, maximum Acceleration Factor is fairly constant. If your applications vary widely in natural connectedness — for instance, if you develop both scientific and commercial systems — you will have to analyze them in separate domains. The maximum Acceleration Factor should stay constant over each domain.

Your project may achieve an acceleration that is greater than any ever recorded in your organization before. But a prudent manager can hardly justify *planning on* such performance. If you collect a sample of Acceleration Factors from past projects in your organization (more about collecting these numbers in Chapter 18), then the nominal and maximum values should guide your project planning.

There is reason to believe that there exists a *global* limit to acceleration. Such a limit has been described by Boehm as an "Impossible Region" for development, as shown in Figure 17-13 [Boehm, 1981]. The Impossible Region represents effectively infeasible manpower strategies. There is a limit to how many man-months of effort can be squeezed into a given elapsed time, and the edge of the Impossible Region marks that limit. Projects that try to squeeze effort of MM man-months into less than $1.9 \times (MM)^{.33}$ months are in the Impossible Region. That doesn't mean they cannot possibly succeed, only that the empirical evidence is strongly against them.

The graph of Figure 17-13 is a weapon in your arsenal to use against unreasonably inflated expectations dropped on you from above. I've often had managers ask for advice on how to deal with blatantly unattainable targets. In many companies, you're just not a team player if you don't accept upper management's target, no matter how outrageous it may be. But the Impossible Region sheds a whole new light on the problem — it gives you some empirical evidence to determine reasonableness. If you're

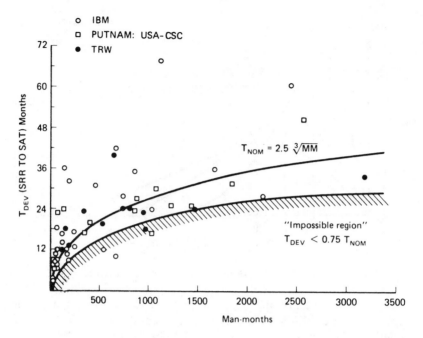

Figure 17-13. The Impossible Region.*

asked to perform within the region, your response is the same as if you were assigned the task of running a three-minute mile. You point to the evidence and say, "We'll sure give it a fling, boss. But you should know that if we do succeed in performing at that level, we'll be the very first to do so." I feel that I've spent half my professional life slogging away in the Impossible Region. I wish I'd had the evidence of Figure 17-13 fifteen years ago.

17.5 The effect of accelerating or relaxing the project schedule

The curves of Figure 17-12 showed three different feasible ways to apply the same manpower (100 man-years), but the three are not equivalent in terms of useful work likely to be delivered. Individual productivity falls off as acceleration increases. In order to make reasonable strategic decisions, you need to know how much this productivity penalty will be. The PNR effort equation provides this information.

I have very carefully withheld the exact equation, because its implications are a little hard to swallow. Before I do show it to you, please be aware that the equation was derived empirically: It's not anybody's theory about how effort *ought to* vary as schedule is compressed; it's the observed pattern of how it *has* varied.

For a given application and a given project team (Difficulty Factor and Technology Factor fixed), the PNR effort equation boils down to this:

*Barry W. Boehm, SOFTWARE ENGINEERING ECONOMICS, © 1981, p. 471. Reprinted by permission of Prentice-Hall, Inc., Englewood Cliffs, N.J.

$$\text{Effort (man-months)} = \frac{\text{Constant}}{t_d^4}$$

Changes in delivery time have an inverse fourth-power effect on effort!

Clearly, you cannot expect this relationship to apply over a very wide range. Doubling delivery time will probably not allow you to decrease effort by a factor of 16. Putnam derived the relationship from data that was rich in examples of development in the area between the t_d nominal and the Impossible Region shown in Figure 17-13. The fourth-power relationship doesn't seem unreasonable as a quantitative description of the cost of approaching the Impossible Region.

Relaxing delivery time allows you to do the same work with less staff. If you accepted the concept that individual productivity falls off as you increase team size, then applying that same concept in reverse means that individual productivity goes up as you reduce team size. So extending delivery time will reduce total development cost *up to a point.* Beyond that point, the following contrary effects begin to increase costs with further extension:

- increasing user-requested changes during the project (the longer the project runs, the more changes will catch the effort in mid-stream)
- decreasing sense of urgency due to an overly relaxed schedule
- increasing cost, due to inflation

Putting all this together produces the view of cost as a function of delivery time shown in Figure 17-14.

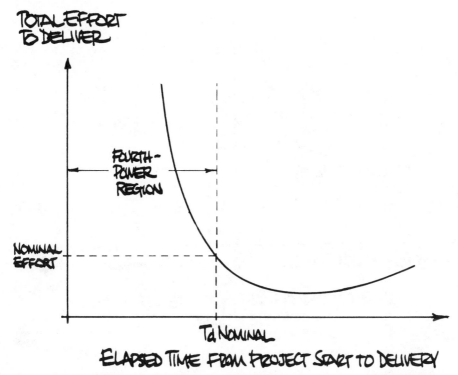

Figure 17-14. Cost of a given system as a function of time allocated for development.

Compressing your schedule to deliver the system before the nominal delivery time exposes you to fourth-power cost penalties. Relaxing the schedule beyond t_d

nominal affords you some net saving, though probably not as dramatic as the effect between t_d nominal and the Impossible Region. Beyond about $2 \times t_d$ nominal, further schedule relaxation increases net cost. The exact characteristic is specific to each domain.

17.6 The effect of reducing function

If, instead of increasing time, you reduce the amount of function to be delivered (the system Bang), you can always implement in the same elapsed time at less cost. Sometimes the savings can be substantial, as the following example will illustrate: Imagine that you have computed Bang for a new development and projected (using your corrected single-factor cost model) that the expected manpower to deliver that much Bang will be 240 man-months. From this, you compute t_d nominal (using Boehm's formula or your own tailored version). Let's say that the resultant t_d nominal is fifteen elapsed months. The cost variation due to delivering more or less Bang in the same fifteen months is governed by a curve of the form of Figure 17-15.

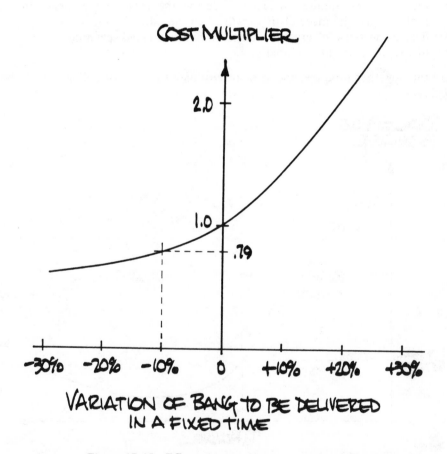

Figure 17-15. Effect of increasing or reducing function.

Putnam's observed fourth-power relationship is reflected in Figure 17-15 for values of Bang to the right of the zero axis. The power relationships throughout the area indicated are greater than one: Reducing load will always reduce cost more than proportionately due to the increasing productivity that results from fewer people interacting.

This often-ignored fact has an important implication for how cost/benefit studies ought to be performed. In most cost/benefit studies, a system function is justified if its likely benefit is greater than its portion of the cost. So, in the example below, Feature D is deemed to be justifiable:

Feature	Percentage of Total Bang	Allocated Cost	Expected Benefit
A	45%	$450,000	$1,100,000
B	30%	300,000	800,000
C	15%	150,000	500,000
D	10%	100,000	120,000

Total expected system cost = $1,000,000
Delivery time fixed at 15 months

The fallacy of this approach lies in the proportional allocation of costs. Proportional allocation only makes sense if there is a linear relationship between cost and the amount of Bang to be delivered within the fixed time.

A better scheme for justifying each element is to compare its expected benefit with *savings to remove.* What might you save by removing Feature D from the system? Your best calculation of the saving comes from use of a locally verified version of Figure 17-15: You pick off the cost multiplier associated with the Bang of the reduced system (original system minus Feature D). In this case, the cost multiplier at 90% Bang is 0.79.

Cost of system minus Feature D   = $1,000,000 × 0.79
                                                      = $790,000

Savings due to removal of D   = $210,000

You save more by not implementing the feature than you would benefit if you did implement it.

17.7 Synthesis: The kind of time-sensitive cost model required

So far in this chapter, I have introduced four different and mutually incompatible time-sensitive models — the work of Putnam, Norden, Boehm, and Parr. Each of these models could be useful in dealing with selected aspects of the manager's manpower and scheduling strategy. What's required now is a synthesis of these different tools into some compatible form.

The result, the prescribed time-sensitive cost model, will be made up of these three components:

1. *A feasible manpower utilization curve,* similar to the graph shown in Figure 17-13, but tailored to your organization. Each point on the graph represents a past project in terms of its manpower and elapsed time from start of project to first full-function delivery. An equation for t_d nominal is derived from the sample of points by solving for the best-fit equation of the form
$$t_d \text{ nominal} = C \times \text{manpower}^E$$

Until you have collected local data of your own, use the Boehm figures $C = 2.5$ and $E = 0.33$. The feasible manpower utilization curve should be annotated with a local Impossible Region at 75% of t_d nominal, or wherever your own empirical data suggests it should lie.

2. *A prototype manpower-loading pattern for projects in your organization.* The result will be similar in appearance to Figure 17-9. You build it by normalizing manpower-loading curves for past projects, as described in Chapter 18. If you have no local data, I suggest you use the Parr approximation for small projects (under fifteen man-years) and the PNR model for larger ones. In either case, start with an average value of the Acceleration Factor, such that the initial slope of the curve is less than three persons per month.

3. *A compression penalty curve of the form of Figure 17-16.* This curve is used to calculate the cost variation that will result from scheduling

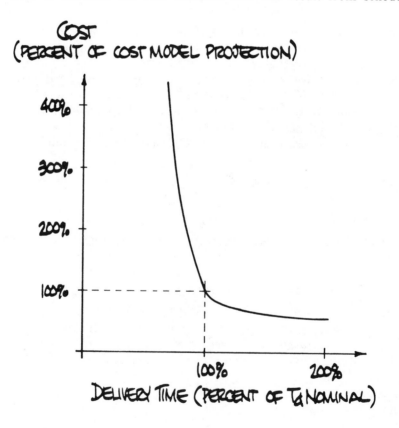

Figure 17-16. Compression penalty curve.

delivery at a time other than t_d nominal. Until you can build your own locally tailored compression penalty curve, use the one in Figure 17-16. (It is important to build your own curve, though, because the one shown here embodies a fourth-power penalty for compression beyond t_d nominal. That may be realistic, as Putnam suggests, but no one in your organization will believe it until you have some local data to support it.)

The time-sensitive model is now used in conjunction with the single-factor cost model to establish delivery time, staff requirements at each month of the project, and cost penalty (or saving) due to the strategic decision to hurry up (or slow down) delivery. Construction and use of the time-sensitive cost model are described further in Chapter 18.

17.8 Selected reference

For a comprehensive selection of papers on time-sensitive cost modeling, see

Putnam, L.H. *Software Cost Estimating and Life Cycle Control: Getting the Software Numbers.* (Tutorial) New York: Institute of Electrical and Electronics Engineers, 1980.

This collection includes key works of Putnam, Parr, and Norden, as well as Ware Myers's excellent survey of time-sensitive modeling techniques.

18

A PRACTICAL SCHEME
FOR PUTTING COST
MODELS TO WORK

So much for the abstract view of cost modeling. How do you put the concept to work for your company? How does the Metrics Group use cost models, what cost models does it use, and what data are they based on? This chapter will begin to answer such questions, and to present a *procedural* view of Metrics Group activities.

18.1 Component cost models

Up to this point, I have talked about a cost model as though it correlated a single predictor, some indication of volume and complexity of work, with total cost. Most of the cost models in the literature do use a single predictor and do project total cost. But you could equally well construct a cost model that projected several outputs, the several components of total cost that you have identified (see Figure 18-1). I shall continue to refer to this as one model, although it might equally well be thought of as *n* models, since there are *n* correlations to keep track of. The advantage of projecting component costs instead of the total is that the statistics of aggregation work for you: The sum of the deviations is less than the deviation of the sum.

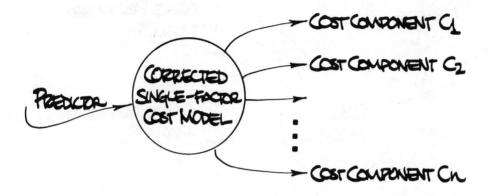

Figure 18-1. Model that projects component costs.

18.2 Multiple projections of each component cost

The kind of predictor that is measurable early in a project is never as strongly correlated to eventual results as the predictors that become available later. In order to assure high EQF estimates (early and strong convergence to actuals), we must consider using early available predictors at the beginning of the effort and then changing each time a stronger predictor becomes available. This implies a cost model driven by a number of predictors, and capable of generating component costs based on each one of them. If the model allows P different predictors and projects C different component costs, then it must keep track of P $\times$ C correlations (see Figure 18-2). If it is a corrected model, it must also maintain P $\times$ C corrections. Again, I'll treat this as a single cost model, rather than P $\times$ C models. Note that the number of correlations and related corrections to maintain has grown sharply, but that the underlying concept has not varied. The methods of Chapter 16 can be applied without change to each component correlation. The total amount of data to keep track of has not grown proportionately, since many of the model formulations share the same data.

For the projection scheme described here, there are three basic predictors:

- Bang (Chapter 9)
- Design Weight (Chapter 11)
- Implementation Weight (Chapter 12)

Each of the component costs to be projected will be correlated with each of the three predictors.

18.3 Key correlations

The fact that a given predictor has a strong correlation to one cost component does not imply that it will have a strong correlation to all the cost components we'll need to project. As an example, the design predictor is very useful for forecasting debugging time, and not at all useful for forecasting user training time. Table 18-1 presents a set of the correlations that should be useful.

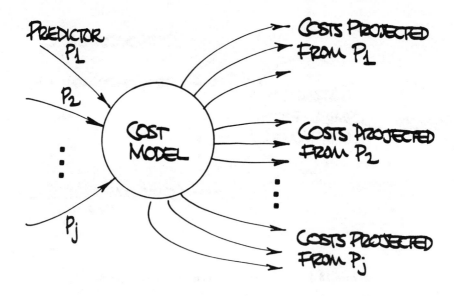

Figure 18-2. Complex cost model.

Table 18-1
Correlations Between Predictors

Predictor	Used to forecast
Bang	Design effort
	Conversion effort
	Acceptance test generation
	Documentation
	User training
Design Weight	Total effort
	Implementation effort
	Debugging effort
	Defects
	Residual defects
	Maintenance characteristic
	Machine time
Implementation Weight	Total effort
	Unit testing effort
	Integration effort
	Acceptance testing
	Defects
	Residual defects
	Maintenance characteristic
	Machine time for testing

One more complication to add: It is entirely likely that you will need to use differently weighted predictors to project different cost components. In the ultimate case, there might be a unique predictor for each correlation. So, Bang1 would be used to project design effort, Bang2 to predict user training time, and so on. The variant predictors would be composed of the same elemental metrics, but combined in different proportions.

18.4 Operations of the Metrics Group

The Metrics Group constructs the component cost models, then collects data on subsequent projects, and uses that data to forecast expected costs for those projects. Activities of your Metrics Group will depend on how you answer the following three questions: What cost models shall we build? What data shall we collect and retain in support of the cost modeling effort? What steps shall be involved in each new forecast? My own suggested answers to these questions are presented in the next three sections.

18.4.1 What cost models to build

In Section 18.2, I described a complex cost model made up of P × C single-factor cost models, where P is the number of predictors, and C is the number of cost categories of total project cost. I suggest that, at least when you first begin your Metrics Group, P ought to be equal to three: The three predictors are Bang, Design Weight, and Implementation Weight. The number of cost categories that the total can be broken down into is a function of the granularity of your project models. In order to identify the categories in your organization, you have to go through this kind of analysis:

- Assemble project models from a small sample of past or ongoing projects.
- Construct a *superset project model,* one that describes all projects in the domain.
- Use the activities of the superset model for cost categories that you will need to track.

The superset model will typically look something like that shown in Figure 18-3. The model has a node for any identifiable activity that occurs in any of the projects. Note that the superset model describes the classes of activity, but doesn't say anything about how such activities will be carried out, since such specific decisions may vary from project to project.

The superset model of Figure 18-3 establishes ten cost categories, the costs of effort to complete each of the ten activities. For such an organization, there are therefore thirty component cost models to construct. These cost models correlate the three predictors with each of the ten cost categories. In addition to cost of effort (manpower), some of the activities may involve cash expenditures or machine time costs. For such cases, there may be additional correlations to keep track of.

Along with the thirty or more single-factor models, you will need to construct the three time-sensitive component models described at the end of Chapter 17.

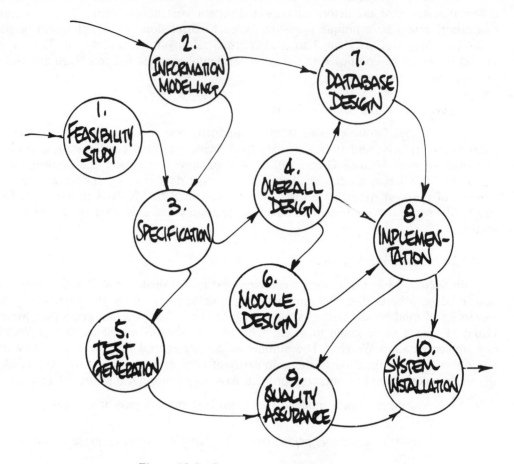

Figure 18-3. Superset project model.

18.4.2 What data to collect and keep

Each hour of effort on each project must be charged against both the superset project model and against the associated component of each one of the system models. This data should be retained in raw form. Data used to compute the composite predictors should also be retained in raw form — it's not sufficient to keep the computed value of Bang, for instance, since the formula for computing Bang may be refined as the data sample matures. The value of each one of the primitive counts must therefore be recorded and entered into the database.

18.4.3 What to do at each forecasting point

There are six basic forecasting points during each project: three when reasonable values of the three principal predictors can be estimated, and three others when those same three predictors become measurable (see Figure 18-4). At each forecasting point, the steps that follow Figure 18-4 are taken.

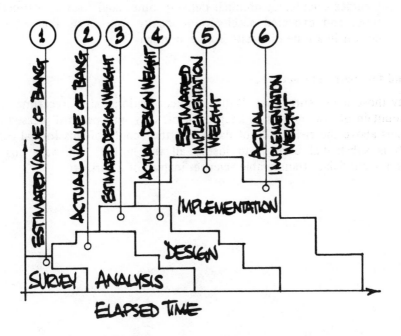

Figure 18-4. Six principal forecasting points.

1. Quantify the predictor(s). This step involves data collection (or estimation) of the elemental metrics and application of predetermined weighting factors to produce an actual (or estimated) value of the composite predictor.

2. Project each correlated dependent cost using the corrected single-factor cost model. The result of each projection is a predicted value and a standard error of estimate (SEE).

3. Override each projection based on an assessment of expected deviation of this project from the data in the model's sample. (This part is a pure estimate.)

4. Calculate total cost as the sum of the components.

5. Calculate total estimating error by adding the absolute values of the component SEEs. (SEEs will typically be expressed in percentages — multiply by the associated value to determine the absolute value.) Adding the component errors is overly conservative in most cases, but is the only reasonable precaution against *hidden dependence* among the component activities. Such hidden dependence would make all components responsive to the same cause (for example, staff turnover) and thus make their errors additive.

6.   Use the prevailing time-sensitive model to constrain the result. This includes calculating nominal delivery time, staff load as a function of time, and expected acceleration penalty for efforts that attempt to deliver in a time different from t_d nominal.

18.5 And for their next act . . .

Pity those poor estimators! With thirty correlations, six forecasting points, and a small mountain of raw metrics to keep track of, they may be hard pressed just to keep their heads above the rising tide of data. But the benefit of this formal cost modeling approach is substantial enough to justify all the bother: Software cost estimating becomes a quantifiable, transferable science, instead of a dark art.

PART IV
Software Quality

Measuring software production without measuring quality of the resultant product will only assure that debugging costs "migrate" out of the project and into the maintenance activity. Conversely, measuring quality of delivered software will cause the reverse process. Costs of coping with product faults will migrate back into the project, where they should have been incurred anyway. It is difficult to imagine a more desirable result. Part IV treats techniques for measuring and improving software quality.

19

IN SEARCH
OF SOFTWARE QUALITY

An old story from my salad days as a design instructor: I was presenting a seminar to a project team on the West Coast. There were about twenty people in the class, including two hardware types. These two had had only a single programming experience between them — a piece of software they had built together some years before. That program was still alive and well, and had earned them considerable renown; throughout its years of use, no one had ever found a bug in it. I asked one of them how he explained this phenomenal success, an apparently bug-free delivery on first try. "Well," he said, "we didn't know bugs were allowed."

19.1 Bugs are a fact of life (aren't they?)

It's common wisdom among software developers that you never get the last bug out of a program. Bugs are accepted as a sad fact of life. We expect to stamp them out one at a time, but never really triumph over them. I am more and more disquieted by

---

*Parts of this chapter are based on an article, "Zero-Defect Development," which was published in *The YOURDON Report,* Vol. 4, No. 5 (November-December 1979), pp. 5-6. Copyright © 1979. Reprinted by permission.

the idea that this fatalistic attitude toward bugs is not a productive element of our approach to the problem, but part of the problem itself. I believe that if we stopped assuring ourselves that bugs were allowed, there would be fewer of them.

Just to get you in the mood for what follows, I am going to introduce a disturbing new term, the *defect*. A defect is a deviation between desired result and observed result. It is very like what we have always called a bug. The difference in connotation, however, is important. A bug is something that crawls of its own volition into your code and maliciously messes things up. It is certainly no reflection on you; it could happen to anyone. But a defect is your own damned fault. Bugs are cute; defects aren't cute at all. Developers sort of like bugs (because developers usually enjoy debugging, which wouldn't be any fun at all without bugs); nobody likes defects. Bugs can be accepted as a fact of life; defects need not be.

> Find out the cause of this effect,
> Or rather say, the cause of this defect,
> For this effect defective comes by cause.
>
> — Hamlet

The first step in trying to develop high-quality software products is to recognize defects for what they are: individual failures to perform. The word *bug* will not appear again in this book. I urge you as well to banish it from your vocabulary and speak of *defects* instead.

19.2 Software quality and the concept of spoilage

Before saying anything about what software quality is, a word about what it is not: Quality is not spending most of your software money on defects. Quality is not the grim state of affairs portrayed in Figure 19-1.

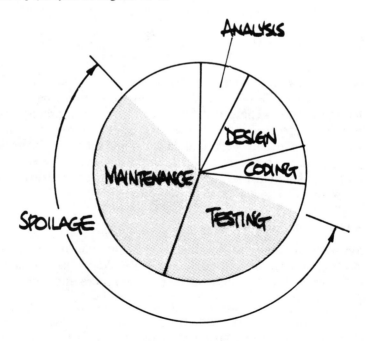

Figure 19-1. Cost of spoilage.

Figure 19-1 expresses the total investment in a given piece of software from inception of the project through its development, through the maintenance cycle, and up to product retirement. The proportions allocated to the different expense categories are taken from industry averages [Boehm, 1976; Phister, 1979; DeMarco, 1981]. The shaded area of the figure shows the portion of the whole that should be considered "spoilage," that is, effort dedicated to diagnosis and removal of the faults that were introduced during the development process. Spoilage represents about 55% of the total lifetime cost of the average system.

Most people have no quibble with treating almost all of testing as spoilage. But why have I allocated so much of the maintenance activity to this category? Isn't the majority of the maintenance dollar spent on enhancement? Yes, undoubtedly. But, for a typical system, enhancement has a lot of built-in spoilage:

- Many so-called enhancements are requirements that always existed, but were not properly elicited by the initial specification process. This is the reason for the hump under the maintenance cost curve of Figure 19-2. For a typical system effort, the hump covers the first 15% of the system's productive life and accounts for as much as half of the lifetime maintenance cost. All or most of the change under the hump represents *analysis failure,* and thus ought to be considered as spoilage.

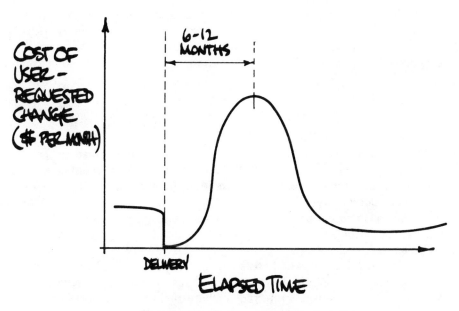

Figure 19-2. Evidence of analysis failure.

- Enhancements are added at a rate of productivity (measured in Bang Per Buck, for instance) that is one or two orders of magnitude lower than the rate during development. For a system that costs $1 million over its lifetime, more than half might be spent in maintenance; yet when the system is retired, less than 5% of the system will have been changed. The cost of changing that 5% was as great or greater than the cost of building the 95% that didn't need to be changed. Poor rate of productivity during the post-delivery period is due principally to *design failure*, and the money you spend to make up for this failure is also spoilage.

Spoilage is the cost of human failure in the development process. Such human failure may include flaws of coding, testing, design, and analysis.

19.3 A quantifiable view of software quality

Software quality is the absence of spoilage. This definition leaves out some of the favorable connotations that often go along with the word quality — elegance, grace, simplicity — but has the advantage of being measurable. (You can't control what you can't measure . . . or have I mentioned that already?) Since it is essential that we exercise control over quality, we need a quantifiable definition.*

Different defects have different costs. If you keep careful track of all defects and the costs to find and correct each one, then you can express quality as

$$\text{Quality} = \frac{\Sigma \text{ Defect Diagnosis and Correction Cost}}{\text{Program Volume}}$$

stated, for instance, in dollars per thousand bits. Small values imply high quality.

While this is an intuitively satisfying approach to quantifying software quality, it is not the generally accepted norm. The still small literature on the subject tends to express quality in terms of "defects per thousand source lines of executable code (KLOEC) delivered." Since you will want to compare your observed quality with that of other organizations, it will pay to keep track of this additional quality measure.

Here are some typical software quality numbers from different sources [Jones, 1981]:

10-50 defects per KLOEC (average for American-produced code)
0.4 defects per KLOEC (internal target for a major manufacturer)
0.2 defects per KLOEC (average for Japanese code)

More disturbing than the high defect rate is that so many companies (particularly in the United States) studiously avoid collecting defect data. At a recent conference on measurement, the speaker asked how many people in the audience of fifty worked in an environment where defects were counted. Not one person raised a hand. Defects are simply out of control in most American companies. And the magnitude of the loss of control is staggering: Correcting software defects accounts for more than $7.5 billion per year in the United States alone.

Measurement of defect rates and costs affords the possibility of real improvement. Figure 19-3, for example, shows the record of defect reduction at Hitachi [Tajima-Matsubara, 1981]. The "spoilage" referred to there includes only post-delivery defect cost, and probably does not include effects of specification error. But look at the progress (Figure 19-3). Defect measurement raises workers' consciousness of the problem, and that by itself helps to reduce the number of defects.

---

*In neglecting the more esoteric aspects of quality, I concentrate here on *quality of the implementation alone*, rather than quality of the design. Design quality is a separate and equally important topic.

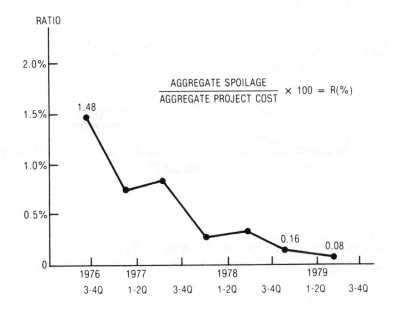

$$\frac{\text{AGGREGATE SPOILAGE}}{\text{AGGREGATE PROJECT COST}} \times 100 = R(\%)$$

Figure 19-3. Quality improvement results from Hitachi.*

It is discouraging to reflect how few companies could draw a graph such as Figure 19-3. Most have no precise idea of just how badly they're doing because they don't collect any data on defects. Systematically ignoring software quality only assures that it will never improve — it's probably getting worse. This is one case in which what we don't know is killing us.

19.4 Quality measurement throughout the project and product lifetime

The most common measures of software quality are oriented toward the delivered product. The problem with this approach is that delivery policy varies so much from one organization to another and from one project to another that the results are not easily comparable. If you're under enormous pressure to deliver a stop-gap system, then of course quality is likely to suffer. It would be handy to measure quality in such a way that we could compare the results from accelerated-delivery projects to those from relaxed-delivery projects. That would involve making a running analysis of quality throughout the project and up to retirement of the product system.

Imagine that you could keep track of all the relevant details of each defect, including its insertion date, removal date, and removal cost. That would allow you to plot curves showing cumulative defect insertion and removal (Figure 19-4).

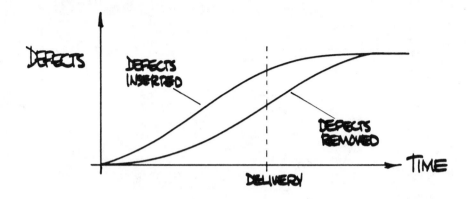

Figure 19-4. Defect rates.

The two curves meet at retirement of the system. The same figure could now be weighted for defect cost, giving Figure 19-5. At any given time, the distance between

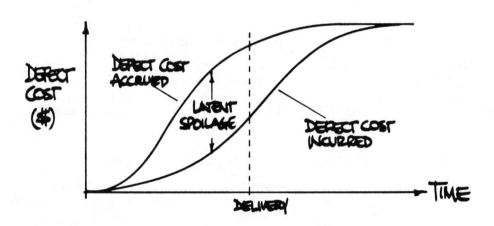

Figure 19-5. Cumulative defect cost.

the two curves is the dollar value (cost to remove) of defects currently in the product. This is what I think of as *latent spoilage*. Plotting latent spoilage on its own graph produces Figure 19-6. Such a graph, if we could draw one for each system produced, would provide a meaningful indication of quality as a function of time throughout the life of the system. The less area under the curve, the higher the quality of the product, regardless of when delivery is made.

Given that most organizations can't even come up with a simple defect count for their present systems, it's not likely they will ever be able to track latent spoilage. But tracking *actual spoilage expenditures* is considerably easier, and almost as useful. All this requires is tracking aggregate defect removal cost over time. The result will take the form shown in Figure 19-7.

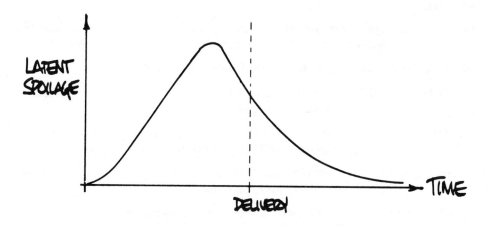

Figure 19-6. Change in system quality over time.

In Figure 19-7, the area under the whole curve is called *Total Spoilage.* The area under the curve and to the left of delivery is called *Project Spoilage,* and that to the right of delivery is called *Product Spoilage.*

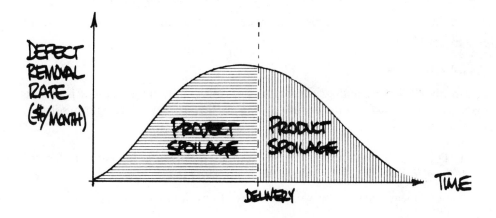

Figure 19-7. Simplified quality metrics.

Coming up with a *final* measure of Product Spoilage may require eight to ten years of observation (observation over the entire system lifetime). That is clearly too long to wait before telling your staff whether it did a good job. We humans are short-term thinkers: We tend to discount the value of any result that won't show up for a long time. So we need some quick indication of what eventual Product Spoilage is likely to be. For most systems, a meaningful predictor of Product Spoilage is the Six-Month Spoilage Rate, the cost of defect removal over the period from delivery until six months after delivery. Provided that total defect density is small — say, two defects per KLOEC or less — the entire shape of the defect discovery curve should be apparent within six months.

19.5 Summary

You need to measure work quality both during and after the project. I specifically recommend that you observe and record the following eight metrics:

Project Detected Defects:	simple count of defects detected prior to delivery
Project Defect Density:	defects detected prior to delivery expressed per thousand bits of Volume.
Project Spoilage:	cost of all defect removal prior to delivery (dollars per thousand bits of Volume)
Delivered Defects:	simple count of defects discovered between product delivery and retirement
Product Defect Density:	delivered defects per thousand bits of Volume (also recorded as defects per thousand lines of delivered executable code)
Product Spoilage:	cost of defect removal from delivery until product retirement (dollars per thousand bits of Volume)
Total Spoilage:	sum of Project Spoilage and Product Spoilage
Six-Month Product Spoilage:	cost of defect removal during first six months after delivery (dollars per thousand bits of Volume)

The costs cited here cover direct labor of diagnosing and repairing each defect, but not the original detection cost.

19.6 Selected references

Since so much of the exciting, successful work on quality improvement is coming from Japan, you might be interested in looking at this survey of Japanese software development techniques:

Tajima, D., and T. Matsubara. "The Computer Software Industry in Japan." *Computer,* Vol. 14, No. 5 (May 1981), pp. 89-96.

For a discussion of measuring all the various kinds of development spoilage, see

Abe, J., K. Sakamura, and H. Aiso. "An Analysis of Software Project Failure." *Proceedings of the 4th International Conference on Software Engineering.* New York: Institute of Electrical and Electronics Engineers, 1979.

20

SOFTWARE
QUALITY CONTROL

Defects are not so much a technological as a *sociological* problem. So the measures we take to control them can be expected to lie largely in the sociological plane, affecting the structure and organization of projects, the allocation of goals, and the fostering of new attitudes.

Before any discussion of what the attitude toward defects ought to be (opposed, basically), it's worth digressing a bit on just what the prevailing attitude is. I think of it as . . .

20.1 Quality prevention

Take a look at Figure 20-1. There you see an approach to defect removal that has got to seem bizarre. The production system coded by your staff is so full of defects that the listings it produces are wrong in hundreds of ways. So you put the whole staff to work correcting the listings. They get out their adding machines and recompute all the totals that the programs have improperly summed. They red-pencil the incorrectly reported sales, and enter by hand the ones that were dropped by the system. They correct bad headings and summaries. They cut and paste to fix the groupings of transactions that the program botched. When they're done, the listings are perfect — admittedly, a bit sloppy with all the red ink and cutting and pasting, but nonetheless correct and meaningful to the users. Of course, it was a lot of work to make all these corrections, but it's a job well done. Your reward is you get to do it all over again next week . . . and the week after . . . and the week after that. . . .

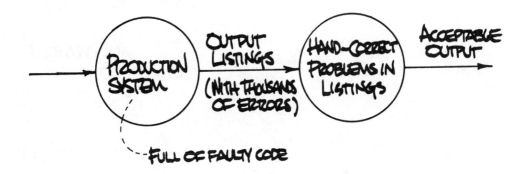

Figure 20-1. Does this make sense to you?

Wait a minute. Why would you ever be correcting the listings? you ask. That would be applying the correction effort in just the wrong place. You wouldn't think of correcting the listings every single week instead of correcting the program once. Nobody's that dumb.

But look at Figure 20-2. It shows *exactly the same situation,* with only a few labels changed. Once again, it portrays your staff laboriously and repeatedly correcting the defective products of a system rather than correcting the system that produced those defective products. Once again, you are performing work in the loop that should be done outside the loop. We spend *billions* of dollars a year correcting system defects without ever realizing that *we're correcting the wrong system.* It's the system for building systems that we should be correcting.

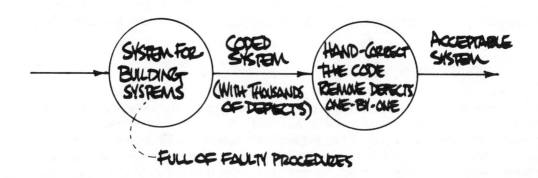

Figure 20-2. Same concept with minor modification.

Think of how the testing process works in your shop: It leads up to that triumphant moment when a programmer can stick a finger in the listing and say, "Ah ha! I've found it! This is the problem." Sorry to be a killjoy, but that isn't the problem at all — it is only a symptom. The real problem is some defective development procedure that allows that defective code to be put there in the first place. We correct the code, but never the root cause. We don't remove defects from the system for building systems, because we never go looking for them. Applying our defect removal skills to the product instead of to the process that built it is the essence of *quality prevention*.

There must be a better way. That better way involves correcting the system for building systems so that it doesn't insert defects (or at least doesn't insert so many defects) in the first place.

20.2 An alternative to defect removal

The alternative to defect removal is *defect abstinence*. If I asked you which was greater, the cost of removing a given defect or the cost of not adding it in the first place, you might respond this way: "Of course it would cost less to build the system without the defect, *if you could,* as opposed to building it with the defect and then paying for defect removal. But the question is academic — we *try* to abstain from defects. The ones we have to remove are those that sneak by in spite of our best efforts."

But do we really even try to abstain from defects? Since almost no one bothers to count them, it's hard to make the point that our industry is terribly defect-conscious. In one software organization that experimented with the concept of "zero defect development," the simple statement "Our goal is zero defects" had a positive effect on work quality (more about this idea in Chapter 22). Many of the programmers reacted with comments along this line: "Oh. So *that's* what our goal is." The statement, all by itself, helped to reduce the defect rate. We concluded that, whatever the goal had been before the program, it certainly wasn't anything approaching defect abstention. Raising consciousness about defects is a simple and necessary step in kicking the defect habit.

What sort of measure would you institute if you were truly defect-conscious, if, for instance, your life depended on low defect rates? With your life on the line, I believe you would be led implacably to consider the approach laid out in the rest of this section. I'm going to suggest it as a meaningful one in even less extreme conditions because in the long run there can be no success in the software field without learning to cope successfully with the defect problem. Before you read further, let me warn you that the method proposed has disturbing overtones: It will encourage you to think about things that most of us would rather not think about at all.

Figure 20-3 presents an idea that our industry has been aware of for many years: The differences among individuals are enormous [Sackman et al., 1968; Myers, 1975; Boehm, 1981]. In any but the smallest project teams, you can expect variations on the order of ten to one in performance. These variations aren't caused solely by the extreme cases; they apply across the whole spectrum of workers. Even if you have no extremely good or extremely poor performers working for you, you will find differences of three to one and four to one in your teams.

> *Rule of Thumb:*   Whatever you measure, expect variations of at least two
>   to one between the half of your team above the median
>   and the half below.

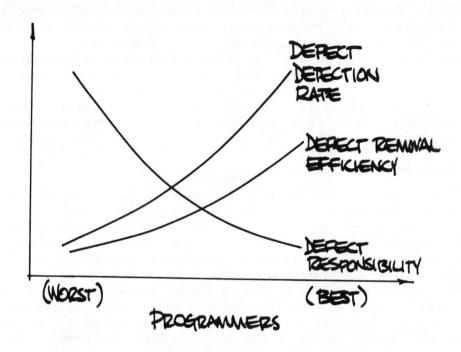

Figure 20-3. Individual differences among programmers.

This rule applies particularly to defect insertion rate (Section 20.3). Poor performers are responsible for an order of magnitude more defects than are the best performers; lower-average performers are responsible for twice as many as upper-average. Keep in mind that defect cost makes up from 35% to 55% of the cost of development, the largest component of development cost.

We've known all this since the early sixties, but we've never come completely to grips with what it implies: that there are people on almost all projects who insert enough spoilage to exceed the value of their production. Let me state that in its baldest form: *Taking a poor performer off your team can often be more productive than adding a good one.* And this does not apply merely to extreme cases. In a team of ten, expect as many as three people to have a defect rate high enough to make them net negative producers. With a normal distribution of skills, the probability that there is not even one negative producer out of ten is virtually nil. If you're unfortunate enough to work on a high-defect project (density of from thirty to sixty defects per KLOEC), then fully half your team may be in this category.

How has this extraordinary situation ever come to be? How is it that you never hear very much about it? Oh, you hear that defects are a big cost item and that people vary widely in their performance rates, but you don't hear much about the problem of the defect-prone developer. There are two basic reasons for this: First of all, defect-prone people do not appear to be bad developers. They are often respected senior project members, hard workers. They may even be the "stars" you've come to depend on when the chips are down, particularly during integration. Defect-prone workers are often excellent at defect removal. (They get so much practice, you see.) Without actually measuring defects, it would never occur to you that such people weren't really helping the project. Secondly, the very idea of measuring the individual is slightly repugnant to most people; there is a vague scent of corporate fascism about the concept and a real fear that people will be insulted and leave. And yet, ignoring the problem benefits no one.

Imagine for the moment that we could succeed in figuring out, first of all, a way to measure and allocate defects fairly (Section 20.3), and second, a way to make the whole idea palatable to the people affected (Section 20.4). Then we find that some of the staff are definitely defect prone. What action to take? Defect-prone people are not useless. When you find some of your workers to be defect prone, it doesn't mean they shouldn't be allowed to work for you, only that they shouldn't be allowed to write code. Assign them to do other things. The people who rank lowest in some of the skills described by Figure 20-3 rank highest in others.

> *Moral:*   The rational response to finding wide variations in skill levels is to *specialize.*

If A is found to be skilled at writing nearly defect-free products, and B is found to be skilled at defect detection and diagnosis, then assign them accordingly: Let A write all the code and B do all the testing. Setting up and managing teams of specialized workers is the subject of Chapter 21.

You may feel more comfortable ignoring the difference between A and B, but the cost of ignorance can be substantial. The result of assigning them homogeneously can be expected to work out something like this:

Table 20-1
Comparison of Two Workers Assigned the Same Tasks

ITEM	WORKER A	WORKER B	A + B
Cost of Labor:			
Coding	$5,000.00	$5,000.00	$10,000.00
Testing	$5,000.00	$5,000.00	$10,000.00
Defect Insertion Rate	0.8 D/KLOEC	7.0 D/KLOEC	
Expected Defects	4.8	42	46.8
Defect Detection Rate	0.7	0.85	
Project Detected Defects	3.36	35.7	
Nominal Project Defect Cost	$1,200.00	$12,500.00	
Defect Removal Efficiency	50%	250%	
Actual Project Spoilage	$2,400.00	$5,000.00	$7,400.00
Residual Defects	1.44	6.3	
Product Spoilage	$4,032.00	$17,640.00	$21,672.00
Total Spoilage	$6,432.00	$23,640.00	$29,072.00

Here I have assumed that each worker codes and tests and repairs his/her own code. I have used middle-range figures to describe their capabilities. The removal cost per defect during the project and after the project (contributions to Project Spoilage and Product Spoilage) are taken from typical industry figures. The ratios of development cost to spoilage are approximately average. Both workers are better-than-average performers in terms of their defect responsibility rates.

A simple reassignment of roles (B does all testing and defect detection and diagnosis, A does original coding and preparation of fixes) gives this result:

Table 20-2
Comparison of Two Workers Assigned Different Tasks

ITEM	WORKER A	WORKER B	A + B
Cost of Labor:			
Coding	$10,000.00	N/A	$10,000.00
Testing	N/A	$10,000.00	$10,000.00
Defect Insertion Rate	0.8 D/KLOEC	N/A	
Expected Defects	9.6	N/A	9.6
Defect Detection Rate	N/A	0.85	
Project Detected Defects	8.16	N/A	
Nominal Project Defect Cost	$2,850.00	N/A	
Defect Removal Efficiency	50%	250%	
Actual Project Spoilage	$2,850.00	$570.00	$3,420.00
Residual Defects	1.44	N/A	
Product Spoilage	$4,032.00	N/A	$4,032.00
Total Spoilage	$6,882.00	$570.00	$7,452.00

The second scenario assumes that the effort of defect removal is shared equally between the two workers, half to worker B (defect diagnosis and reporting) and half to worker A (defect repair), and that each performs with the same efficiency as before.

The two scenarios involve the same initial implementation cost, but result in drastically different software quality. Switching roles improves quality by more than 75% (Total Spoilage is reduced to about a quarter of what it would have been with the first assignment).

The two different work allocations demonstrate the difference in cost between removing defects and abstaining from them. There were 36 more defects inserted in the first plan than in the second. The cost of removing those 36 defects, as required in the first plan, was a little more than $18,000. The cost of not inserting them (second plan) was $0.00.

Of course, I haven't yet addressed the hard part: How do you collect accurate defect rates and efficiencies, and do it without upsetting the people involved? But note the results if you do achieve this end. Not only is the quality improved, but *each person's value to the project has increased.* No one need feel embarrassed to have been assigned tasks that make optimal use of individual strengths. Even a worker B, temporarily chastened to learn that all his testing and diagnostic skills barely made up for a high defect insertion rate, will know (once you've assigned him properly) that his previous low value to the project was due to *management failure,* rather than to any failure of his own.

People are different: To ignore their differences and to assign them homogeneously is to default on the most important function of management. Measuring defect rates will prove to you that a quarter or more of your staff should not be coding at all, and that some of the best coders should not be allowed to test.

20.3 Quality accounting

Measuring defects is the most productive way to raise defect-consciousness. Allocating defect responsibility to individuals or to small teams (the walkthrough participants, for instance) will provide an objective mechanism for improving quality and for specializing skills. Keeping track of defects and defect responsibility is what I call "quality accounting." Clearly, this is a delicate matter and it has to be managed delicately. The key questions are these:

- Who shall collect defect data?
- What protocol shall govern the use of defect data?
- What data shall be collected about each defect?
- How shall defect responsibility be determined?
- How shall defect data be collected?

Each of these questions is addressed in its own subsection below.

20.3.1 Who shall collect defect data?

People under measurement have some very valid concerns about the whole process. You must be able to assure them that the data collectors are fair (have no vested interests in the results); competent (are practiced in meaningful measurement); and trustworthy (are determined to protect the data they collect for use only within the limits agreed upon).

Defect data collection ought to be a Metrics Group responsibility. Your staff can expect members of the group to be measurement professionals who are politically isolated from the project and from the line of command immediately above the project. Members of a free-standing Metrics Group have no vested interest in the results of what they measure. Moreover, they can protect the data from misuse by ensuring that the public protocol for valid use of the data (Subsection 20.3.2) is observed. In case there is no formal Metrics Group, defects should nonetheless be measured by someone from outside the area being measured, perhaps a worker from the standards area or a consultant.

20.3.2 What protocol shall govern the use of defect data?

There must be a published protocol governing the use of defect data. The purpose of this protocol is to allay the legitimate worries about misuse of the data. The underlying philosophy of the protocol is this: *Data collected on an individual basis can be used only for the benefit of the individual.* Upon finding that a given project worker is defect prone, the measurer can share the data with that worker and with no one else: "Fred, you're rather defect prone. Over four months of coding, you introduced 79 defects that cost altogether more than $53,000 to remove. The average worker introduced less than $2,600 worth of defects while doing approximately the same work. You know this, and I know it, but nobody else is going to know it." Getting himself reassigned to a different specialty is Fred's own business. Of course, his every inclination is to do just that. Once he comes to trust the data, he will use it to maximize his own contribution to the effort. He is motivated to do this by *his own self-esteem,* a far stronger motivation than any that management could apply.

The only defect data that may be legitimately shared is global data, defect rate and spoilage figures for the project team or organization as a whole. The measurers must assure that data is not reported on projects nor on subprojects that are small enough to reflect on individuals.

The protocol should be an official policy of the organization, and it should be *personally binding* on those collecting the data. The measurers have to treat the data they collect as privileged, and thus subject to the same restrictions as information shared in the attorney-client relationship or related to a priest in the confessional. All parties must understand that misuse of the data brings dishonor to the data collector. The personal guarantee of the measurer is the only one that is likely to persuade anyone concerned about misuse.

20.3.3 *What data shall be collected about each defect?*

Initial data collection on each defect begins with detection of the defect symptom. At that time, the defect is logged by the Metrics Group and given a number. A history record is opened for that defect, and maintained until the defect is removed. At that time, it should contain all the following information:

> History Record =   Defect-Number + Detection-Date +
> Symptom-Description + Detector's-Name +
> {Hours-Charged + Date + Worker-Name + Category-of-Work} +
> Removal-Date + Total-Cost-of-Defect +
> Analysis-of-Cause +
> {Responsibility-Cost + Person-Charged}

Once the defect is repaired and the record completed, it becomes the secure property of the Metrics Group.

20.3.4 *How shall defect responsibility be determined?*

Defect responsibility cannot be *allocated;* it must be *accepted.* There is no way to charge defects to individuals or to small groups of individuals without their concurrence. Any defect that is not accepted by anyone is, by default, charged to the whole project.

In the defect history record, more than one person can be charged for the cost of a defect. If the defect was present already in the design model, for example, then responsibility is split between designer and coder. If the code was inspected, the responsibility is split evenly among the inspection participants. This adds a new dimension to the review process: *Review exposes participants to potential defect liability.* When an inspection is over, the inspected code no longer belongs to the coder — it belongs to all of the inspection participants. They are collectively responsible for it if it fails.

A frequent defense against defect responsibility is, "It was the analyst's fault. The specification made me do it (or at least didn't prohibit what I did)." More than half of the cost of Product Spoilage falls into this category, at least in organizations using traditional specification methods. Some Project Spoilage as well can be pinned on the analyst. It's perfectly reasonable to involve the analyst in quality accounting — in fact, you won't succeed in charging any defects to the implementors if the analyst isn't subject to the same kind of liability. But analysis defects should be kept separate, treated as a different category of defect, because they are never exclusively the analyst's fault. They are a reflection on the analyst-user relationship.

20.3.5 *How shall defect data be collected?*

Defect data is collected as a by-product of fault detection by someone other than the person or team responsible for the code. You can't expect the individual to note and record his own defects and then allow them to be charged against him. Any flaw that is caught and corrected by the person responsible ought not to be thought of as a defect at all. Similarly, flaws detected in walkthroughs and inspections should not be logged or charged. The bottom-line requirement for any discrepancy to be considered a defect is that it be detected by someone outside of the development effort.

After product delivery, the user and the maintenance organization detect and track defects. Contributions to Product Spoilage are therefore properly recorded by someone suitably removed from the original development. But what about *Project* Spoilage? The requirement that defects be detected by a non-developer insures that no Project Spoilage data can be collected for a project in which the developers do all their own testing. Building a meaningful Project Spoilage profile is possible if and only if *the test function is isolated and performed by people outside the development team.* In most environments, only the final testing is performed by a separate test team, and so only a portion of the data on Project Spoilage can be collected.

There are excellent reasons to separate the entire testing function from development and assign it to a team of testing specialists. This idea is the principal subject of Chapter 21. In addition to the justifications presented there, I add this one: Project Spoilage is an excellent indicator of the defect propensity of the development. When Project Spoilage is high, Product Spoilage will also be high. Learning only at the end of the project that quality is poor assures that you won't be able to take effective steps to improve it. If you separate the testing function entirely, using the approaches described in the next chapter, then the first Project Spoilage evidence will be available before the development is even half done.

20.4 The human factor

You can't undertake any system of quality accounting without broad acceptance of the concept by the people to be measured. But such acceptance is not impossible to obtain. If you shrug off the entire idea as likely to be devastating to the morale of your staff, you are missing a key point: *Not* measuring quality has a disastrous effect on morale. Of all the gripes I hear at seminars, the most frequent is, "Nobody in my organization cares about quality, only about quick delivery of even the shoddiest product." The real question for management ought not to be, Shall we measure? but rather, Can we afford the continuing morale cost of not measuring?

It is possible to collect defect data without determining responsibility for each defect. The data can be useful, just not as useful. Although it provides only some of the advantages of full quality accounting, a no-fault defect recording scheme is probably the correct way to begin in any organization. It allows the measurers to build skills and establish a track record before attempting full quality accounting. By the time you start quality accounting, your staff should have confidence in the competence, fairness, and incorruptibility of the measurers.

For quality measurement to succeed, the measurers must be perceived to be competent. In all the hullabaloo during the 1960s about the evil of measuring lines of code, many managers concluded that programmers were anti-measurement. That was a wrong conclusion, I believe. We never objected to being measured, only to being *mismeasured.* Raw counts of lines of code gave no real indication of the value contributed by the individual, so it was useless data. Useless data cannot be put to any good end — it can only be misused. But when the measurers are competent and the data proves useful, the concept of quality measurement can be made palatable to the people involved.

Quality accounting should be set up on a pilot basis after no-fault defect measurement has been demonstrated on at least one project. It must be sold to the staff, not imposed upon them. A good way to test the concept might be through the kind of training exercise or "Coding War Game" described at the end of the next chapter.

As a last comment about the human response to increasing emphasis on quality, I offer this incident from *The Right Stuff*, Tom Wolfe's history of the American space program. The incident involves a trip by the astronauts to the Convair plant. The purpose of the trip was to "say a few words" to the workers:

> The idea, much encouraged by NASA, was that the personal interest of the astronaut would infuse everyone working for the contractors with a greater concern for safety, reliability, efficiency.

> Oddly enough, it seemed to work. Gus Grissom was out in San Diego in the Convair plant, where they were working on the Atlas rocket, and Gus was as uneasy at this stuff as Cooper was. Asking Gus to "just say a few words" was like handing him a knife and asking him to open a main vein. But hundreds of workers are gathered in the main auditorium of the Convair plant to see Gus and the other six, and they're beaming at them, and the Convair brass say a few words and then the astronauts are supposed to say a few words, and all at once Gus realizes it's his turn to say something, and he is petrified. He opens his mouth and out come the words, "Well . . . do good work!" It's an ironic remark implying: "because it's my ass that'll be sitting on your freaking rocket." But the workers started cheering like mad. They started cheering as if they had just heard the most moving and inspiring message of their lives: *Do good work!* After all, it's little Gus's ass on top of our rocket! They stood there for an eternity and cheered their brains out while Gus gazed blankly upon them. . . . Not only that, the workers — the workers, not the management, but the workers! — had a flag company make up a huge banner and they strung it up high in the main work bay, and it said: DO GOOD WORK.*

People want desperately to know that the quality of their work matters. Quality accounting is the strongest possible statement that it does. It speaks a message that management has almost never spoken before, a message that your developers *need* to hear: DO GOOD WORK.

---

*T. Wolfe, *The Right Stuff* (New York: Farrar, Straus & Giroux, 1979), pp. 147-48.

21

IMPROVING
SOFTWARE QUALITY

A prevalent line of reasoning on the subject of software product quality runs this way: Poor product quality is a sign of inadequate testing. Improving quality is as simple as increasing the investment in testing. While this idea is intuitively appealing, the facts don't bear it out at all. Incredibly, the testing investment is an *inverse* indicator of product quality. In one sample after another, we see that a heavy investment in testing is a symptom of poor quality, not a cure. For instance, the following data were derived from the Yourdon 1978-80 Project Survey by dividing all projects into two sets based on defect density, and then calculating testing cost as a percentage of the total for each set as follows:*

Projects delivering better-than-median product quality spent 20.6% of effort in testing.
Projects delivering worse-than-median product quality spent 28.4% of effort in testing.

---

*Interestingly enough, a similar trend could be noted in productivity. The set of better-than-median producers spent significantly less time in testing than the set of worse-than-median producers.

This evidence indicates (and I believe) that the *major determinants of quality are for the most part already in the software before testing even begins.*

A common model of the defect insertion/removal process assumes that all untested code produced in a given environment has approximately the same incidence of defects, and that testing removes these defects at a more or less fixed rate expressed as a percentage of still-remaining defects found per unit of time. Most quality improvement strategies in the past have been implicitly based on this model.

A far more realistic model for the process assumes that no amount of testing can remove more than $N\%$ of the defects present, where N is a natural limit, probably on the order of fifty percent. In this model (Figure 21-1), the only explanation for wide variations observed in quality of tested code is that the incidence of defects in the *untested* code must vary enormously as a function of coding and review techniques. This second model implies that the only effective way to improve the quality of tested code is to reduce the insertion of defects in the code prior to testing. A quality improvement strategy based on this concept is the subject of this chapter.

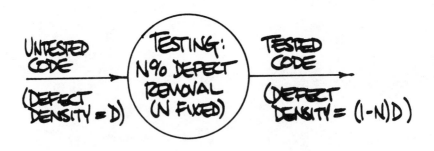

Figure 21-1. *N*% testing.

21.1 Task allocation for maximizing quality

Software testing is essential because it removes a particularly irksome kind of defect, the kind that brings the system to a halt. But, in terms of its effect on defect density, testing borders on the irrelevant. Quality of delivered code in the United States varies over the range of 0.016 defects per KLOEC to 60 defects per KLOEC, a factor of nearly 4,000. A factor of more than 30 separates the quartile just below median from the quartile just above. If testing can only hope to remove half the defects in a given product, then its effect is relatively negligible. The quality improvement battle will have to be fought out on a different battleground: The only way to make a drastic improvement in the quality of the code that comes out of the testing process is to make a drastic improvement in the quality of the code that goes into the testing process.

Some organizations regularly deliver systems with defect rates of under 0.4 defects per KLOEC. Individuals and teams in those organizations regularly produce untested code with fewer than 0.8 defects per KLOEC. The different methods used in low-defect environments are not as important as the different *incentives.* The incentives are strongly directed toward optimizing quality prior to testing.

How do you create such incentives? You begin by separating the testing function from the rest of development.

21.1.1 Why separation of testing?

Separation of testing is not a new idea, and it's not originally my idea. But the rationale offered here is just a bit different from what you usually hear. Most often the justification for a separate test group is that it improves the efficiency of testing (which it does). My reason for advocating the same idea is its much more important effect on the not-yet-tested code. When the people responsible for writing and inspecting code are not allowed to test that code, then their last chance to prove the excellence of their work is past when they submit it for testing. In this environment, they tie all their self-esteem to producing defect-free code directly from the coding/inspection process. This is exactly the attitude required to improve quality.

Note that this is not at all the attitude that prevails in a more traditional structure. If programmers do some or all of the testing on the code they produce, then self-esteem is tied only to the final result. Each programmer is allowed to make a tradeoff between pre-test effort and test effort. Now here's the key point: Programmers tend to allocate their time *based on which of the two activities they enjoy more.* The more pleasure they take in testing, the less concerned they are about building quality into the untested code. In fact, their concern works directly against that goal — they are subconsciously dismayed at the thought of coding defect-free products, because it might take all the fun out of testing. All of this provides some insight into an effect that systems people have puzzled over for years, an effect that might be named . . .

The Paradox of On-Line Testing

Every instinct tells you that testing on-line ought to be more efficient. And it is, in a way. The mean time to track down a given defect is demonstrably less if you track it on-line. But one study after another has set out to prove that on-line tested code is of higher quality than batch-tested code, and they all came up with either no proof at all, or (maddeningly) evidence that just the opposite was true. How is it possible that on-line methods improve test efficiency, but not quality?

Programmers allocate their time differently when they use on-line test methods. On-line testing is more fun and more efficient, so they allocate proportionately more of their time to it, and less to careful code production and inspection. Unfortunately, testing still only removes $N\%$ of the defects in the code. On-line testing removes that $N\%$ in less time and with less effort, but it doesn't seem to change the value of N. The result is that the code produced is of lower final quality. If you want to take advantage of the efficiency of an on-line testing tool, you have to take it out of the hands of the coder.

Most of the organizations that separate testing functions from development don't separate them entirely. They take one of these compromise positions:

- The developers do all testing right up to delivery. A separate test organization (often called quality assurance) performs acceptance testing or a final quality test just prior to user-conducted acceptance testing.

- The developers do all unit testing and system testing. A separate test team takes over for the integration effort.
- The developers do unit testing on each module. The test team does the rest.

These compromises may improve test efficiency — the more testing you remove from the developers' hands, the better tested the product will be — but they do not help to improve the quality of the critical efforts that precede testing. If you're going to succeed in making drastic quality improvements, you have got to take the extreme position: Developers are not allowed to do any testing at all on the work they produce. They don't integrate, they don't system test, they don't even unit test. Partial separation of testing is like partial chastity: It defeats the intentions of the underlying concept.

Total separation of testing creates strong new incentives to maximize the quality of untested code. It also affords a good mechanism for defect data collection during the project, so that meaningful Project Spoilage figures can be produced. That makes two more good reasons to set up a testing group that is completely separate from development. But there were already significant reasons for doing that anyway. We've known for years that people can't test their own code and ought not to be allowed to try. The case for separate testing (Section 21.3) was already irrefutable. Yet I am convinced from talking to managers all over the world that almost no one is doing it. Why on earth is a technique that everyone endorses so universally ignored?

21.1.2 We've been talking about this for years — Why don't people do it?

Separate testing has not been broadly implemented for a number of complex and almost frightening reasons. You will have to understand them if you're ever going to make much progress in quality improvement. I offer three as the most important ones.

Development projects often don't really care about quality. This is not to say that the developers are bad people or sloppy workers. They don't care about quality because the people above them don't care about quality. DP management is given to frequent sermonizing about the importance of quality, but much if not all of the time it's nothing but sham. The proof that they don't really care is that they aren't willing to pay for quality by taking the time to develop high-quality products. Given the choice between delivering a product on schedule with 25 defects per KLOEC or delivering it two months late with 0.6 defects per KLOEC, most managers show their true colors. You can prove conclusively that removing all those defects after delivery will cost more (by nearly an order of magnitude) than removing them during the project. *But the money comes out of a different pocket.* DP management makes the correct decision, given the way incentives are set up for them. This problem has only one remedy: careful measurement of Product Spoilage with enough emphasis placed on the results to encourage the manager to make quality-related decisions in the true best interest of the company.

Half-way test separation has some unpleasant side effects. Separation of only the final testing will improve defect detection efficiency, but will have no effect on initial defect insertion rate. For many projects, the result is unacceptable. Knowing near the end of a project that you have 1,500 defects in 60,000 lines of code is a disaster — you never have time for such a massive defect removal effort. But you can't deliver a product with so many *known* defects. You might be better off not knowing. There is probably a practical limit to how much defect repair you can hope to do anyway. Correcting 1,500 defects is almost surely an impossible task. The first few hundred corrections would so contort the design that each subsequent repair would insert more problems than it corrected. The solution to this problem is to separate all testing, and thus take a giant step toward reducing the initial defect insertion rate.

Programmers enjoy testing; they don't want that enjoyable task to be taken away. This is the most insidious reason of all. Programmers don't really enjoy testing, but only one of the three component tasks of testing. (Exercising the code in order to provoke new defect symptoms and repairing defects after diagnosis are not particularly intriguing tasks.) It's diagnosis that people enjoy. Defect diagnosis has some of the thrill of the hunt. And, sadly, the amount of diagnosis is limited by the number of defects. Testing with few defects or no defects at all is like hunting without game. When the defects you're hunting are your own, you have a blissfully easy way to keep the game well stocked — you use quick-and-dirty coding methods and no inspections. The solution to this problem is to keep developers from doing any testing of their own work.

21.2 The adversary team concept

Part I of this book advocated a division of traditional project function into two pieces (Figure 21-2), development and measurement. The reason for that division was to take advantage of truly different incentives that ought to be applied to the two func-

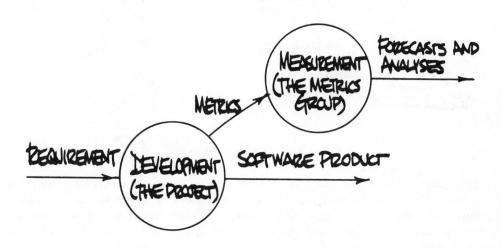

Figure 21-2. Initial division of function.

tions. Now I am advocating a further division into three separate functions as shown in Figure 21-3. This final organizational structure involves three teams:

- The *constructors* are responsible for analysis, design, and code of software products, as well as for repair of any defects reported back to them.

- The *testers* are responsible for all defect detection and diagnosis.
- The *measurers* (Metrics Group) are responsible for all quantitative data collection, metric analysis, and forecasting.

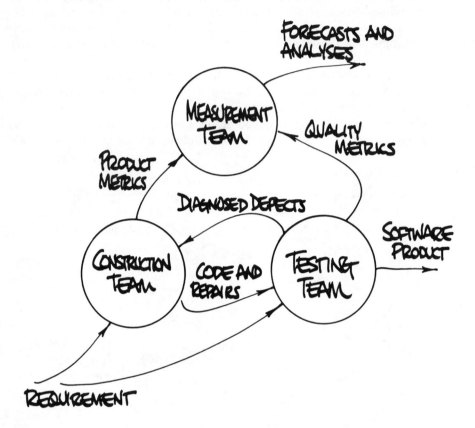

Figure 21-3. Adversary teams.

This partitioning is necessary because the three teams have distinctly different goals. The different goals often guide project members in different, even opposite, directions. Any single project team that includes all three functions will have irresolvable goal conflicts. By dividing the effort as shown in Figure 21-3, you establish three teams with no internal goal conflicts. Each of the teams has its own well-understood, attainable, and easily measured goal.

The goal of the construction team is to deliver the maximum net Bang per dollar of project cost. Included in this cost is not only construction expense proper, but also the entire cost of Project Spoilage. The cost of all defect diagnosis and repair is charged to the developers. The cost of testing to provoke defect symptoms is not charged to the developers.

The goal of the test team is to find the maximum number of defects in submitted products. Team members try to maximize the number of truly new defects detected per dollar spent trying to provoke symptoms. Success of the test team is judged by comparing Project Spoilage to Product Spoilage:

$$\text{Test Team Efficiency} = \frac{\text{Project Spoilage}}{\text{Product Spoilage}}$$

and expressing the result in terms of the cost (percent of Bang) of the defect detection effort. Since the system life may be long compared to the time testers can wait to know how well they have succeeded, an approximation of Product Spoilage based on spoilage during the first six months from delivery is used to provide quicker feedback to the team.

The goal of the measurement team (the Metrics Group) is to define and collect useful metrics, and to use these to forecast results with a maximum EQF.

Goals of the construction team conflict with those of the test team. The constructors want there to be little or no Project Spoilage, and testers want there to be as much as possible. This is a healthy conflict as long as it governs the relationship between two teams — within a single team, such a conflict would be counterproductive.

Since the goals of the different teams are at odds with each other, I characterize the three teams as *adversaries.* They need not be enemies, but they should understand that the success or failure of one team does not dictate the success or failure of either of the others. The reason for setting up adversary relationships within a development organization is the same as the reason for setting up an adversary relationship between the prosecution and the defense in court: The system as a whole works better to achieve its overall goals if we do it that way.

Organizing adversary teams for construction and testing provides an ideal way to exploit the different individual skills described in Chapter 20. What you end up with is a variation on the Chief Programmer Team structure. This concept (now almost totally abandoned) also tried to exploit individual differences, but its problems — over-reliance on a single individual, difficulty in finding anyone to qualify as Chief Programmer, difficulty in managing around the Chief Programmer — tended to outweigh the advantages. The more conservative specialization of the three adversary teams gives most of the advantages without most of the problems.

21.3 How the separated teams work

Once development is divided into construction and testing functions, the teams take different approaches to quality improvement. If the goals are set up properly, the teams will discover for themselves the best ways to maximize their performance. The purpose of this section is to survey some of the approaches that have proved useful in such an environment.

21.3.1 Black Team testing

The now-legendary "Black Team" was a separate test group that worked in a particularly quality-conscious environment at IBM. The team was unique at the time in that it made active use of its adversary position. According to the (possibly apocryphal) stories, team members took positive delight in destroying code that had been written by perfectly nice people. They were fiendish. They stressed the code in ways that would never occur to anyone whose mind wasn't horribly devious and more than a little bit nasty. They reduced poor programmers to tears. They prided themselves on being able to make almost any program crash a few dozen different ways before breakfast. And, worst of all, they *loved* doing all these awful things.

For Black Team members, the real pleasure wasn't defect diagnosis; it was defect detection. They felt this so strongly that they began to use some strange terminology in talking about tests. They would say, for instance, that a test had *failed* if it didn't provoke a new defect symptom. The test-your-own-code school is positively offended by this notion. They feel that a test should only be considered a failure if it does provoke defect symptoms. A person testing his own code is most pleased when "all tests pass," meaning no defects. Clearly, the Black Team had a very different attitude about the purpose of a test. This different attitude, that a test is an utter failure if it doesn't make the system show defect symptoms, is one of the main reasons that the Black Team was so successful.

By taking pleasure in other people's failings, the Black Team provoked a kind of backlash. Programmers became determined not to allow any defects to slip through into testing. The revenge of the programmers was to give the Black Team extraordinarily clean code, and then observe their frustration when they couldn't make it crash.

21.3.2 A tool for the construction team

With so many defects to practice on, our industry has developed an impressive body of tools for defect detection and diagnosis. These have become the tools of the Black Team. But what comparable techniques are available for use by the construction team?

The most effective construction team method is the *formal code inspection*. T.C. Jones, from his study of the defect history of some 10 million lines of installed code [Jones, 1981a, 1981b], has concluded that code inspection can remove as many as 85% of all defects. No other single defect detection technique has achieved more than 50% efficiency.

Inspections can be time consuming, but *virtually always pay back more than they cost*. In the Yourdon 1978-80 Project Survey, those companies that used code inspections or walkthroughs performed with a net productivity that was 38% higher than that of the companies that used no such methods. The payoff from inspections is quick and dramatic. They reduce spoilage so much that most practitioners think of inspections as a tool for enhancing productivity rather than quality.

21.3.3 Defect seeding

Defect seeding was first proposed in the early 1960s at Bell Laboratories and later described in some detail by Tom Gilb [Gilb, 1977]. The scheme involves intentional insertion of defects into code just prior to testing. Careful documentation of seeded defects is required to substantiate their source (for defect accounting purposes) and to make sure they aren't inadvertently left in the product.

Seeding can be used to derive an early statistical indicator of how well defect detection is proceeding.* The percentage of seeded defects that remain undetected is an indication of the percentage of unseeded defects remaining. Clearly, the whole scheme breaks down if the sample of defects inserted is not representative of the kinds of

---

*It works in much the same way as the banding of samples of animals to determine kill rates: Band *n* whales and note the number of banded whales killed; when you find that 73% of the banded whales have been killed in a year, you have a good indication that 73% of the world whale population has been wiped out that year by the nations that kill whales.

defects typically encountered. In order to make the seeding representative, you will need to collect statistics about classes of defects and the relative frequency of defects from each class. (Before your own statistics are available, you might use those documented in [Glass, 1981]. That reference also suggests a workable set of defect classes.)

With an adversary team organization, seeding defects has an advantage beyond its use as a measurement technique. The test team is assured that there will be a reasonable number of defects present. When the construction team gets its inspection procedures working properly, seeded defects may become a real necessity, just to keep the test team awake.

Defects ought to be seeded by the Metrics Group, or at least by someone not on either of the other teams. Seeding should simulate true defect incidence, and not attempt to outwit the test team with extraordinarily creative defects.

21.3.4 Adversary incentives

The most obvious example of separated test teams at work today is the Validation and Verification (V&V) industry that has sprung up, mostly in California. These V&V companies provide testing services on a contract basis. They charge according to a negotiated formula, typically one that calls for greater charges as more unique defects are detected. They are more or less "defect bounty hunters."

You can run your test team on a bounty hunting basis. I don't mean you have to pay a cash bonus for each unique defect they turn in, although in some organizations this might be feasible and productive. Whether a detected defect has monetary significance or not, you should keep track exactly as though you were paying by the defect. (I doubt it would improve the incentives particularly if the winning high school basketball team was paid a prize for each point of margin, but keeping score is absolutely essential to maintaining the interest of the participants.)

What incentive system might help to motivate the construction team in the same way that bounty hunting helps to motivate the test team? The following is an admittedly exotic scheme that has been used successfully by at least one enterprising company:

Royalties for Low-Spoilage Software

Compute the expected cost of Product Spoilage for a piece of new software, using its Volume and the Average Observed Spoilage in your organization per unit of Volume. Discount this number by whatever percent you determine is a realistic target for quality improvement. The remaining figure represents the expected cost of Product Spoilage for the program or system. Use a profile of spoilage cost incurred by year to project how much of the total spoilage cost will be incurred in each year. Measure actual spoilage. If actual spoilage is less than the projected figure in a given year, the difference is a direct cash saving, due entirely to the excellent quality performance of your construction team. Pay them a percentage of the saving as a royalty. (Or at least make a big fuss over how much money the company saved due to attention to quality.)

If you're inclined to reject that idea as the author's excursion to someplace other than the real world, well, join the club. But how realistic is it to ignore the cost of poor quality or the savings due to high-quality performance? How realistic is it that our programmers never hear a word about the quality of the product they deliver, no matter how excellent or how atrocious it may be?

21.3.5 Developing key quality skills

In 1976 and 1977, Glenford Myers ran some controlled experiments in inspection and walkthrough techniques, and described the results in an article [Myers, 1978]. As you might imagine, the experiments involved the use of a program with known defect incidence. Programmers were set to work on defect detection and removal using inspections. (In a subsequent work, Myers evaluated some testing techniques in the same fashion.) The following quote is taken from the discussion section at the end of Myers's paper:

> Comments were solicited from the participants and most of the participants felt that the experiment had a high *educational* value. At the end of the experiment, each participant was given a copy of the 15 known errors. In the normal environment, one does not have the opportunity to test a program and then receive immediate feedback on the errors overlooked. . . .

The purpose of the experiment, of course, had nothing to do with its educational value. But why shouldn't programmers have a chance to test and hone their skills in a controlled environment? All it takes is an initial investment in preparation of a testing or inspection *clinic,* to be run in this fashion:

1. The Training Department develops the clinic from one or more pieces of production code (known to have run successfully for enough years to imply very low residual defect rate). The trainer collects enough design and program documentation to support people reading the code for the first time. The code of superordinate and subordinate modules should also be included in the package.

2. The trainer inserts defects from a profile of empirically observed defect incidence by type. (Alternately, actual defects already removed from the code are put back in.)

3. Teams of programmers not familiar with the program take the clinic by inspecting the product. The trainer may precede this activity with a brush-up session on inspections.

4. At the end of their inspection, the participants are given an annotated list of the actual defects, and encouraged to go back over their performance to see why they missed any.

A similar clinic for testing can be put together at a very modest cost.*

---

*I am indebted to Hal Eckel of Owens Corning Fiberglas for sharing with me his work on clinics to improve the skills of analysts, designers, and programmers.

21.3.6 Coding War Games

A more elaborate form of quality clinic is the *Coding War Game*. My own experience with this concept is limited to games organized and run by Yourdon inc., but there is no reason why they could not be put on by anyone. The Coding War Game works like this:

1. The trainers develop a specification and design for a truly tiny application (say, five small modules).

2. After extensive walkthroughs/inspections of these products for correctness and clarity, the trainers actually code, inspect, and test a version of the application. The purpose of this step is to serve as a final verification of the specification and the design, and to determine broad time requirements for implementation. The coded result is discarded.

3. The clinic is limited to six or eight participants at a time.

4. Participants are formed into two teams of equal number. Each team codes and inspects a complete implementation of the product. Time for this activity is limited, but more than adequate.

5. The teams exchange products.

6. Team A tests Team B's product, while Team B tests Team A's. All defects are formally recorded and charged. Each true defect bears the cost of diagnosis (by the test team) and repair (by the construction team). The trainers serve as arbitrators of defect allocation.

7. Testing continues for a fixed time.

8. Spoilage and defect density are computed for both teams. The winner is the winner.

A war game typically takes a day, with some reading of the specification the evening before. It should be conducted with great fanfare (noisy scoring, great emphasis on team performance). If it isn't fun, you're not doing it right.

21.4 Selected references

The best work I know on the subject of software testing is

Myers, G.J. *The Art of Software Testing.* New York: John Wiley & Sons, 1979.

For a description of walkthrough and inspection methods, see

Fagan, M.E. "Design and Code Inspections to Reduce Errors in Program Development." *IBM Systems Journal,* Vol. 15, No. 3 (July 1976), pp. 182-211. [Reprinted in *Writings of the Revolution: Selected Readings on Software Engineering.* E. Yourdon, ed. New York: Yourdon Press, 1982, pp. 123-48.]

E. Yourdon. *Structured Walkthroughs.* New York: Yourdon Press, 1978.

22

ZERO DEFECT
DEVELOPMENT

People are conditioned to believe that error is inevitable. We not only accept error, we anticipate it. Whether we are designing circuits, programming a computer, planning a project, soldering joints, typing letters, completing an account ledger, or assembling components, it does not bother us to make a few errors, and management plans for these errors to occur. We feel that human beings have a "built-in" error factor.

However, we do not maintain the same standard when it comes to our personal life. If we did, we would resign ourselves to being shortchanged now and then as we cash our pay checks. We would expect hospital nurses to drop a certain percentage of newborn babies. We would expect to go home to the wrong house by mistake periodically. As individuals we do not tolerate these things. Thus we have a double standard — one for ourselves, one for the company.

The reason for this is that the family creates a higher performance standard for us than the company does. . . .

Many companies spend ten, fifteen, and even twenty percent of their sales dollar on scrap, rework, warranty, service, test, and inspection. The errors that produce this waste are caused directly by the personnel of the company, both employees and management. To eliminate this waste, to improve the operation, to become more efficient, we must concentrate on preventing the defects and errors that plague us. The defect that is prevented doesn't need repair, examination, or explanation. The first step is to examine and adopt the attitude of defect prevention. This attitude is called, symbolically: Zero Defects.

— Philip Crosby*

The zero defects attitude is a performance standard for companies that approximates the kind of performance standard created by the family. This chapter will describe an approach to zero defects that is tailored for the software development environment.

22.1 Defect clustering

Zero defects is not just a slogan that you pay lip service to in the attempt to achieve a surrogate goal of few defects. Zero defects is, at least for the individual project member, a reasonably attainable goal. That doesn't mean you should expect to deliver entire systems containing tens of thousands of lines of code absolutely without defects. But it does mean that *the great majority of modules can be made utterly defect-free;* that is, they will be retired after a long productive life, during which they never had need of defect repair. Many, perhaps even most, project workers can expect to deliver zero defect work.

The IMS program product from IBM is an existence proof of such results: Out of 425 modules that make up the product, more than 300 are still defect-free [Jones, 1981]. IMS, as a whole, was not defect-free. So the other 125 modules accounted for all the defects. Defect density was extremely uneven over the product. In fact, it was so uneven that *7.3% of the modules accounted for 57% of the defects.* A similar effect was noted in OS/360, in which 47% of the APARS (field-detected defects) were traced to 4% of the modules [Myers, 1979].

Early elimination of defect clustered modules is one of the main thrusts of zero defect development. The technique for spotting them is derived from this surprising ramification of defect clustering: "The probability of the existence of more errors in a section of a program is proportional to the number of errors already found in that section" [Myers, 1979]. This idea is presented graphically in Figure 22-1. Myers's statement is one more refutation of that common mental model of defect characteristics (all code starts with approximately the same degree of defect; the more you test, the cleaner it gets) that I referred to in the previous chapter. It should give you pause next time a programmer tells you something like this: "Harry and I have been testing our modules for the last few weeks. So far, I've already tracked down and removed twelve of my errors, and Harry has not found any of his (not a great tester, old Harry, heh, heh, heh). He's probably got at least twelve to find." Nothing could be further from the truth. The next defect found is highly likely to be in the module from which twelve have already been removed. And it will then be even more likely that defects are still remaining.

---

*P.B. Crosby, *Quality Is Free: The Art of Making Quality Certain* (New York: McGraw-Hill, 1979).

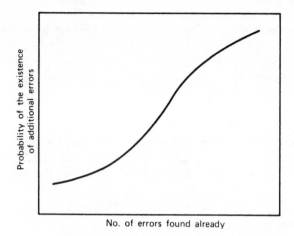

Figure 22-1. The errors-found/errors-remaining relationship.*

After I had introduced the Myers curve in one of my seminars, a student offered this observation: "When you see a roach climbing up the wall of a restaurant, you don't say, 'There goes *the* roach.' You say, 'The place is infested.' "

22.1.1 *Relating early and late defects*

The relationship shown in Figure 22-1 is meaningful at a fixed moment of time (say, delivery day). The number of errors already found (horizontal axis) are the ones detected prior to that moment, and the "additional errors" expected (vertical axis) are the ones you will probably detect from that moment on, during the rest of the product's lifetime. So, the curve shows a relationship between defects detected early and those to be detected later.

You could concoct a figure like Figure 22-1 for any well-defined moment in the project, for instance, end of unit testing, end of system testing, end of acceptance testing. And in each case, the curve would show the same basic trend. Early defects are a strong predictor of later defects; the more defects already detected in a given piece of code, the more you should expect to find in it.

22.1.2 *A strategy based on defect clustering*

A basic strategy derived from the defect clustering effect is this: Don't spend money "cleaning up" code that has already shown itself to be defect prone; get rid of it. Coding cost is nearly irrelevant compared to the cost of repairing defect-prone modules. Set a defect threshold and when any module exceeds that threshold, throw it away. Give the recoding assignment to a different developer.

Since early defects are a predictor of late defects, the clue to delivering zero defect products is to discard work in progress that has already shown a tendency toward defects.

---

*G.J. Myers, *The Art of Software Testing* (New York: John Wiley & Sons, 1979), p. 15. Reprinted by permission.

22.1.3 The compilation indicator

Now here is a radical proposition for you to consider: Since the earliest and most easily detected defects are compilation errors, is it possible that the number of compilation errors can be related to the number of expected errors remaining?

The answer is a qualified yes. Depending on how you collect the data, you can treat compilation failure as an early indicator of defects remaining. In one extensive study, T.C. Jones found that the average module was compiled thirty to fifty times during development, but that those modules that later turned out to be defect prone (more than one hundred defects per KLOEC) had had to be compiled more than twice as often during development (more about the compilation indicator, how to measure it and how to use it, in just a bit).

22.1.4 Some healthy skepticism

There is something terribly counterintuitive about the defect clustering and the Myers curve shown in Figure 22-1. (Probabilistic effects are often counterintuitive.) Participants in my seminars sometimes find the concept impossible to swallow. And almost everyone gets grumpy when I assert that the effect even applies when a compilation indicator is used as the predictor. Since much of what follows is derived from this fact, I urge you not to reject it outright, but to make the small investment required to investigate the effect in your own environment. Defect data mounts up very quickly.*
With only a trivial cost of measurement, you can collect massive amounts of data. Then, rather than accept Figure 22-1 as revealed truth, you can build your own family of such curves:

- project-detected defects compared to defects detected after delivery
- unit test defects compared to system test defects
- first six months of spoilage compared to subsequent spoilage
- compilation defects compared to rest of project-detected defects

Of course, this data is not collected only to substantiate the Myers curve; its principal use is for predicting quality characteristics of systems in development.

22.2 The zero defect development program

A workable zero defect development program involves combining the quality accounting scheme of Chapter 21 with a careful exploitation of the defect clustering effect. The elements of such a program are these:

1. There is a stated goal of zero defects in the delivered product. This applies to intermediate as well as final products.

2. There is complete organizational separation of development, testing, and measurement, as shown in Figure 22-2.

3. The product passed from developers to testers is *uncompiled code.* It should be in automated form, but never yet submitted to a compiler. In this scheme, the compiler permissions are held only by the testers (developers have no access to it).

---

*This deplorable fact becomes a positive advantage when you set out to collect the data.

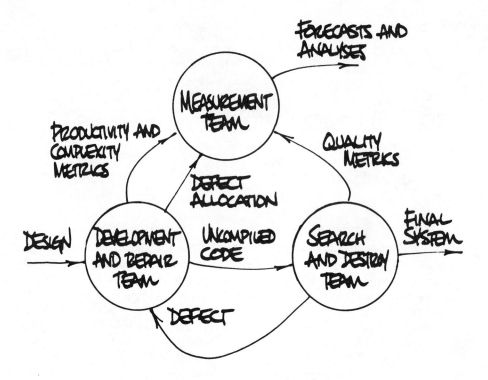

Figure 22-2. Organizational separation in zero defect development.

4. Compilation errors are treated as defects. Failure to compile perfectly is treated as one defect, no matter how many defects the compiler detects or seems to detect (since a single flaw can sometimes generate multiple error messages). Modules should be compiled separately if possible, so that the compilation defects can be assessed for each module.

5. Compilation defects are used as feedback to indicate degradation in the effectiveness of the inspection process.

6. Repeated failures to compile perfectly are an early indication that code is defect prone, and are a basis for rejection and recoding.

The major tool in producing zero defect work is, again, the formal inspection. Inspections, we all know, can be a powerful mechanism for assuring quality. But inspections tend to have less effect as their use becomes standard. People get bored and complacent, and their inspection skills lose the fine edge. In order to keep the inspection process tuned and efficient, we require an immediate feedback whenever it fails. Compilation defects provide this feedback. When the inspection accepts zero defects as its goal, any compiler-detected error is clearly a sign of inspection failure.

A second advantage of inspecting uncompiled code is that there is less *cognitive dissonance* − in this case, due to the preconceived notion that it's not worth looking for defects since there probably aren't any. Cognitive dissonance can be caused by the compiler's stamp of approval: NO ERRORS. Everyone knows that there are classes of defect that the compiler misses, but its approval is nonetheless an indicator of meticulous compliance with one of the established standards (syntax), and is a strong implication that the code is very methodically and carefully constructed.

The most important advantage of working with uncompiled code is that coders are not allowed to indulge the dead-end fancy that it's perfectly all right to produce defect-ridden code and then use the compiler to clean it up. I often hear this attitude expressed in this fashion: "My time is expensive, much more expensive than a few runs of the compiler. Why not let the compiler do that part of the work that it is much more efficient at than I am? That will give me more time to work on the things that only a human can do."

There is no question that compilers are much more efficient at removing syntax errors than people are. The cost of detecting a missing semicolon in a walkthrough is probably an order of magnitude greater than the cost of letting a compiler detect it. But the attitude that it's okay to start out with a product that is full of errors is unacceptable; the incidence of compiler-detectable defects is higher (not very important) and the incidence of undetectable defects is also higher (all-important).

The cost of removing syntax errors is irrelevant, whether the compiler does it or the walkthrough team does it. It's the defects the compiler cannot hope to catch that really matter. Those can be demonstrably decreased by an inspection process that benefits from immediate feedback on its effectiveness in detecting at least one class of defect. The small loss in syntax correction efficiency is a reasonable price to pay for such a powerful feedback mechanism.

22.3 Setting up a zero defect experiment

Building high quality into software costs money, but poor quality also costs money. In most cases, the cost of building it right the first time is considerably less than fixing it forever after. But the tradeoff between quality and original investment varies. Systems with extremely short expected lifetimes are poor candidates for a heavy investment in any quality-improvement program. At least your first attempt to apply the zero defect concept should be directed toward a system for which quality matters, that is, one with a long projected life and/or a requirement for particularly high reliability.

Some managers are concerned that zero defect development may be too radical a measure if applied to an entire project. I urge such managers to consider trying out the concept, not on a project basis, but on a module basis. This involves designating certain key modules *in advance* as target zero defect modules. For these modules alone, the product transferred from developer to tester is uncompiled code. For these modules alone, compilation errors are treated as defects and used as a specific feedback on inspection effectiveness. This approach allows you to try the idea out in a limited way, and to collect data on its effectiveness before applying zero defect development on any broader scale.

22.4 A final note

Good grief, it's the end of the book. Have I made my point? Was the meaning clear? Has anyone read the whole thing? Isn't there *much, much* more to say about software quality and function weighting and complexity measurement and organization of the development process and . . . ?

But it's too late for all that now. Through the window beside my terminal, there is barely a glimmer of twilight left in the sky over the Hudson River — the last hour of the last project day. Time left only to say thank you for coming all this way with me. And may you always enjoy the satisfaction of *doing good work*.

APPENDIX A
A Sample Set of Models

Appendix A presents a sample set of models developed as part of a small-scale project. The object of the project was to produce statistical and management tools in support of the Metric Function. The automated portion of the implemented system was called Fourth-Generation Metric Support Package (MSP-4). The sections include

Section A1: Specification Model
Section A2: Project Model
Section A3: Design Model
Section A4: Metric Analysis of Models

Section A1
MSP-4 Specification Model

A1.1 Context of the study

The requirement was to construct a package of automated aids to support functions of the Metrics Group. The context of the specification study is shown in Figure A-1. A partial data dictionary (containing definitions of net input and output data flows) is presented below:

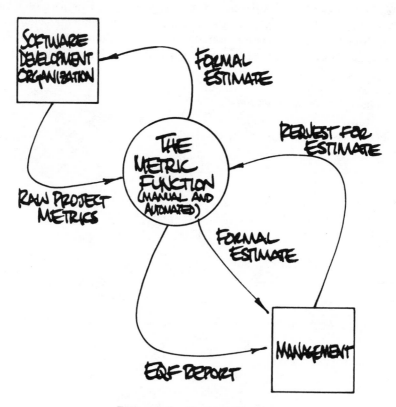

Figure A-1. Context diagram.

A1.1.1 Context-level data dictionary

Request-For-Estimate =
     Project-ID + { Cost-Components-To-Be-Estimated }

Formal-Estimate =
     Project-ID + Domain +
     { Cost-Component-Name + Cost-Component-Projected-Value + Standard-Error }

Raw-Project-Metrics =
    Project-ID + { Metric-Name + Metric-Value +
                Charge-Categories + Audit-Trail }

        Charge-Categories = * what task or piece of the system should work be recorded against *
                        = Specification-Model-Component +
                          Project-Model-Component +
                          (Design-Model-Component)
        Audit-Trail   = Worker-ID + Measurer-ID + Date-Of-Measurement +
                          Date-Of-Work + Assessed-Tolerance + (Notes)

EQF-Report =
    Report-Date + Estimating-Group-Name + Number-Sample-Points +
    { Project-EQF-Detail } + Aggregate-EQF
        Project-EQF-Detail =
                    Project-ID + Project-Overall-EQF +
                    { Date-Of-Initial-Estimate +
                    Estimated-Metric-Name + EQF-For-Named-Metric }

A1.2 First-level partitioning

The initial partitioning of the subject area is presented in Figure A-2. The man-machine boundary appears there as the communication between MSP-4 (bubble 7) and the rest of the diagram. All bubbles, with the exception of bubble 7, are entirely manual.

A1.2.1 Partial first-level data dictionary

Data dictionary entries describing all the net flows across the man-machine boundary are below:

Analysis-Request =
    Report-Name + ([Domain | Project-ID]) * request a specific report   *

Correction-Request =
    [New-Factor-Entry   * assign correction value to a project *
    | Multiple-Regression-Request   * how well do factors explain variance? *
    | Analysis-Request   * display reports   *]

Correction-Result =
    [Acknowledgment | Error-Msg   * response to factor entry   *
    | Multiple-Regression-Result   * equation relating factors to variance *
    | Cost-Model-Report   * one of n possible reports   *]

Correlation-Request =
    Domain + Dependent-Factor + Independent-Factor
    * analyze all projects in domain and report on DF-to-IF relationship   *

Correlation-Result =
    Count-Of-Projects-Analyzed + Correlation-Equation + Scatter + (Display)
        Correlation-Equation = Multiplier + Predictor + (Power) + Offset
                                * expressed as a prediction line equation   *
                                * of the form: $\text{Cost} = M \times \text{Predictor}^P + \text{Offset}$ *
        Scatter   = * standard error of estimate   *
        Display   = * graphic showing data points + prediction line *

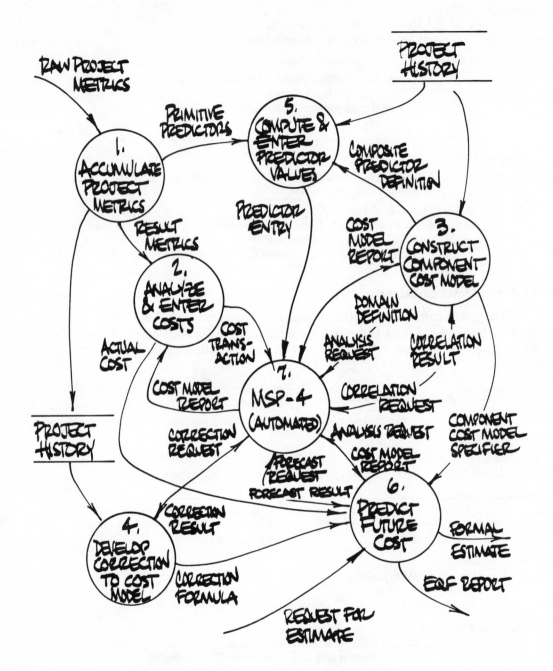

Figure A-2. Diagram 0: The Metric Function.

Cost-Transaction =
　　[Analysis-Request 　　　　* display a selected report 　　　　　　　*
　　| Cost-Data-Entry 　　　　　* allocate cost by category 　　　　　　*]
　　　　Cost-Data-Entry = 　　　Project-ID + { Cost-Category + (Cost-Value) }
　　　　　　　　　　　　　　* null value requests deletion of metric 　　　*

Cost-Model-Report =
    [Domain-Summary   * list of projects within domains   *
    | All-Project-List   * all projects: ID, domain(s), total cost   *
    | Cost-Report   * cost by category for a given project   *
    | Project-Report   * listing of costs, predictors, and factors   *
    | Metric-Census   * which projects have values of each metric   *
    | Effort-Over-Domain   * effort by category for each project   *]

Domain-Definition =
    Domain + { Project-ID }
    * define this domain to be made up of the following projects   *
    * also used to add or subtract projects from an existing domain   *

Forecast-Request =
    Project-ID + Domain + Dependent-Factor + Independent-Factor
    * use value of IF for this project together with trend over the domain   *
    * to project a value of the DF   *

Forecast-Result =
    Dependent-Factor-Value + Scatter

Predictor-Entry =
    Project-ID + { Predictor-Name + (Predictor-Value) }
    * null value requests deletion of metric   *

Raw-Project-Metrics = { Project-ID + { Metric-Name + Metric-Value } }

A1.2.2 Commentary

Since lower-level DFDs of the manual procedures are excluded from this example, the following comments may be necessary to round out your understanding of MSP-4.

1.   *Accumulate project metrics:* Metrics Group personnel observe and record values of in-progress, as well as completed, projects. The raw data (entire content of Raw-Project-Metrics, as defined above) is saved by project in the Project History database. This raw data may be used (functions 3, 4, and 5) to develop new composite metrics and predictors and to correct the single-factor cost model results.

2.   *Analyze and enter costs:* Result metrics (principally units of effort charged against a project) are accumulated until completion of tasks. When a given task, a component of the project model, is judged to be complete, the aggregate cost is entered through one or more cost transactions. There may be more than one, for instance, if the effort of completing the task has to be charged against more than one component of the system. All effort is charged against two or three categories: It is charged against a project model component (task), against a specification model component (primitive function), and possibly against a design model component (module). Charge against a task may involve translation of the project model used by the developers into the terms of the superset project model, thus allowing component costs of one project to be compared to component costs of another.

3. *Construct component cost model:* Cost dependency theories are developed and tested. A new theory may involve creation of a new composite metric (a variation on Bang, for instance). Values of the new metric, once computed and entered, are tested for statistical correlation to cost components. This test involves use of MSP-4: A Correlation-Request, which asks for statistical analysis of the component-cost-to-composite-metric relationship, is submitted. MSP-4 reports back (Correlation-Result) by giving the equation of the best-fit line through the data points in the domain, and an indication of how widely the points scatter around that line. Promising relationships are documented and passed on to the forecasting process, bubble 6, below.

4. *Develop correction to cost model:* Development factors that are not included in any composite predictor are tested to see if they might explain variation between predicted and actual cost. Numeric values are assigned to these factors after analysis of the Project History records. These quantified factors (New-Factor-Entry) are entered into the computer. MSP-4, in response to a Correction-Request, will perform a multiple regression to show the likely relationship between any set of quantified candidate factors and variation from the prediction line. As useful Correction-Formulas are developed, they are passed on to the forecasting process.

   Variations due to acceleration of the project — adding more people to reduce time to develop — are also studied here and may result in development of Correction-Formulas for use by the forecasters.

5. *Compute and enter predictor values:* For each composite predictor defined by the cost model constructors (bubble 3), actual values must be calculated from on-going, as well as past, projects. This may involve analysis of Project History. Values are entered (Predictor-Entry) into MSP-4.

6. *Predict future cost:* Formal estimates are produced in response to requests from management. This involves breaking down total cost into components and extrapolating component costs through the use of specific cost modeling techniques developed in bubble 3. MSP-4 is used as a computational tool to aid this effort. The system does the actual extrapolation. The manual process involves correcting the extrapolated value for the truncated factors and for acceleration, and summing projected component costs to produce a Formal-Estimate of the total. Metrics Group members log their estimates and compare them to actual results (as they become known) to issue a periodic report (EQF-Report) on effectiveness of the estimating process.

A1.3 A second-level partitioning

Data flow diagram 7 (Figure A-3) portrays the further partitioning of MSP-4, the automated portion of the system.

A1.3.1 Partial data dictionary for the second level

Most of the interfaces shown here have been defined above. The only newly introduced terms are

Multiple-Regression-Request =   Domain-ID + Dependent-Parameter-Name +
                                 { Independent-Parameter-Name }

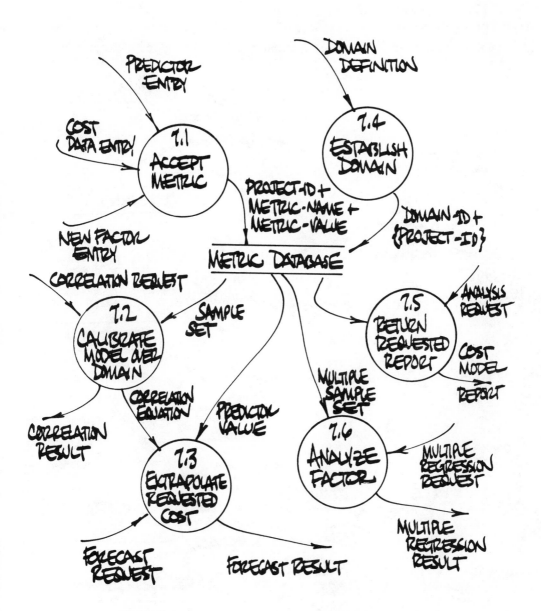

Figure A-3. Diagram 7: MSP-4 metric support system.

Multiple-Regression-Result = Domain-ID + Count-of-Projects +
Dependent-Parameter-Name + Constant-Factor +
{ Independent-Parameter-Name + Multiplier }

Multiple-Sample-Set = { Project-ID + { Metric-Name + Metric-Value } }

Sample-Set = * empirical data points from projects in the domain *
  = { Project-ID + Predictor-Value + Cost-Component-Value }

Metric-Database = * see Section A1.5 *

A1.4 Third-level figures

Two third-level DFDs are included without comment (Figures A-4 and A-5).

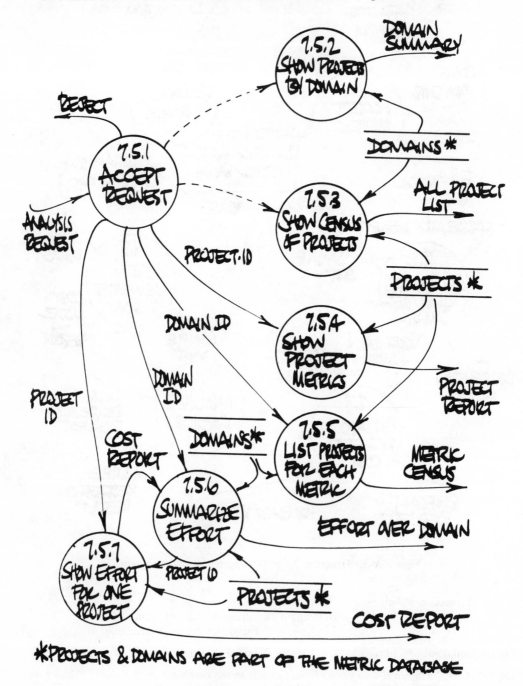

Figure A-4. Diagram 7.5: Return Requested Report.

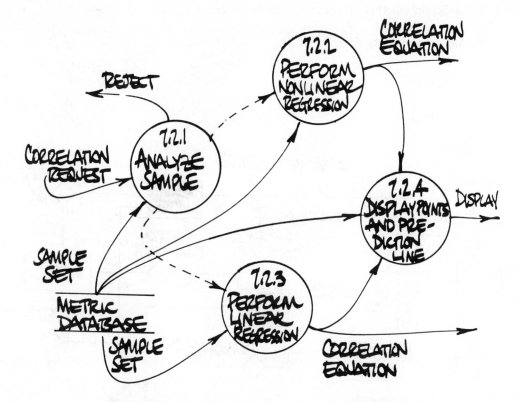

Figure A-5. Diagram 7.2: Calibrate Model Over Domain.

A1.4.1 Partial data dictionary for the third level

Domain-Summary	=	{ Domain-ID + { Project-ID } }
All-Project-List	=	{ Project-ID + { Domain-ID } + Total-Cost }
Project-Report	=	Project-ID + { Metric-Name + Metric-Value }
Metric-Census	=	{ Metric-Name + { Project-ID } }
Effort-Over-Domain	=	Domain-ID + { Project-ID + { Cost-Category-Name + Accrued-Cost } }
Cost-Report	=	Project-ID + { [Cost-Category-Name | Category-Group-Name] + Accrued-Cost }

A1.5 The retained data model

Shown in Figure A-6 is the retained data model for MSP-4. Most of the data retained by the system is associated with one of the fourteen objects shown in the model. Cost data is associated with more than one object (intersection data). By convention, intersection data is associated with the relationship between those objects, "Charges," in this case.

The complete retained data model would consist of the diagram plus a description of each node (object or relationship). The description would, in each case, consist of

- unique name
- definition (or policy-based description)

- data content (list of associated data elements)
- data structure
- data dependency description

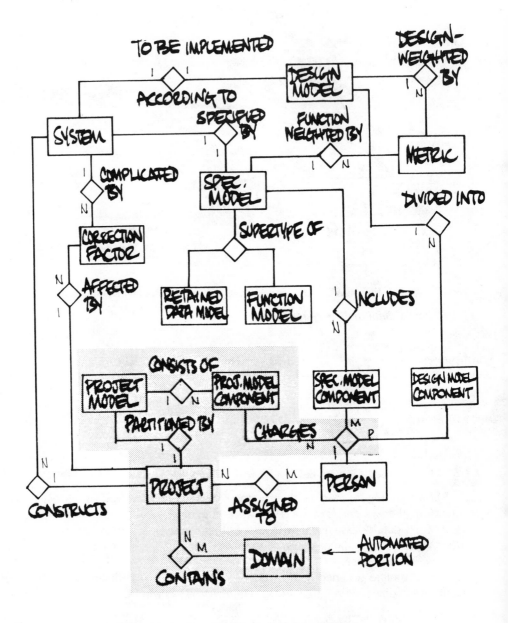

Figure A-6. Retained data model for MSP-4.

Only part of the retained data model is to be automated, the part shown in the shaded area in Figure A-6. This can be compressed into the following form (Figure A-7). Notational conventions for the retained data model are discussed in Appendix B.

Figure A-7. Retained data model (automated portion).

A1.6 The state transition model

Shown in Figure A-8 is a state transition diagram describing the twenty distinct processing states of MSP-4 and the events that cause state transitions. Most of the events are operator actions — in particular, entry of a function-select character in response to a displayed menu of alternatives. In the figure, single letters are the prompts entered at the terminal in response to menus; and unlabeled transitions imply "doneness," that is, all work associated with the state has completed normally.

Section A2
MSP-4 Project Model

A2.1 MSP-4 custom methodology

In Figure A-9, the MSP-4 project has been decomposed into nine component activities, each one connected by production of a binary deliverable. Since the project is small, no further partitioning is warranted. The deliverables are described below.

Specification: complete structured specification (as described by [DeMarco, 1978]) plus one-page text overview

Algorithm package: clear statement of selected numerical algorithm for computation of simple linear regression, simple nonlinear regression, standard error of estimate, and multiple nonlinear regression

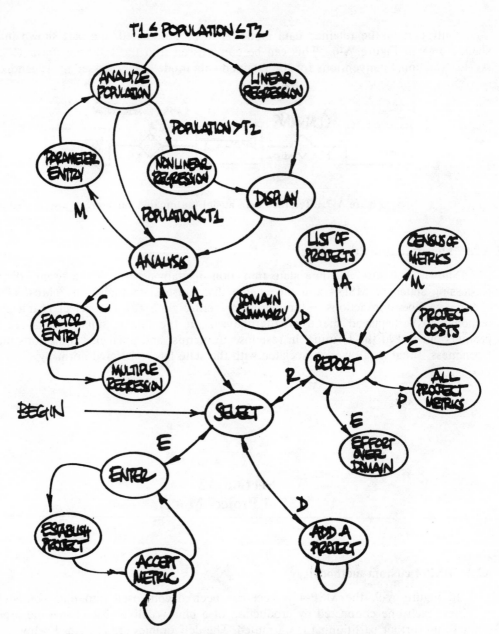

Figure A-8. Coordinated prompting states of system and user.

Design package: complete packaged design as described in [Page-Jones, 1980].

Charter: as described in [Yourdon, 1982]

Cost/benefit report: as described in [Yourdon, 1982]

User manual: as described in [Yourdon, 1982]

Coded component: ready-to-compile module (it may be a revised module, as will be the case if the module has already been rejected by activity 7)

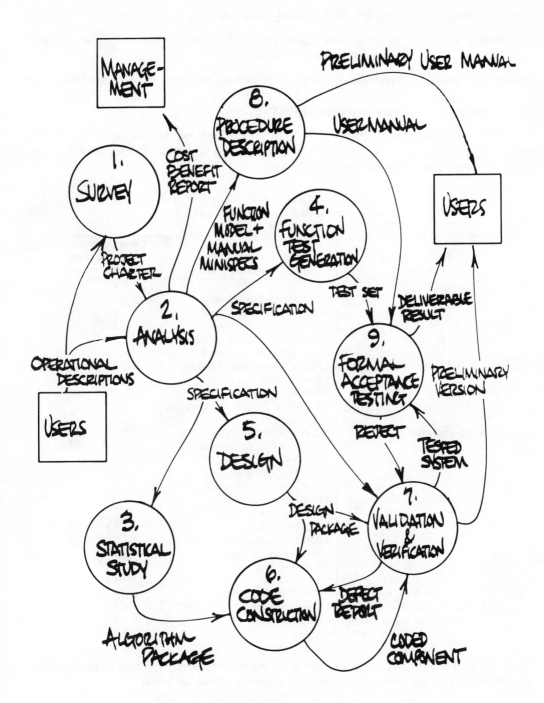

Figure A-9. MSP-4 component activities.

Defect report: defective module(s) plus test that provoked defect plus test result plus written defect analysis

Tested system: complete MSP-4 ready for acceptance testing

Preliminary version: partial system made available to user community plus narrative description of limitations

Deliverable request: final MSP-4 system plus user manual plus Acceptance Test report

A2.2 Cost accounting categories for MSP-4

The superset model assumed for this development organization is the one described in [Yourdon, 1982]. All effort charged to activities of the MSP-4 project must be mapped into cost categories as follows:

Table A-1
Cost Accounting for MSP-4 Activities

MSP-4 Activity Number	Cost Category Names from Superset Model	Corresponding Activity Number of Superset Model
1. Survey	Effort.Survey	1
2. Analysis	Effort.Analysis.Old Physical	2.1
	Effort.Analysis.Old Logical	2.2
	Effort.Analysis.New Logical	2.3
	Effort.Analysis.New Physical	2.4
	Effort.Analysis.Cost/Benefit	2.5
	Effort.Analysis.Option Selection	2.6
	Effort.Analysis.Constraint	2.7
	Effort.Analysis.Packaging	2.8
3. Statistical Study	(No correspondence — unique to this project)	
4. Function Test Generation	Effort.Test Gen.Test Plan	5.1
	Effort.Test Gen.Performance Test	5.2
	Effort.Test Gen.Normal Test	5.3
	Effort.Test Gen.Error Test	5.4
	Effort.Test Gen.Packaging	5.5
5. Design	Effort.Design.Derivation	3.1
	Effort.Design.Evaluation	3.2
	Effort.Design.Internal	3.3
	Effort.Design.Database	3.4
	Effort.Design.Packaging	3.5
6. Code Construction	Effort.Selection	4.1
	Effort.Coding	4.2
7. Validation & Verification	Effort.Validation	4.3
8. Procedure Description	Effort.Procedure Description	7
9. Formal Acceptance Testing	Effort.Final Test	9

Note: MSP-4 will report costs charged to a project by category, or by category group. For instance, you can request a report in any of the following ways:

Category	Result
Effort.Design.Packaging	hours logged in this one specific activity
Effort.Design	hours logged in any activity of DESIGN family
Effort	hours logged against the project

Section A3
MSP-4 Design Model

A design model for the MSP-4 system is presented on the following pages. The design is made up of 51 modules:

MSP-4 MODULE LIST

Number	Module Name	Number	Module Name
1.	MSP-4	27.	Get Next Project
2.	Solicit Next Function	28.	Solicit Sub-Function
3.	Record Project Metrics	29.	Calibrate Cost Model
4.	Report On Metrics	30.	Solicit Parameter Name
5.	Analyze Metrics Over Domain	31.	Display Result
6.	Establish Domain Of Projects	32.	Evaluate Correction Factors
7.	Update Or Reject Set	33.	Get Domain Containing Project
8.	Solicit Next Update	34.	Regress Over Sample
9.	Record One Metric	35.	Forecast Result
10.	Get Metric Value	36.	Construct Display of Domain
11.	Construct Display Of Metrics	37.	Clear Display
12.	Get Next Metric	38.	Add Cell To Display
13.	Solicit Change To Domain	39.	Present One Screen Of Display
14.	Ask Report Type	40.	Read Display Cell
15.	Read New Metric	41.	Replace Display Cell
16.	Get Next Project In Domain	42.	Determine Display Position
17.	Summarize Domain	43.	Get Cost By Category
18.	Show Effort Over Domain	44.	Add Or Delete Project
19.	Show Cost Report	45.	Update Or Reject Domain
20.	Show Project Report	46.	Compute Forecast
21.	Show Metric Census	47.	Construct Sample
22.	List Projects	48.	Display Sample
23.	Ask Domain Name	49.	Display Result
24.	Cost One Project	50.	Regress Linear
25.	Get Next Cost Category	51.	Regress Nonlinear
26.	Ask Project ID		

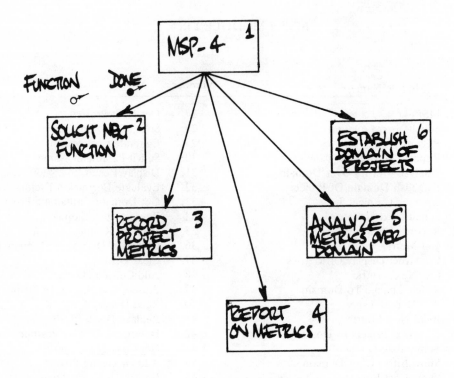

Figure A-10. Structure chart 1: MSP-4.

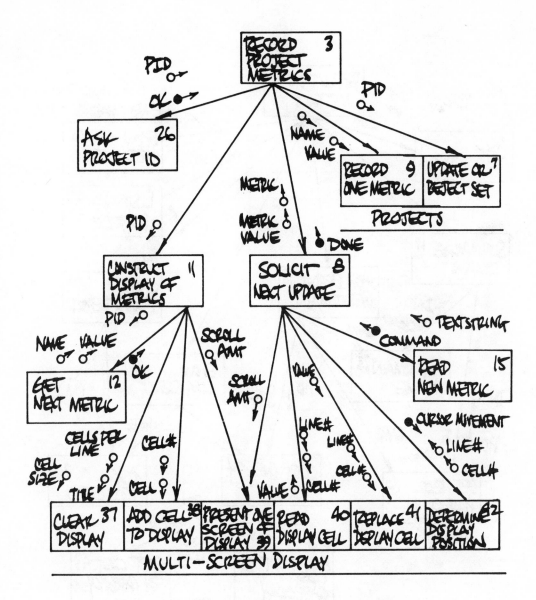

Figure A-11. Structure chart 3: Record Project Metrics.

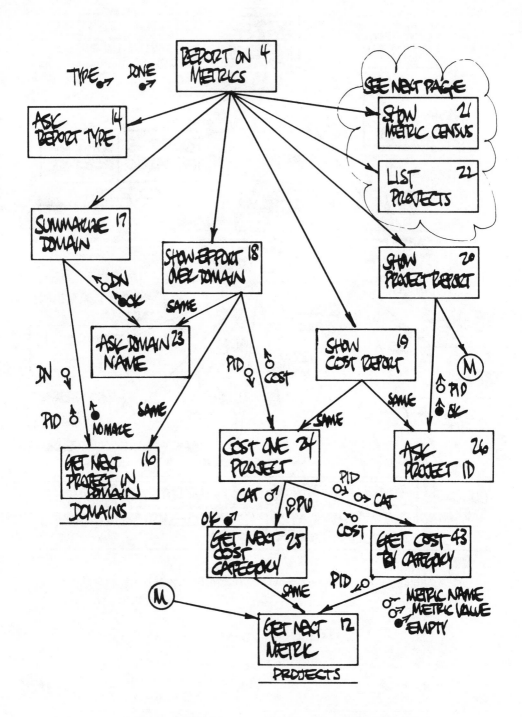

Figure A-12. Structure chart 4: Report On Metrics.

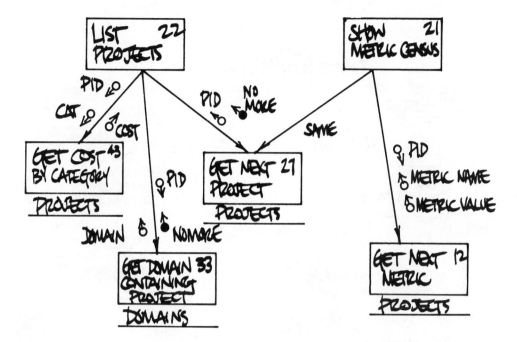

**Figure A-13. Structure chart 21: Show Metric Census.
Structure chart 22: List Projects.**

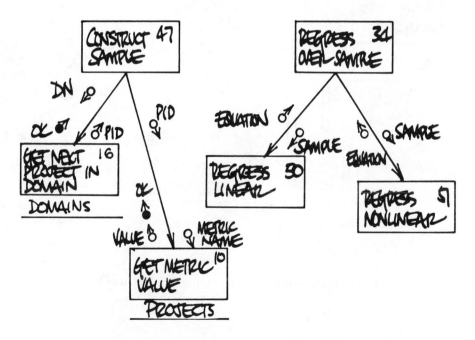

**Figure A-14. Structure chart 34: Regress Over Sample.
Structure chart 47: Construct Sample.**

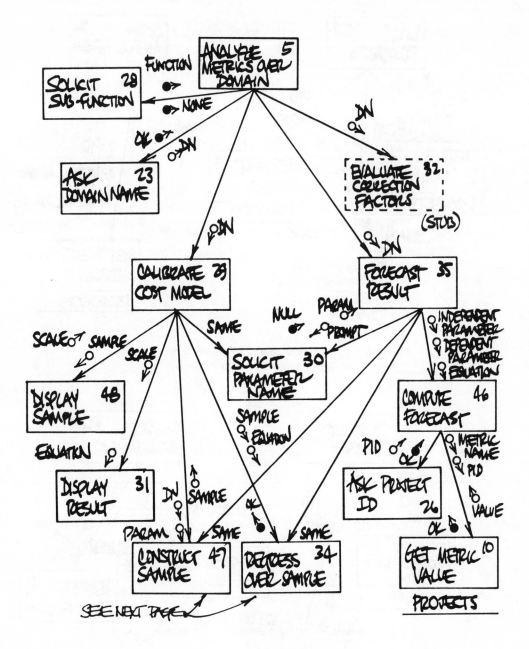

Figure A-15. Structure chart 5: Analyze Metrics Over Domain.

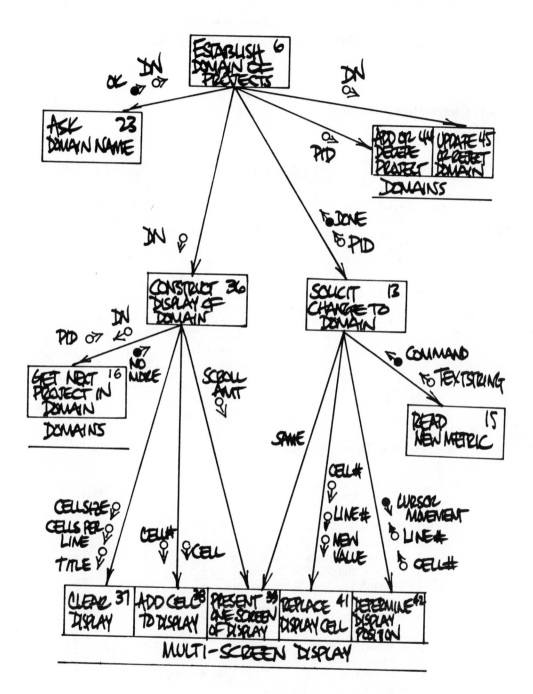

Figure A-16. Structure chart 6: Establish Domain Of Projects.

Section A4
Metric Analysis of the Models

A4.1 Computation of Bang

Primitive	Tc	Class	Bang Increment		
7.1	6	Simple Update	7.8 ×	.5 =	3.9
7.2.1	7	Edit	9.8 ×	.8 =	7.8
7.2.2	6	Computation	7.8 ×	2.0 =	15.6
7.2.3	6	Computation	7.8 ×	2.0 =	15.6
7.2.4	13	Display	13.0 ×	1.8 =	23.4
7.3	13	Arithmetic	24.1 ×	.7 =	16.8
7.4	4	Simple Update	4.0 ×	.5 =	2.0
7.5.1	10	Synchronization	16.6 ×	1.5 =	24.9
7.5.2	4	Tabular Analysis	4.0 ×	1.0 =	4.0
7.5.3	6	Tabular Analysis	7.8 ×	1.0 =	7.8
7.5.4	6	Tabular Analysis	7.8 ×	1.0 =	7.8
7.5.5	5	Tabular Analysis	5.8 ×	1.0 =	5.8
7.5.6	8	Tabular Analysis	12.0 ×	1.0 =	12.0
7.5.7	5	Tabular Analysis	5.8 ×	1.0 =	5.8
7.6	12	Computation	21.5 ×	2.0 =	43.0
Total					196.2

A4.2 Computation of Design Weight

Module	Tokens	Decisions	Weight
1. MSP-4	2	2	2.6
2. Solicit Next Function	4	2	7.1
3. Record Project Metrics	5	3	10.7
4. Report On Metrics	2	3	3.3
5. Analyze Metrics Over Domain	4	4	9.0
6. Establish Domain Of Projects	4	3	7.9
7. Update Or Reject Set	6	3	13.4
8. Solicit Next Update	10	3	23.2
9. Record One Metric	5	2	9.5
10. Get Metric Value	4	3	7.9
11. Construct Display Of Metrics	10	1	20.7
12. Get Next Metric	4	2	7.1
13. Solicit Change To Domain	8	2	17.4
14. Ask Report Type	4	3	7.9
15. Read New Metric	3	3	5.4
16. Get Next Project In Domain	3	3	5.4
17. Summarize Domain	4	3	7.9
18. Show Effort Over Domain	5	3	10.7
19. Show Cost Report	3	2	4.9
20. Show Project Report	6	4	15.3

Module	Tokens	Decisions	Weight
21. Show Metric Census	4	2	7.1
22. List Projects	6	3	13.4
23. Ask Domain Name	2	1	2.6
24. Cost One Project	5	2	9.5
25. Get Next Cost Category	6	1	10.7
26. Ask Project ID	4	1	6.3
27. Get Next Project	2	3	3.3
28. Solicit Sub-Function	3	1	4.4
29. Calibrate Cost Model	8	3	9.6
30. Solicit Parameter Name	3	1	4.4
31. Display Result	10	3	26.0
32. Evaluate Correction Factors	0	0	0.0
		(stub)	
33. Get Domain Containing Project	3	3	5.4
34. Regress Over Sample	3	1	4.4
35. Forecast Result	9	3	22.7
36. Construct Display Of Domain	7	2	14.6
37. Clear Display	3	0	4.0
38. Add Cell to Display	2	2	2.9
39. Present One Screen Of Display	4	3	7.9
40. Read Display Cell	3	2	4.9
41. Replace Display Cell	3	2	4.9
42. Determine Display Position	3	1	4.4
43. Get Cost By Category	6	1	10.7
44. Add Or Delete Project	1	2	1.2
45. Update Or Reject Domain	3	2	4.9
46. Compute Forecast	8	2	17.4
47. Construct Sample	8	2	17.4
48. Display Sample	9	3	22.7
49. Display Result	10	2	23.2
50. Regress Linear	4	2	7.1
51. Regress Nonlinear	5	2	9.5
Total			494.8

APPENDIX B
Notational Conventions for Specification and Design Models

B.1 Function model: Network component

The network of functions (also called a data flow diagram or DFD) that is at the heart of a function model is composed of the four basic notational elements shown in Figure B-1.

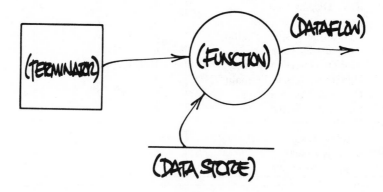

Figure B-1. Function model network notation.

These elements are defined as follows:

- A *data flow* is a pipeline through which packets of known (and defined) data composition flow.

- A *function* is a transformation of arriving data flows into departing data flows according to some set of transforming rules (user policy).

- A *data store* is a repository in which data items are retained (in accordance with user policy) over a period of time.

- A *terminator* is a person, organization, machine, system, or business entity that lies entirely outside the function model and is an immediate producer or receiver of modeled data.

The function model may require a number of networks (DFDs), which together make up an integrated set. The rules for integrating the set are the following:

- *There is always one diagram that describes the entire system;* that is, it shows the transformation of all arriving system data flows into all departing system data flows. This network is typically called the *context diagram.* The context diagram usually portrays the whole system without partitioning, as shown, for instance, in Figure B-2.

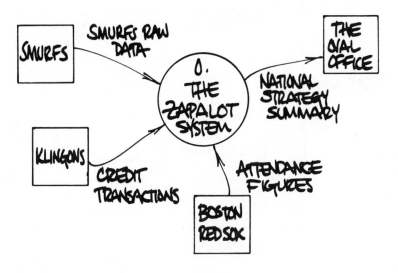

Figure B-2. Context Diagram.

- *Each component function shown on any network is further described by a lower-level network (called a child diagram), or by a written description (called a minispecification or minispec).* The child diagram or minispec bears the same number as that of the parent function. Figure B-3 shows a parent network and one of its children.

- *Each function on each network is constrained by a rigorous data conservation rule:* The data shown arriving at the function must be both necessary and sufficient to allow generation of the data shown departing from the function.

- *Each child network describes the same subject matter as the associated function of the parent;* that is, it describes transformation of the same net arriving data into the same net departing data. See, for example, the net equivalence of the data into and out of function 3 in Figure B-3; and the data into and out of its child diagram.

- *Each interface (data flow) shown on each function network must be named and defined in the interface dictionary (data dictionary).*

B.2 Function model: Interface dictionary component

All modeled data flows and data stores must be defined in the interface dictionary. If the interface has components, then its definition consists of a census of those components that make up the whole, together with a description of how the components are related. If the interface is elemental (has no component pieces), then its definition consists of a statement of what values or ranges of values the element may take on.

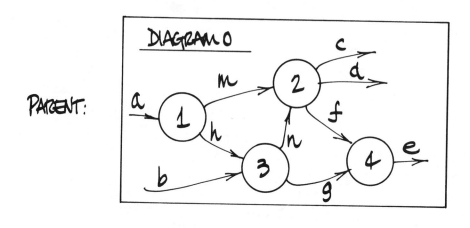

Figure B-3. Parent and child diagrams.

In describing relationships that apply among data items, the following notation is used:

=   the item being defined *is made up of* the following components

+   one component is always present *together with* another

[ ]   *one and only one* of the enclosed items is present; the items are separated by a | character

{ }   the enclosed item is present *zero or more times*

( )   the enclosed item is *optionally* present

The relational operators may be used in successively lower- and lower-level definitions, as in the following example:

Overdue-Accounts-Report	= Heading + { Account-Detail } + Summary
Heading	= Branch-Number + Date + (Time)
Account-Detail	= Account-Number + Date-Of-Last-Transaction + Overdue-Amount + [Officer-Name | Officer-ID]
Summary	= Number-Of-Overdue-Accounts + Total-Dollar-Amount

B.3 Retained data model

The notational convention for drawing a retained data model is shown in Figure B-4. The elements of the model are the following:

- An *object* is something whose existence is simulated by the system.
- A *relationship* is an association between two or more objects.

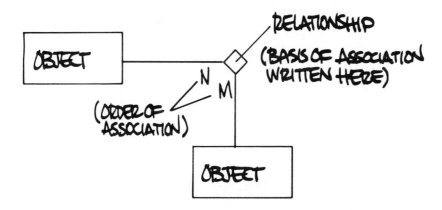

Figure B-4. Retained data model notation.

Each relationship is annotated with *the basis of association* (how the objects are related) and the *order of the association* (how many instances of the first object are associated with how many instances of the second).

The set of connected objects and relationships is called the *object diagram.* It is only part of the retained data model; the other components are

- a *policy-based description* of each object or relationship
- a *statement of data content,* the data attributes of each object or relationship
- a *data structure,* or statement of the format and organization of attributes
- a *statement of dependencies* that apply among objects and relationships

B.4 State model

The notational convention for drawing a state model is shown in Figure B-5. The elements of a state model are defined as follows:

Figure B-5. State model notation.

- A *state* is a characteristic set of stimulus-response relationships that determine a system's behavior.
- A *transition* is an event that causes a system to modify its state and adopt a new pattern of behavior characterized by the new state.
- An *entry point* is a system's initial state.

B.5 Design model

The notational convention for drawing a design model is shown in Figure B-6.

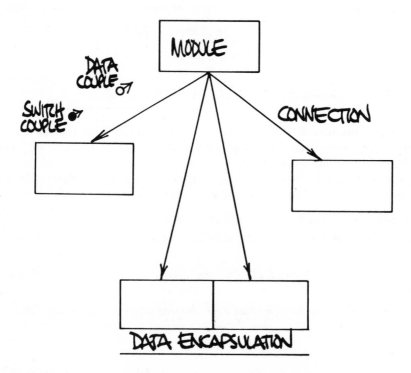

Figure B-6. Design model notation.

The elements are defined as follows:

- A *module* is a contiguous block of code with a single identifier by which it can be referenced as a unit.
- A *connection* is a reference by one module to some other module or to some item contained in the other module.
- A *couple* is a data item that is shared by two or more modules.
- An *encapsulation* is a small block of data accessible as local data by a limited set of modules.

B.6 Selected references

Each of the notational conventions presented here is taken from some other work. For a more complete description of function model notation, see

DeMarco, T. *Structured Analysis and System Specification.* New York: Yourdon Press, 1978.

For more information on the retained data model, see

Flavin, M. *Fundamental Concepts of Information Modeling.* New York: Yourdon Press, 1981.

On the state model, refer to

IEEE Standard Digital Interface for Programmable Instrumentation. New York: Institute of Electrical and Electronics Engineers, 1978.

For details on the design model, see

Yourdon, E., and L.L. Constantine. *Structured Design: Fundamentals of a Discipline of Computer Program and Systems Design,* 2nd ed. Englewood Cliffs, N.J.: Prentice-Hall, 1979.

APPENDIX C
A Tailored Primer on Statistics

The purpose of this appendix is to describe a very limited set of statistical terms and techniques, specifically those terms and techniques used in the text. In presenting the ideas of *regression* and *analysis of convergence,* I shall make more use of graphics than of the underlying statistical mathematics. As a result, this section should give you a sufficient feel for the subject to complement your reading of the text, but you may need some further aid to actually apply the concepts.

C.1 Regression

Take a look at the two graphs presented in Figures C-1 and C-2. Each shows a causal relationship between two variables. In Figure C-1, the relationship is *deterministic:* If you know precisely the value of the independent parameter (current), you know

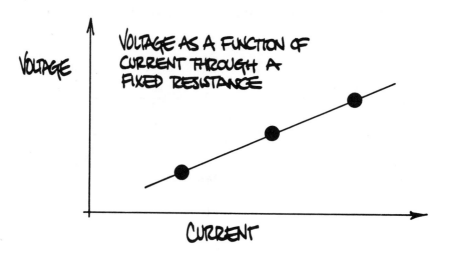

Figure C-1. Deterministic relationship.

equally precisely the value of the dependent parameter (voltage). In Figure C-2, on the other hand, the relationship is *stochastic:* If you know precisely the value of the independent parameter (years of experience), you know equally precisely what value of the independent parameter (salary) is your best guess for a given value of years of experience, but actual values will be scattered in some orderly way above and below this best-guess value.

Figure C-2. Stochastic relationship.

The line that connects the points in Figure C-1 might be called a *prediction line*. It describes for any value of current what the associated voltage will be. You can use the line to "predict," for instance, what voltage will result from putting a current of five amps through the resistance. Because the relationship is deterministic (no scatter), drawing the line is trivial — all you need is a sufficiently good eye to connect the points with a smooth curve or (in this case) a straight line.

Drawing the prediction line of Figure C-2, however, is a bit more complicated. Since there is some scatter, no one line passes directly through all the points, but there must be a line that in some sense is the *best fit* to those points. The process of drawing a best-fit line through scattered data points is called *regression analysis*.

C.1.1 Simple regression

Simple regression is the procedure used to find a best-fit line that describes the relationship between *two* variables. Before applying regression analysis, however, we'll need to answer two basic questions: What kind of a line (straight line, parabola, sine wave, and so forth) shall be fit to the data? What constitutes "best fit"? There is no single correct answer to the first of these questions. Each regression must be preceded by some analysis of the supposed relationship between the two variables in order to choose a kind of line. If you choose a straight line, then you'll be doing a *linear* regression when you determine which particular straight line best fits the data. If you choose an exponential curve, you'll be doing *nonlinear* regression when you determine the values of the best-fit curve parameters. There are as many other kinds of simple regression as there are prototype lines to be fit to the data. Figure C-3 shows two correctly drawn regression lines through the data. The first is the best-fit straight line, and the second, the best-fit exponential.

The determination of best fit usually involves minimizing the sum of the squares of the vertical distances (deviations) between the line and the data points. So, in Figure C-4, the best-fit straight line is the one whose slope and initial vertical position cause a minimum value of $D1^2 + D2^2 + D3^2$. There is a rather abstruse statistical

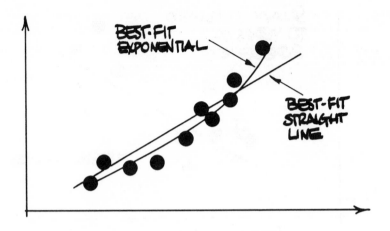

Figure C-3. Two correct regression lines.

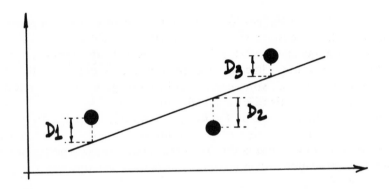

Figure C-4. Best-fit line.

justification of this least-sum-of-squares criterion of good fit, but for our purposes, it hardly matters: The prediction line determined by minimizing the sum of the squares of the deviations is invariably the *best-looking fit*. The mathematical formula that describes best fit is just a handy way to characterize the judgment of the eye.

Simple regression helps you to exploit the relationship between two, but no more than two, variables. Simple regression is fine for single-factor cost modeling, since each cost component to be studied is assumed to depend upon a single predictor (upon Bang, for instance). Most predictors are composites of weighted sums of other parameters. Once you've determined a workable formulation for your predictor, simple regression will be all you'll need, since you'll treat the predictor from that point on as a single parameter. But for the purpose of original weighting of the predictor, you can make profitable use of the technique of *multiple regression*.

C.1.2 Multiple regression

Multiple regression is an extension of the technique of simple linear regression into three or more dimensions. If you suspect that a particular unknown depends on the values of, for example, two variables, you can make the same kind of analysis that you'd have made if it depended on only one, *but you'll be working with planes instead of lines.* Imagine data points plotted in three dimensions (Figure C-5). Multiple regres-

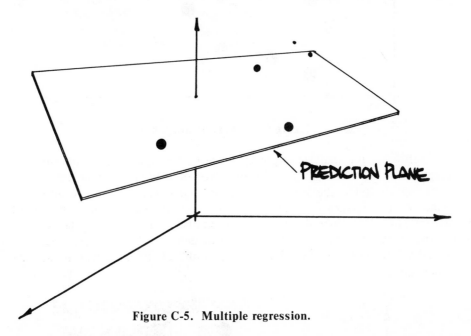

Figure C-5. Multiple regression.

sion analysis will now involve finding the best-fit plane to match the data. The determination of best fit is based on minimization of the sum of the squares of the vertical distances between the data points and the prediction plane. Once you've found the best-fit plane, you can use it to predict the value of your unknown from your knowledge of the values of the two known parameters.

You can apply the same logic to relationships with any number of parameters, though the trick of visualizing the prediction equation as a line or plane cannot be extended into four or more dimensions.

C.2 Analysis of convergence

Once you've performed a regression analysis, what have you got? The technique of regression guarantees to provide the best-fit prediction line for any supposed relationship, but it makes no guarantee about the absolute degree of fit. You can use regression even when there is no very strong relationship between variables, as in Figure C-6. The technique will always give some answer, but the quality of the answer for purposes of projection will vary with the scatter of the data. The more the data points scatter around the line, the less confidence you should have in any projection based on the line. Analysis of convergence is a technique for quantifying scatter around a prediction line, and for determining how much confidence you should place in a projection from that line. This process involves analyzing the data points to see how well the prediction line would have predicted each one.

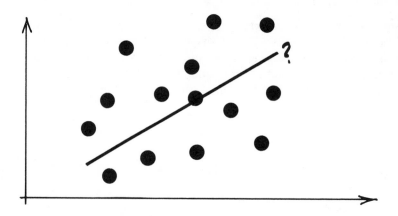

Figure C-6. Weak relationship.

A useful tool for analysis of convergence is the *standard error of estimate*. A simple, graphic way to think of the standard error of estimate is this: Imagine tolerance lines running alongside the prediction line at equal distances above and below; now widen the vertical distance from prediction line to tolerance line until the band between the two tolerance lines includes 68% of the points. This vertical distance (S in Figure C-7) is the standard error of estimate. If your data are well behaved (points normally distributed about the line), then doubling the width of the band will include about 95% of the data points.

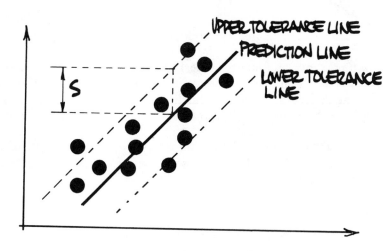

Figure C-7. Standard error of estimate.

Suppose regression and analysis of convergence present you with this situation:

$$\text{Effort}_i = 5.0 + 1.3 \times \text{Predictor}_i \pm 12.6$$

(all units are man-months)

where 12.6 man-months is the standard error of estimate. Suppose further that you need to estimate this effort for a system with a predictor value of 100. The projected value of Effort_i is 135 man-months $(5.0 + 1.3 \times 100)$. How much confidence are you justified in placing in this estimate? In order to answer this question, consider ranges around the projected value and use the definition of the standard error to assign confidence levels:

For a confidence level of 68%, expect effort in range 122.4 < Effort < 147.6
For a confidence level of 95%, expect effort in range 109.8 < Effort < 160.1

APPENDIX D
Sample Program
to Compute Code Volume

The program presented here will compute Volume of a Pascal source file in UCSD format. The program is itself written in UCSD Pascal. This program is provided only as a sample of its kind and carries no warranty, explicit or implicit, with respect to accuracy or completeness.

```pascal
program volume;
const    OK = 0;            TOKENSIZE = 20;
         QUOTE = '''';  MAXVOCABULARY = 500;

type     list =
              record
              count: 0 .. MAXVOCABULARY;
              word: array [0 .. MAXVOCABULARY] of string [TOKENSIZE];
              end;
         shortstring = string [TOKENSIZE];
         maxstring = string [255];

var      vocabulary: list;
         token: shortstring;
         line: maxstring;
         filename: string;
         source: text;
         totaltokens, uniquetokens: integer;

{$I remove}          {include procedure to remove comments}
{$I getnext}         {include function to deliver next token from input stream}
{$I lowercase}       {include procedure to replace upper with lowercase}
{$I strip}           {include procedure to strip out delimiters}
{$I unique}          {include function to determine if word ever encountered before}
{$I link}            {include procedure to link unique word into list}
{$I log2}            {include function to compute log base 2 of a number}

begin
repeat
         write ('Source File = ');
         readln (filename);
         {$I-} reset (source, filename); {$I+}
until ioresult = OK;
uniquetokens := 0;
totaltokens := 0;
vocabulary.count := 0;
while not eof (source) do
         begin
         readln (source, line);
         removecomments (line);
         lowercase (line);
         strip (line);
         while getnexttoken (token, line) do
              begin
              totaltokens := totaltokens + 1;
              if unique (token, vocabulary) then
                   begin
                   link (token, vocabulary);
                   uniquetokens := uniquetokens + 1;
                   end;
              end;
         end;
writeln ('Unique tokens = ', uniquetokens, '; Total tokens = ', totaltokens);
writeln ('Volume of ', filename, ' = ', totaltokens * log2 (uniquetokens));
end.
```

```pascal
procedure removecomments (var textline: maxstring);

    {Note:  only removes UCSD-style comments (enclosed in braces)}
    const    BEGINCOMMENT = '{';
             ENDCOMMENT = '}';
    var      teststring, nextline: maxstring;
             index, endex: integer;
             quoting, foundcomment: boolean;
    begin
    repeat
      quoting := FALSE;
      foundcomment := FALSE;
      index := 0;
      while ((index < length (textline)) and not foundcomment) do
          begin
          index := index + 1;
          if textline[index] = QUOTE then
              quoting := not quoting
          else if textline [index] = BEGINCOMMENT then
              if not quoting then
                    foundcomment := TRUE;
          end;
      if foundcomment then
          begin
          teststring := textline;
          delete (teststring, 1, index);
          endex := pos (ENDCOMMENT, teststring);
          if endex > 0 then
              delete (textline, index, endex + 1)
          else {comment runs over end of line}
              begin
              textline := copy (textline, 1, index - 1);
              repeat
                  readln (source, nextline);
              until pos (ENDCOMMENT, nextline) > 0;
              delete (nextline, 1, pos (ENDCOMMENT, nextline));
              textline := concat (textline, nextline);
              end;
          end;
      until not foundcomment;
    end;
```

```pascal
function getnexttoken (var token: shortstring; var line: string): boolean;
    {module to isolate and deliver next operand or operator}

    var spacepointer: integer;
        phrase: maxstring;
    begin
    while pos (' ', line) = 1 do
        delete (line, 1, 1);
    spacepointer := pos (' ', line);
    if pos (QUOTE, line) = 1 then
        begin
        delete (line, 1, 1);
        if pos (QUOTE, line) > 0 then
            begin
            phrase := copy (line, 1, pos (QUOTE, line) -1);
            delete (line, 1, length (phrase) + 1);
            end
        else
            begin
            phrase := line;
            line := '';
            end;
        end
    else if spacepointer > 0 then
        begin
        phrase := copy (line, 1, spacepointer - 1);
        delete (line, 1, spacepointer);
        end
    else
        begin
        phrase := line;
        line := '';
        end;
    getnexttoken := (length (phrase) > 0);
    if length (phrase) > TOKENSIZE then
        token := copy (phrase, 1, TOKENSIZE)
    else
        token := phrase;
    end;


procedure lowercase (var textline: maxstring);
    {convert to lowercase -- beware:  implementation dependent}

    var   index: integer;
    begin
    for index := 1 to length (textline) do
        if ((textline[index] >= 'A') and (textline[index] <= 'Z')) then
            textline [index] := chr (ord (textline [index]) -
                    (ord ('A') - ord ('a')));
    end;
```

```pascal
procedure strip (var progline: maxstring);

    {module to strip away punctuation}

    var    index: integer;
    begin
    while pos (':=', line) <> 0 do
        line [pos (':=', line)] := '=';
    for index := 1 to length (progline) do
        if progline[index] in [':', ';', ',', '(', ')', '[', ']'] then
            progline [index] := ' ';
    end;
```

```pascal
function unique (newword: shortstring; wordlist: list): boolean;

    {module to determine if a given word has ever been encountered before}

    var    index: integer;
    begin
    unique := TRUE;
    for index := 1 to wordlist.count do
        if newword = wordlist.word [index] then
            unique := FALSE;
    end;
```

```pascal
procedure link (newword: shortstring; var wordlist: list);

    {module to add a token to list of known tokens}

    begin
    wordlist.count := wordlist.count + 1;
    wordlist.word [wordlist.count] := newword;
    end;
```

```pascal
function log2 (number: integer): real;

    {return log base two of argument}

    begin
    log2 := ln (number) / ln (2);
    end;
```

References

[Bailey-Basili, 1981]

Bailey, J.W., and V.R. Basili. "A Meta-Model for Software Development and Resource Expenditures." *Proceedings of the 5th International Conference on Software Engineering.* New York: Institute of Electrical and Electronics Engineers, 1981, pp. 107-16.

[Boehm, 1976]

Boehm, B.W. "Software Engineering." *IEEE Transactions on Computers,* Vol. C-25, No. 12 (December 1976), pp. 1226-41. Reprinted in *Classics in Software Engineering,* E. Yourdon, ed. New York: Yourdon Press, 1979, pp. 325-61.

[Boehm, 1981]

———— . *Software Engineering Economics.* Englewood Cliffs, N.J.: Prentice-Hall, 1981.

[Chen, 1978]

Chen, E.T. "Program Complexity and Programmer Productivity." *IEEE Transactions on Software Engineering,* Vol. SE-4, No. 3 (May 1978), pp. 187-94.

[Christensen-Fitsos-Smith, 1981]

Christensen, K., G.P. Fitsos, and C.P. Smith. "A Perspective on Software Science." *IBM Systems Journal,* Vol. 20, No. 4 (1981), pp. 372-88.

[Crosby, 1979]

Crosby, P.B. *Quality Is Free: The Art of Making Quality Certain.* New York: McGraw-Hill, 1979.

[Curtis, 1979]

Curtis, B. "In Search of Software Complexity." *Workshop on Quantitative Software Models for Reliability, Complexity, and Cost: An Assessment of the State of the Art.* IEEE Catalog No. TH0067-9. New York: Institute of Electrical and Electronics Engineers, 1979, pp. 95-106.

[Curtis-Sheppard-Milliman, 1979]

————, S.B. Sheppard, and P. Milliman. "Third Time Charm: Stronger Prediction of Programmer Performance by Software Complexity Metrics." *Proceedings of the 4th International Conference on Software Engineering.* New York: Institute of Electrical and Electronics Engineers, 1979, pp. 356-60.

[DeMarco, 1977]

> DeMarco, T. *Report on the 1977 Productivity Survey.* New York: Yourdon inc., September 1977.

[DeMarco, 1978]

> ———— . *Structured Analysis and System Specification.* New York: Yourdon Press, 1978.

[DeMarco, 1981]

> ———— . *Yourdon 1978-80 Project Survey Final Report.* New York: Yourdon inc., September 1981.

[Dolotta-Mashey, 1976]

> Dolotta, T.A., and J.R. Mashey. "An Introduction to the Programmer's Workbench." *Proceedings of the 2nd International Conference on Software Engineering.* New York: Institute of Electrical and Electronics Engineers, 1976, pp. 164-68.

[Feller, 1957]

> Feller, W. *An Introduction to Probability Theory and Its Applications.* Vol. I. New York: John Wiley & Sons, 1957.

[Feuer-Fowlkes, 1979]

> Feuer, A.R., and E.B. Fowlkes. "Some Results from an Empirical Study of Computer Software." *Tutorial on Models and Metrics for Software Management and Engineering.* New York: Institute of Electrical and Electronics Engineers, 1979.

[Gane-Sarson, 1977]

> Gane, C., and T. Sarson. *Structured Systems Analysis: Tools & Techniques.* New York: Improved System Technologies, 1977.

[Gilb, 1977]

> Gilb, T. *Software Metrics.* Cambridge, Mass.: Winthrop Publishers, 1977.

[Glass, 1981]

> Glass, R.L. "Persistent Software Errors." *IEEE Transactions on Software Engineering,* Vol. SE-7, No. 2 (March 1981), pp. 162-68.

[Halstead, 1977]

> Halstead, M.H. *Elements of Software Science.* New York: Elsevier North-Holland, 1977.

[Hoare, 1981]

> Hoare, C.A.R. "The Emperor's Old Clothes." *Communications of the ACM,* Vol. 24, No. 2 (February 1981), pp. 75-83. Reprinted in *Writings of the Revolution: Selected Readings on Software Engineering.* E. Yourdon, ed. New York: Yourdon Press, 1982, pp. 187-99.

[Jones, 1981a]

> Jones, T.C. *Programming Productivity: Issues for the Eighties.* IEEE Catalog No. EHO 186-7. New York: Institute of Electrical and Electronics Engineers, 1981.

[Jones, 1981b]

        ———— . "Program Quality and Programmer Productivity: A Survey of the State of the Art." ASM Lectures, November 1981.

[Kidder, 1981]

        Kidder, T. *The Soul of a New Machine.* Boston: Atlantic Monthly/Little, Brown, 1981, p. 113.

[Mayer-Stalnaker, 1968]

        Mayer, D.B., and A.W. Stalnaker. "Selection and Evaluation of Computer Personnel — the Research History of SIG/CPR." *Proceedings of the 1968 ACM National Conference.* New York: Association for Computing Machinery, 1968, pp. 657-69.

[McCabe, 1976]

        McCabe, T.J. "A Complexity Measure." *IEEE Transactions on Software Engineering,* Vol. SE-2, No. 12 (December 1976), pp. 308-20.

[Myers, 1975]

        Myers, G.J. *Reliable Software Through Composite Design.* New York: Petrocelli/Charter, 1975.

[Myers, 1978]

        ———— . "A Controlled Experiment in Program Testing and Code Walkthroughs/Inspections." *Communications of the ACM,* Vol. 21, No. 9 (September 1978), pp. 760-68.

[Myers, 1979]

        ———— . *The Art of Software Testing.* New York: John Wiley & Sons, 1979.

[W. Myers, 1978]

        Myers, W. "A Statistical Approach to Scheduling Software Development." *Computer,* Vol. 11, No. 12 (December 1978), pp. 23-35.

[Norden, 1963]

        Norden, P.V. "Useful Tools for Project Management." *Operations Research in Research and Development.* New York: John Wiley & Sons, 1963.

[Orr, 1981]

        Orr, K.T. 5th International Conference on Software Engineering, 1981. Unpublished panel on methodologies.

[Page-Jones, 1980]

        Page-Jones, M. *A Practical Guide to Structured Systems Design.* New York: Yourdon Press, 1980.

[Parr, 1980]

        Parr, F.N. "An Alternative to the Rayleigh Curve Model for Software Development Effort." *IEEE Transactions on Software Engineering,* Vol. SE-6, No. 3 (May 1980), pp. 291-96.

[Phister, 1979]

Phister, M., Jr. *Data Processing Technology and Economics,* 2nd ed. Santa Monica, Calif.: Santa Monica Publishing Co. and Digital Press, 1979.

[Putnam, 1978]

Putnam, L.H. "Example of an Early Sizing, Cost and Schedule Estimate for an Application Software System." *Proceedings of COMPSAC '78.* New York: Institute of Electrical and Electronics Engineers, 1978.

[Putnam, 1980]

————— . *Software Cost Estimating and Life-Cycle Control: Getting the Software Numbers.* IEEE Catalog No. EH0 165-1. New York: Institute of Electrical and Electronics Engineers, 1980.

[Putnam-Fitzsimmons, 1979]

—————, and A. Fitzsimmons. "Estimating Software Costs." *Datamation,* 3-part series, Vol. 25, No. 9 (September 1979), pp. 89-98; Vol. 25, No. 10 (October 1979), pp. 171-78; Vol. 25, No. 11 (November 1979), pp. 137-40. Reprinted in *Writings of the Revolution: Selected Readings on Software Engineering.* E. Yourdon, ed. New York: Yourdon Press, 1982, pp. 326-44.

[Ross-Brackett, 1977]

Ross, D.T., and J.W. Brackett. "Structured Analysis for Requirements Definition." *IEEE Transactions on Software Engineering,* Vol. SE-3, No. 1 (January 1977), pp. 6-15.

[Sackman-Erikson-Grant, 1968]

Sackman, H., W.J. Erikson, and E.E. Grant. "Exploratory Experimental Studies Comparing Online and Offline Program Performance." *Communications of the ACM,* Vol. 11, No. 1 (January 1968), pp. 3-11. Reprinted in *Writings of the Revolution: Selected Readings on Software Engineering.* E. Yourdon, ed. New York: Yourdon Press, 1982, pp. 368-82.

[Shen-Conte-Dunsmore, 1982]

Shen, V.Y., S.D. Conte, and H.E. Dunsmore. "Software Science Revisited: A Critical Analysis of the Theory and Its Empirical Support." Unpublished paper, 1982.

[Shooman, 1979]

Shooman, M.L. "Tutorial on Software Cost Models." *Workshop on Quantitative Software Models for Reliability, Complexity, and Cost: An Assessment of the State of the Art.* IEEE Catalog No. TH0067-9. New York: Institute of Electrical and Electronics Engineers, 1979, pp. 1-19.

[Tajima-Matsubara, 1981]

Tajima, D., and T. Matsubara. "The Computer Software Industry in Japan." *Computer,* Vol. 14, No. 5 (May 1981), pp. 89-96.

[Teichroew-Hershey, 1977]
Teichroew, D., and E.A. Hershey, III. "PSL/PSA: A Computer-Aided Technique for Structured Documentation and Analysis of Information Processing Systems." *IEEE Transactions on Software Engineering,* Vol. SE-3, No. 1 (January 1977), pp. 41-48. Reprinted in *Classics in Software Engineering.* E. Yourdon, ed. New York: Yourdon Press, 1979, pp. 389-407.

[Thompson-Chelson, 1979]
Thompson, W.E., and P.O. Chelson. "Software Reliability Testing for Embedded Computer Systems." *Workshop on Quantitative Software Models for Reliability, Complexity, and Cost: An Assessment of the State of the Art.* IEEE Catalog No. TH0067-9. New York: Institute of Electrical and Electronics Engineers, 1979, pp. 201-208.

[Walston-Felix, 1977]
Walston, C.E., and C.P. Felix. "A Method of Programming Measurement and Estimation." *IBM Systems Journal,* Vol. 16, No. 1 (January 1977), pp. 54-73. Reprinted in *Writings of the Revolution: Selected Readings on Software Engineering.* E. Yourdon, ed. New York: Yourdon Press, 1982, pp. 389-408.

[Warnier, 1976]
Warnier, J.D. *Logical Construction of Programs,* 3rd ed., trans. B.M. Flanagan. New York: Van Nostrand Reinhold, 1976.

[Weinberg-Schulman, 1974]
Weinberg, G.M., and E.L. Schulman. "Goals and Performance in Computer Programming." *Human Factors,* Vol. 16, No. 1 (February 1974), pp. 70-77.

[Wirth, 1981]
Wirth, N. 5th International Conference on Software Engineering, 1981. Unpublished keynote address.

[Yourdon, 1982]
Yourdon, E. *Managing the System Life Cycle: A Software Development Methodology Overview.* New York: Yourdon Press, 1982.

[Yourdon-Constantine, 1979]
_____, and L.L. Constantine. *Structured Design: Fundamentals of a Discipline of Computer Program and Systems Design,* 2nd ed. Englewood Cliffs, N.J.: Prentice-Hall, 1979.

Index

Abe, J., 204
Acceleration Factor, 175, 178, 180-81, 186
Adaptation Factor, 122
Adapted code, discounting of, 122
Adversary team concept, 219-21
Aiso, H., 204
Albrecht, A.J., 91
Alexander, C., 48
Asynchronous models, 94-95

Bailey, J.W., 154, 163, 167, 169-70
Bang, 80-91, 102, 140, 145, 157, 167, 171, 175, 184-85, 189, 190-92, 220
  algorithms for computation of, 90
  computation of, for MSP-4, 254
  formulating, for data-strong systems, 89
  formulating, for function-strong systems, 84-88
  tailoring of, 90-91
Bang Per Buck, 60, 90-91, 115, 199
  maximizing, 60
Basili, V.R., 154, 159, 163, 167, 169-70
Binary deliverables, 137-38
Black Team testing, 221-22
Boehm, B.W., 154, 163-64, 170, 178, 180-81, 199
Brackett, J.W., 81
Bugs, 197-98

Census of interfaces, 43
Chelson, P.O., 126
Chen, E.T., 119-20
Chen's Number, 119-20
Chief Programmer Team, 221
Christensen, K., 117, 128
Chump, 115
COCOMO, 163-64

Code, metrics derived from. *See* Volume, of code; Complexity, of code.
Code Complexity. *See* Complexity, of code.
Code Volume. See Volume, of code.
Coding War Games, 214, 225
Compilation Rate, 123-24
Complexity, of code, 118-22, 127, 163
Component cost models, 189
Composite predictors, 192. *See also* Bang, Design Weight, Implementation Weight.
Composite requirements model. *See* Specification model, composite.
Compression penalty curve, 186
Constantine, L.L., 101, 130, 261
Convergence of data points to prediction line, 157, 164-67
  analysis of, 166, 265-67
Cost accounting, 143-44
  categories for MSP-4, 246
Cost/benefit analysis, 183-85
Cost migration, 114-15, 145, 195
Cost model
  as abstract model, 151-53
  component, 189
  construction of, 155-57
  decomposition of, into categories, 156, 191-92
  definition of, 149, 153-54
  parameters of, 160-61
  transportable, 154-55. *See also* Single-factor cost model; Time-sensitive cost model.
Cost theory, 83-84
  formulation of, 156
Coupling, 96, 123
Crosby, P.B., 227

279